THE DOUBLEDAY
CHILDREN'S
ENCYCLOPEDIA

GENERAL EDITOR: JOHN PATON
PROJECT EDITOR: ROBERTA WIENER

VOLUME 2
DESERT *through* **LEATHER**

DOUBLEDAY
NEW YORK   LONDON   TORONTO   SYDNEY   AUCKLAND

PUBLISHED BY DOUBLEDAY
a division of Bantam Doubleday Dell Publishing Group, Inc.
666 Fifth Avenue, New York, New York 10103

DOUBLEDAY
and the portrayal of an anchor with a dolphin
are trademarks of Doubleday, a division of
Bantam Doubleday Dell Publishing Group, Inc.

The publisher would like to thank Roberta Wiener,
project editor, for her extensive research
and revision of this work.

Library of Congress Cataloging-in-Publication Data
The Doubleday children's encyclopedia/general editor, John Paton, project
editor, Roberta Wiener.—1st ed. in the U.S.
p. cm.
Summary: Presents facts on more than 1300 subjects from Aardvark
to Zoo.
1. Children's encyclopedias and dictionaries. [1. Encyclopedias
and dictionaries.] I. Paton, John, 1914–. II. Wiener, Roberta.
III. Title: Children's encyclopedia.
AG5.D74 1990
031—dc20   89-77208   CIP   AC

ISBN 0-385-41210-X
ISBN 0-385-41211-8 (lib. bdg.)

Copyright © 1989 by Grisewood & Dempsey Limited

THE SUBJECT SYMBOLS

Each entry in this encyclopedia has its own easily-recognized symbol opposite the heading. This symbol tells you at a glance which area of interest the entry falls into—is it animals, history, or science? Below are the 16 subject areas we have used. At the back of the work there is a list of articles divided into subject areas.

ANIMALS Descriptions of behavior, homes, and individual species; mammals, birds, reptiles, fishes, insects, etc.

MACHINES AND MECHANISMS Explanations of everything from simple machines to jet engines, plus descriptions of their inventors.

TRAVEL AND TRANSPORTATION The history and development of aircraft, ships, ralroads, cars, motorcycles, etc.

HUMAN BODY How the body works, the process of birth, aging, diseases, immunity, genetics, etc.

BUILDINGS The history and development of architecture, modern construction and design, famous buildings.

OUR EARTH How the Earth was formed, and how it is still changing; its deserts, mountains, oceans, rivers, etc.

HISTORY Great events and great figures from ancient civilizations up to the present.

COUNTRIES AND PLACES Descriptions, flags, maps, essential statistics, etc. for all countries, plus places of interest.

PLANTS AND FOOD From microscopic plants to gigantic trees—what they are, how they grow, the food they provide.

THE ARTS Drawing, painting, sculpture, crafts, ballet, modern dance, drama, theater, TV, cinema, etc., plus the great artists.

PEOPLES AND GOVERNMENT Descriptions of peoples of the world, the things they do and the way they govern their countries.

LANGUAGE AND LITERATURE How language is constructed, plus descriptions of great playwrights, novelists, poets, etc.

SPORTS AND PASTIMES Competitive sport, great athletes and sporting stars, plus descriptions of many hobbies.

ASTRONOMY AND SPACE Birth of the Universe, the solar system, galaxies, space exploration, etc.

SCIENCE How science is applied in everyday life, the elements, sources of energy, important scientists, etc.

RELIGION, PHILOSOPHY, AND MYTH How these have changed through history and the ones that have survived.

Desert

Not all deserts are hot and sandy. Some are cold, and some are rocky. But all are very dry. Some scientists say that a desert is any area where less than 3 in. (8 cm) of rain falls in a year. Other scientists call a place a desert when there is more rain than this, but where it evaporates quickly in the sun or sinks rapidly into the ground.

Many big deserts are in the tropics, often inland on large continents where rainbearing winds cannot reach them.

There are three main types of desert. The first is rocky, where any soil is blown away by the wind. The second has large areas of gravel. The third is made up of great sand dunes, burning hot by day and bitterly cold at night.

Cold deserts are found in northern Canada, Greenland, the northern Soviet Union, and Antarctica. Very few plants and animals can survive in these regions because they are so cold and icy. Cold deserts are dry because they have no liquid water—it is all in the form of ice.

It is difficult for plants and animals to live in desert conditions. Some plants, like the CACTUS, store

LARGEST DESERTS		
	sq. miles	(sq. km)
Sahara	3,243,000	(8,400,000)
Gt. Australian	1,499,610	(3,885,000)
Libyan	499,870	(1,295,000)
Gobi	299,922	(777,000)
Rub'al Khali	249,935	(647,500)
Kalahari	119,660	(310,000)
Kara Kum	109,971	(284,900)
Atacama	24,994	(64,750)
Mohave	14,996	(38,850)

▼ *Wind-sculpted dunes in the Sahara Desert in Morocco. Not all deserts are sandy; many are stony and barren.*

DESERT

▼ Many animals keep cool in the desert by hiding away during the daytime, coming out after the Sun sets. To conserve water, desert animals sweat very little.

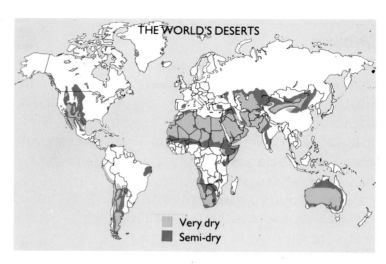

THE WORLD'S DESERTS

Very dry
Semi-dry

▼ The sand grouse soaks its feathers in a waterhole and takes the water to its thirsty young.

◄ The peregrine falcon preys on small desert animals. It is one of the fastest flying birds.

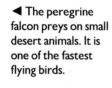

moisture in their fleshy stems. Others have seeds that lie apparently lifeless in the ground for long periods. When a shower of rain falls, they burst into life and can flower and produce new seeds within weeks. Many desert animals shelter from the sun by day and come out only at night. Some never drink, but get all the moisture they need from their food.

The world's largest desert is the SAHARA in Africa. The driest desert is the Atacama in South America, where it may not rain for several years. The Mohave Desert and the Painted Desert lie in the western United States.

▼ There are two types of camel, the Bactrian (two-humped) of the Gobi Desert and the Arabian (one-humped).

▲ The Gila monster is a poisonous lizard. Its poison travels along grooves in its teeth while it is biting its victim.

▲ Dingoes are wild dogs, descended from dogs brought to Australia by the first settlers to arrive there.

Detergent

The word *detergent* means any substance that will clean things. *Soap* is a detergent. But today the word detergent usually means synthetic, or man-made, detergents such as most washing powders. Detergents are similar to soap, but soap leaves behind filmy deposits, such as the familiar bathtub ring. Detergents can reach soiled areas better than soaps and do not leave deposits.

Detroit

Detroit, Michigan, is one of the most important cities in the country, and one of the largest. It is the home of the American automobile industry. Many of the biggest car manufacturers have factories there. Because Detroit is on the GREAT LAKES, it is easy to transport the raw materials that are needed to make cars to it. Detroit was built first by the French, but the British captured it in 1760. It became an American city only in 1796, 13 years after the REVOLUTIONARY WAR.

Diamond

Diamonds are CRYSTALS. They are harder than anything else in the world. They are formed by great heat and pressure deep beneath the surface of the earth. Diamonds are made of pure CARBON, the same mineral that is found in ordinary coal. They are usually colorless and have to be cut in a special

The Cullinan diamond, named after its finder, Thomas Cullinan, was the largest ever found. It was discovered in 1905 near Pretoria, South Africa. The huge uncut stone was about 5 in. (13 cm) across and weighed more than 1½ lb. (.75 kg). In 1908, the diamond was cut by expert diamond cutters in Amsterdam and finished up as 105 separate stones. One big diamond cut from the Cullinan is called the Star of Africa. It is in the British royal scepter. Another is in the State Crown, and others are in jewelry worn by Queen Elizabeth II.

The world's most famous colored diamond is the large Hope diamond. It is deep blue and came originally from India. The Hope is now in the gem collection of the Smithsonian Institution in Washington, D.C. Although diamonds are usually colorless, they are found in a variety of colors in shades of blue, yellow, pink, and champagne.

◄ *A cut and uncut diamond. The finished diamond has usually lost about 50 percent of its original weight after cutting and polishing.*

way to catch the lights and "sparkle." A diamond cutter is very skilled and uses tools tipped with diamonds, for only another diamond is hard enough to cut a diamond. Diamonds are used in industry for drilling and cutting.

Dickens, Charles

Charles Dickens (1812–1870) was a great English writer. His books give us a vivid picture of life in Victorian England in the middle 1800s. Several of his stories are about children, especially poor children and orphans. Dickens tried to improve the lives of the poor by making their suffering more widely known through his books. He also created some of the liveliest and best-known characters in English literature. Some of his most famous books are *Oliver Twist*, *David Copperfield*, *Great Expectations*, and *A Christmas Carol*.

Dickinson, Emily

Emily Dickinson (1830–1886) was one of America's greatest poets and one of the most important of the 1800s. Her poems can be hard to understand. She wrote about the difficulty of understanding the world, and of how quickly and strangely life passes. She was a very reserved person, who refused to publish any of her poems during her life and who never married. She lived all her life at her parents' home in Massachusetts. Few certain facts about her solitary life are known.

Dictator

A dictator is the leader of a country who rules with absolute power and authority. In ancient Rome, a dictator was a magistrate who was given absolute power to deal with emergencies, when decisions had to be made quickly. Today the term is used to describe a tyrant who takes away people's rights and freedoms and rules by force. Often those who try to oppose a dictator are killed, imprisoned, or forced to leave the country until a time when the dictator is overthrown.

▲ *Charles Dickens wrote all his novels in weekly or monthly installments for magazines.*

▼ *An illustration from Charles Dickens' novel* Oliver Twist, *which portrayed the harsh conditions suffered by orphans in Britain at the time.*

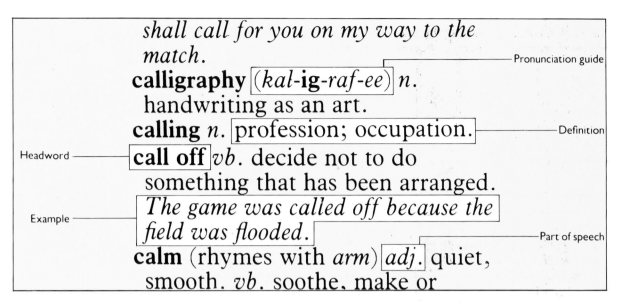

shall call for you on my way to the match.

calligraphy *(kal-ig-raf-ee)* *n.* handwriting as an art.

calling *n.* profession; occupation.

call off *vb.* decide not to do something that has been arranged. *The game was called off because the field was flooded.*

calm (rhymes with *arm*) *adj.* quiet, smooth. *vb.* soothe, make or

Pronunciation guide
Definition
Headword
Example
Part of speech

Dictionary

A dictionary is a book that tells us what words mean. The words are arranged in alphabetical order from A to Z. Often the meanings, or definitions, include the history of the words and how they are used and pronounced. Dictionaries may vary in size from many volumes to dictionaries small enough to slip into your pocket. Dr. Samuel Johnson (1709–84) made one of the first large dictionaries of English words.

▲ *A dictionary definition has a number of standard parts, though not every dictionary includes them all. After the word itself, called the* headword, *comes a pronunciation guide and the part of speech, usually abbreviated (n., adj.). Next comes the definition, or what the word means. Finally, other forms of the same word may be listed.*

Diesel Engine

Diesel engines are a type of INTERNAL COMBUSTION ENGINE in which fuel is burned inside the engine. Diesel engines are named after their inventor, Rudolf Diesel, who built his first successful engine in 1897 to replace the steam engine. Diesel engines use a cruder, heavier fuel oil than gasoline. They are cheaper to run than gas engines, but they are heavier and more difficult to start, so until recently they were not widely used in cars. They are used to drive heavy machines such as trains, tractors, ships, buses, and trucks. A properly-working diesel engine causes less pollution than a gasoline engine.

A diesel engine is similar to a gas engine. But instead of using a spark from a spark plug to ignite the fuel, the diesel engine uses heat that is made by a piston squeezing air inside a cylinder. When air is

▼ *London taxis are driven by diesel engines, which are cheaper to run and cause less pollution.*

A Cheap Day Return saves getting the car out.

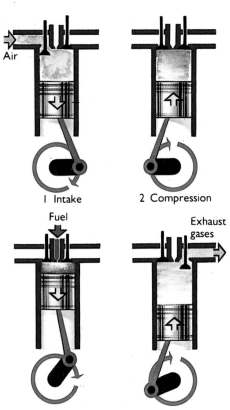

1 Intake   2 Compression

3 Injection and power   4 Exhaust

▲ *How a diesel engine works. As the piston goes down (1), air is drawn into the cylinder. When the piston goes up, the air is squeezed and becomes very hot (2). When the piston gets to the top, oil is squirted in and bursts into flame. The hot gases expand and push the piston down (3). When the piston goes up again, it pushes the spent gases out through the exhaust valve.(4).*

very tightly compressed, or pushed into a much smaller space than it filled before, it gets very hot. This heat sets fire to the diesel oil, which burns instantly, like a small explosion. The burning oil heats the air and forces it to expand again to push the piston down and thus drive the engine.

Many RAILROADS began using diesel engines after World War II. European railroads badly damaged in the war took the opportunity to modernize their engines and replaced the old steam locomotives with diesel ones. Diesel engines were first used regularly on the railroads of the United States in the 1930s. Today, diesel-electric locomotives are in use all over the world. In these engines, the diesel motor is used to make electricity. The electricity then drives the train.

Digestion

Digestion is the way in which the food we eat is broken down into substances that can be used by the body. It takes place in the digestive tract, or *alimentary canal*, a long tube that runs from the mouth to the anus. Digestion starts in the mouth, where the teeth and special chemicals in the saliva help to break down the food. The food then passes down a

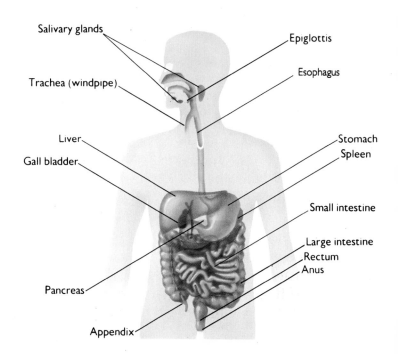

▶ *The human digestive tract. The alimentary canal in an adult is 25 to 35 ft. (8 to 10 m) long.*

tube called the *esophagus*. Muscles in the esophagus push and squeeze the food down into the STOMACH. There, acids and more chemicals help to turn the food into a creamy liquid. Then a muscle at the lower end of the stomach opens from time to time to release food into the small intestine.

Inside the small intestine, bile from the LIVER and juice from the pancreas help to break down the food still further. Much of it passes through the thin walls of the intestine into the bloodstream. The remainder goes into the large intestine. There, liquids and salts are absorbed until only solid waste material is left. Bacteria in the large intestine digest any remaining food products. The final waste product is passed out of the body as *feces*.

> Indigestion is a pain in the stomach which some people feel after eating. It may be caused by eating too fast or by the stomach producing too much acid. People who worry a lot tend to produce a lot of acid in their stomach. Some of this may rise up in their throat and cause a burning feeling. This acid may also damage the lining of the stomach and lead to stomach ulcers (open sores).

Dinosaur

The word *dinosaur* means "enormous lizard." These creatures lived between 65 and 225 million years ago, long before there were any people on earth. They developed from primitive REPTILES.

There were two main groups of dinosaurs—the *saurischians* and the *ornithischians*. The ornithischian dinosaurs were all plant-eaters and most of them moved on all fours. Some of these, like *Stegosaurus* and *Triceratops*, were large and lumbering, but had bony armor to protect them from the teeth and claws of the great meat-eating dinosaurs.

The saurischian group contained both plant-eaters and meat-eaters. The plant-eaters included the largest dinosaurs, the biggest of which scientists are calling "*Ultrasaurus*." The remains of this creature are incomplete, but they include a huge arm and shoulder girdle which show that it was about 26 ft. (8 m) tall at the shoulder—four times the height of a tall man! It probably weighed as much as 130 tons, even heavier than the blue whale. But these great beasts were harmless plant-eaters.

Perhaps the most famous of the dinosaurs are the great carnivores, or meat-eaters. *Tyrannosaurus*, which was 45 ft. (14 m) from snout to tail, stood on its hind legs. Its toes had claws as long as carving knives. Saber-like teeth—some nearly the length of

> During the age of the dinosaurs, 200 million years ago, the continents were all joined together in one great land mass. This is why dinosaurs have been found in every continent except Antarctica. About 300 different species of dinosaur have been found, but some of these are known only from a single tooth or a small bone fragment.

> The largest flying creature that we know about was a pterosaur that glided over parts of North America about 70 million years ago. Scientists calculate from its fossil remains that it had a wingspan of about 36 ft. (11 m)—more than half the distance from home plate to the pitcher's mound!

Triceratops

Tyrannosaurus

▲ *Many of the dinosaurs of the late Cretaceous Period could survive an attack from great meat-eaters such as* Tyrannosaurus. *The ostrich dinosaurs such as* Struthiomimus *could run very fast, while the ceratopsian* Triceratops *and the ankylosaur* Ankylosaurus *had strong armor and weapons such as spikes and clublike ends to their tails.*

a man's hand—lined the jaws. No flesh-eating beasts that ever lived on land were larger or more menacing than these monsters.

No one knows why all the dinosaurs, great and small, died out about 65 million years ago.

Discrimination

There are a few harmless forms of discrimination, but most kinds are bad. If you have a photographic club, anyone who is not interested in photography is excluded. That is harmless discrimination. The oldest form of discrimination is in religion. People who did not belong to the popular religion were punished. For example, until 1829, Roman Catholics in Britain could not vote or sit in Parliament.

Other forms of discrimination are being fought today. One kind is *racism*—discriminating against people because of their race. In the United States blacks were discriminated against for many years. South African *apartheid* is a kind of discrimination.

Ankylosaurus

Struthiomimus

Robinson

Another form of discrimination is by sex. In some countries, women are still barred from some jobs just because they are women.

Disease

Diseases make us ill. Some diseases are caused by BACTERIA, or germs, that invade our bodies. Other diseases are caused by VIRUSES. Sometimes diseases can be passed down from parents to their children in the genes that they are born with.

Our bodies fight against diseases through our immune systems. Special CELLS, such as white blood cells, fight the invading organisms. Our bodies also produce antibodies to fight diseases such as measles and chicken pox. These antibodies stay in our systems when we catch these diseases and prevent us from having the same diseases again. This means that we are immune to these diseases.

Doctors have developed many ways of helping us fight diseases with drugs and inoculations.

HOW DISEASES ARE SPREAD

Bacteria and viruses are often spread when we cough or sneeze.

Hands should always be washed thoroughly before preparing food.

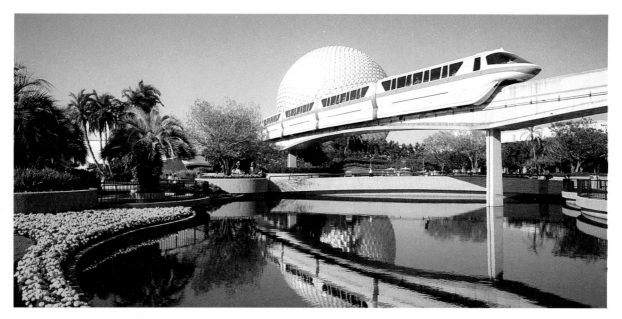

▲ *A monorail at the Epcot Center at Disney World amusement park in Orlando, Florida. Walt Disney opened the first of his parks, Disneyland, in California in 1955.*

▲ *Walt Disney, shown here with his most famous creation, Mickey Mouse, began as a commercial artist and made the first of his short films with sound,* Steamboat Willie, *in 1928.*

Disney, Walt

Walt Disney (1901–1967) was an American filmmaker best known for his cartoons and films for children. Disney characters, especially Mickey Mouse and Donald Duck, are famous all over the world. Walt Disney began his work in the 1920s. His cartoon artists, or animators, produced characters and settings that moved realistically. Full-length Disney cartoon features such as *Snow White and the Seven Dwarfs*, *Pinocchio*, and *Bambi* are still popular everywhere.

Distillation

When water boils, it turns into steam. When the steam cools, it turns back into water again. the steam from a boiling pot *condenses* into drops of water when it hits a cool window. But the water on the window is not quite the same as the water in the kettle. It. is *pure* water. When salt seawater is boiled, pure fresh water condenses from the steam. The salt is left behind in the boiler. This boiling and cooling of liquids to make them pure is called distilling. An apparatus used for distilling is called a still. Large stills are used in some places to turn seawater into fresh water.

Distillation is often used to separate liquids that are mixed together. The mixture is heated, and the

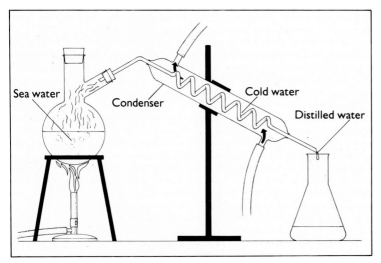

◄ *To distill water in a simple laboratory experiment, the water in the flask is heated. Steam rises into the cold condenser. Cold water circulating around the condenser cools the steam, which turns back into a liquid and collects as distilled water in the beaker.*

liquid that boils at the lowest temperature evaporates first and is separated from the other liquids. Then the liquid with the next lowest boiling point is condensed off, and so on. This is called *fractional distillation*, and it is used to separte the materials in the crude OIL that comes from oil wells. Distilling is also used in making alcoholic drinks such as whiskey.

> Two thousand years ago, Greek sailors made drinking water from seawater by distillation. They boiled seawater and hung sponges in the steam. Then they squeezed pure distilled water out of the sponges.

District of Columbia

The District of Columbia is the site of the city of WASHINGTON. It has been the capital of the United States since 1800. Because it is under the control of the Federal Government, it is the only part of the country that does not belong to any state. All the important offices of the government are here: the WHITE HOUSE, where the president lives; the CONGRESS, where the House of Representatives and the Senate meet; and the Supreme Court. The Lincoln Memorial, the Washington Monument, and the Jefferson Memorial honor three great presidents.

The city was chosen as the capital by GEORGE WASHINGTON in 1791. To honor the first president, the city was named after him.

DISTRICT OF COLUMBIA

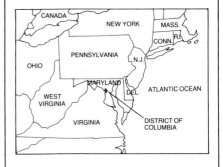

Population: 626,000
Area: 67 sq. miles (173 sq. km)
State flower: American beauty rose
State bird: Wood thrush
State tree: Scarlet oak
Founded: 1791

Djibouti

The small republic of Djibouti is in northeastern Africa beside the Red Sea. It is about the size of Massachusetts. Much of the country is desert, and

DJIBOUTI

Government: Republic
Capital: Djibouti
Area: 8,500 sq. miles (22,000 sq. km)
Population: 297,000
Language: French
Currency: Djibouti franc

▲ *The dodo was said to have a cry like a gosling. It laid one white egg in a nest of grass.*

there are few natural resources. About a third of the people are nomads who rear goats, cattle, and camels. The country's capital, also called Djibouti, is a port that handles exports from neighboring ETHIOPIA. Djibouti gained independence from France in 1977.

Dodo

About 400 years ago Dutch explorers landed on Mauritius, a lonely island in the Indian Ocean. They found doves, fish, and large flocks of birds as big and as fat as turkeys. These birds had no true wings and could not fly. In time, people called them dodos, from the Portuguese word *doudo*. This word means "simpleton" or stupid person.

Sailors quickly learned that dodos were good to eat. Ships that visited Mauritius sailed off with holds full of salted dodo meat. Rats and dogs from the ships started eating dodo eggs and chicks.

By the 1690s, all the dodos were dead. Only drawings, bones, and one stuffed bird remained.

Dog

People have been keeping dogs for perhaps 10,000 years. Most dogs are kept as pets, but some do useful work like herding sheep or guarding buildings.

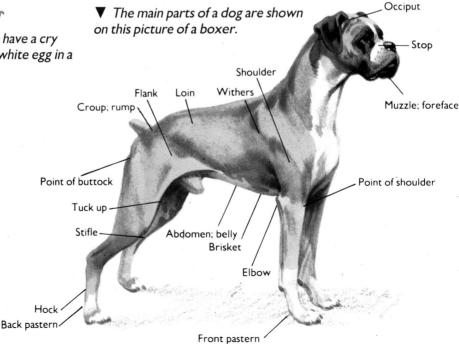

▼ *The main parts of a dog are shown on this picture of a boxer.*

Occiput
Stop
Muzzle; foreface
Shoulder
Withers
Loin
Flank
Croup; rump
Point of shoulder
Point of buttock
Tuck up
Stifle
Abdomen; belly
Brisket
Elbow
Hock
Back pastern
Front pastern

The first dog was probably descended from a WOLF and looked much like a wolf. Today there are more than 100 breeds of dog of many colors, shapes, and sizes. The St. Bernard is the largest breed. A St. Bernard may weigh nearly twice as much as a man. The Yorkshire terrier is one of the smallest dogs. A fully grown Yorkshire terrier may weigh less than a small jar of jelly.

Most of the modern breeds of dog were developed to be good at special kinds of work. Airedales and other terriers make fine rat hunters. Labrador retrievers bring back ducks shot by hunters and also make excellent guide dogs for blind people. Collies round up sheep. Dachshunds were once used for hunting badgers. Dobermans are ferocious guard dogs.

All puppies are born blind and helpless, and at first feed only on their mother's milk. But small dogs are fully grown in a year or so. Most kinds of dog live for about 12 years.

Dogs are nearsighted and can see only a few of the colors we can see. But a dog's sense of smell is thousands of times better than ours. Customs officers use specially trained dogs to sniff out illegal drugs. It is not necessary to open cases or crates—one sniff is enough for a dog, even if the drugs are packed in metal containers.

Doll

Children all over the world play with dolls. Dolls may be made of wood, china, plastic, or many other substances. The very first doll may have been just a forked twig that looked a bit like a human being. Homemade dolls can cost nothing, but doll collectors pay a lot of money for rare old dolls.

Dolphin and Porpoise

Dolphins are small whales. Although they never leave the sea, they are mammals. They breathe air and are warm-blooded. They have sharp teeth, and their heads end in beaklike mouths. Porpoises, close relatives of the dolphins, have no beak and the front of the head is rounded. Because the dolphin is a friendly creature, it has been well known since ancient times. Dolphins are intelligent and communicate with each other by means of whistles and clicks. Tame dolphins can learn many tricks.

▶ *Dolphins and porpoises are small whales. The bottle-nosed dolphin has a shorter, more upturned beak than the common dolphin.*

Common dolphin

Bottle-nosed dolphin

Dome

▲ *Domes, large and small, decorate the church of Santa Maria della Salute in Venice. The word dome comes from the Latin* doma, *meaning "roof" or "house."*

Domes are roofs like giant upturned mixing bowls. Some domes are made from bricks or stones. Other domes are made of concrete, steel, or plastic. Domed roofs cover famous churches such as St. Sophia in Istanbul, St. Peter's in Rome, and St. Paul's Cathedral in London, and non-religious buildings such as the Capitol in Washington. The world's largest dome is the Louisiana Superdome in New Orleans. It is as wide as the length of two football fields.

The Romans were the great dome builders. In A.D. 112 they built the Pantheon in Rome. Its dome is 142 ft. (43 m) in diameter and 142 ft. (43 m) high.

▼ *The Domesday Book recorded who owned land, how much land they owned, how many people worked the land, how many animals they owned, and how many pastures, mills, and fish ponds they had.*

Domesday Book

Twenty years after the Norman Conquest of England, William the Conqueror ordered that a great survey of property owners in England should be made. It was called the Domesday Book (or Doomsday), because it spared no one and there was no appeal from it. William wanted to find out how much land people held so that he could be sure that he was getting all the taxes that were due him. The survey was completed in 1086 and can be seen in the Public Record Office in London.

Dominica

This small island country in the Caribbean Sea was a British colony until it became independent in 1978. The main products are bananas, coconuts, and citrus fruits.

Dominican Republic

The Dominican Republic occupies the larger part of the island of Hispaniola in the Caribbean Sea. The rest of the island is occupied by Haiti. The main crop is sugar. About 75 percent of the people are of mixed black and white descent. Most of them live and work on farms.

Donkey

Donkeys are small and sturdy relatives of the HORSE. They are descended from the wild asses of Africa. A donkey has a large head with long ears. It has a short mane, and its tail ends in a tuft of hair.

Donkeys are sure-footed and can carry heavy loads over rough ground. They have long been used as pack animals and are still at work in southern Europe, North Africa, Asia, and Latin America.

DOMINICA

Government: Republic
Capital: Roseau
Area: 290 sq. miles (751 sq. km)
Population: 74,000
Language: English
Currency: East Caribbean dollar

DOMINICAN REPUBLIC

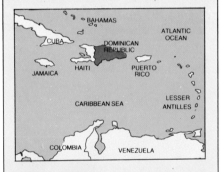

Government: Republic
Capital: Santo Domingo
Area: 18,816 sq. miles (48,734 sq. km)
Population: 6,200,000
Language: Spanish
Currency: Peso

◀ *Donkeys can carry very heavy loads for their size. They are patient and hardworking, and have been used as pack animals for centuries.*

▶ *One of the best known legendary dragons was the one said to have been slain by St. George, the patron saint of England. The story inspired this painting by Paolo Uccello.*

When we read about Sir Francis Drake's exploits, it is hard to imagine how small his ships were. When he set out to pillage Spanish possessions in the West Indies, his two ships weighed just 71 tons and 25 tons. The *Golden Hind*, in which he sailed around the world, was a large merchant ship of its day—it displaced about 100 tons. The *John F. Kennedy* aircraft carrier displaced 87,000 tons.

Dragon

Dragons are storybook monsters, but once many people believed that they really lived. Artists showed them as huge snakes or lizards with wings of skin and terrifying claws. They were supposed to breathe fire and swallow people and animals whole.

Fighting dragons called for great bravery. Legends tell how Hercules, St. George, and other heroes killed these evil monsters.

Not everyone thought dragons were wicked. The Chinese looked upon the creatures as gods.

Drake, Francis

Sir Francis Drake (about 1540–1596) was a sea captain who helped to make England a great sea power. In the 1570s, he led sea raids against Spanish ships and ports in the Caribbean Sea. He also became the first Englishman to sail around the world. In 1588, he helped to destroy the Spanish Armada.

▲ *Sir Francis Drake got his first command as captain of a ship at the age of 24.*

Drawing

Drawings are pictures or designs, usually made as lines with pencil, pen, or some similar material other than paint.

Drawing has been a natural human activity since prehistoric times, when people began to express

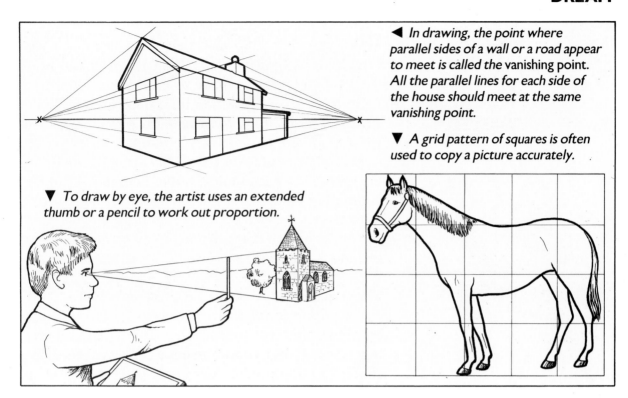

◄ In drawing, the point where parallel sides of a wall or a road appear to meet is called the vanishing point. All the parallel lines for each side of the house should meet at the same vanishing point.

▼ A grid pattern of squares is often used to copy a picture accurately.

▼ To draw by eye, the artist uses an extended thumb or a pencil to work out proportion.

their thoughts and ideas on the stone walls of caves. All children draw naturally. Many famous artists have included drawings in their best work. Some drawings are very precise and realistic. Every detail is picked out. In others, a powerful effect is produced by using very few lines and little detail. LEONARDO DA VINCI made scientific drawings and sketches for his paintings. Other painters who were also expert at drawing include Pieter Bruegel (the Elder), Paul Cézanne, and Pablo PICASSO.

Dream

Dreams occur when our brains are active while we are asleep. Some dreams are of everyday occurrences. Others may be just a series of jumbled images. On waking, we may or may not remember what we have dreamed. A frightening dream is called a nightmare.

We do not know exactly why people dream. Dreams may be sparked off by indigestion or similar physical cause, such as a cramped sleeping position. External noises may also cause dreams. Some dreams are very common. These include dreams of falling, or being chased, or of lakes or water.

▼ A profile of an armored warrior drawn by Leonardo da Vinci in about 1480. Leonardo did numerous sketches and studies from nature.

▲ Foxgloves are still cultivated for the drug digitalis, which is used in the treatment of heart disease.

Drug

Drugs are chemicals that affect the way the body works. Doctors give drugs to patients to help them fight disease. Antibiotics attack certain kinds of germs. These drugs help to cure people suffering from pneumonia and other illnesses. Drugs like aspirin help to deaden pain. The strongest painkillers are called anesthetics. Some people need drugs containing VITAMINS or other substances their bodies must have.

Certain drugs come from plants or animals. For instance, the foxglove gives us a drug called digitalis. This makes weak hearts beat more strongly. Many other drugs are made from MINERALS.

Some people take drugs such as cocaine, cannabis, or alcohol just because they give a pleasant feeling. Some of these drugs can be addictive (habit-forming) and cause illness or even death.

Drum

Drums are the most important of those MUSICAL INSTRUMENTS that are played by being struck. The sound is made by hitting a tightly stretched sheet of skin or plastic called a drumhead. A kettledrum has one drumhead stretched over a metal basin. A bass drum or a snare drum has two drumheads, one across each end of a large open "can."

▼ Tribal drums were once used in Africa to send messages in a drum code from village to village. Today they are used chiefly for ceremonial occasions.

Duck

These web-footed water birds are related to swans and geese. Ducks look somewhat like small geese with short necks.

The two main groups of ducks are dabbling ducks and diving ducks. Dabbling ducks feed on the surface of the water. They may put most of their body under the water, but they do not dive. Dabbling ducks include the mallards that swim on pools and rivers in the northern half of the world. (Farmyard ducks were bred from mallards.) Other dabbling ducks include teal and widgeon, and the pretty wood duck.

Diving ducks dive completely underwater in their

Teal
female
male

Mandarin
female
male

female

Pintail
male

Shoveler
female
male

Mallard
male
female

Eider
female
male

hunt for food. Most diving ducks live at sea. These ducks include the eider duck from which we get eiderdown. Sawbills are also diving ducks. Their long, slim beaks have inside edges like the teeth of a saw. Sawbills are good at grasping fish. The long-tailed duck is a diving duck that can fly at 70 miles (112 km) an hour.

▲ *The best known of the surface-feeders, or dabbling ducks is the mallard. The teal is another suface-feeder and is the smallest European species. The shoveler is characterized by its spoon-shaped bill. The male pintail has a long pointed tail, and the eider duck gives us the soft breast feathers known as eiderdown. The mandarin originated in China and is now found wild in other parts of the world.*

Dye

Dyes are substances that people use to color TEX-TILES and other materials. Some dyes come from plants. Cochineal, a red dye, comes from the cochineal insect. Most dyes are now made from chemicals. To dye an object, dip it in water containing dissolved dye. If the dye is *fast*, the object will keep its dyed color no matter how often you wash it.

Eagle

Eagles are large birds of prey. Most hunt small mammals and birds. Some catch fish or reptiles. The harpy eagle and the monkey-eating eagle catch monkeys. Each of these great birds measures more than 6 ft. (2 m) across its outspread wings. These eagles are the largest in the world.

Many eagles soar high above the ground. Others perch on a tree or rock. When an eagle sees its prey, it swoops suddenly and pounces. It seizes its prey with its sharp claws and tears off pieces of flesh with its strong, hooked beak.

The short-toed eagle, below and left, has white underparts. The booted eagles, left, show the light and dark forms of the bird. The bald eagle is the symbol of the United States.

Booted eagle

Short-toed eagle

Bald eagle

Ear

Our ears help us to hear and to keep our balance. Each ear has three main parts. These are the outer ear, middle ear, and inner ear.

The outer ear is the part we can see, and the tube leading from it into the head. Sounds reach the outer ear as vibrations, or waves, in the air. The cup-like shape of the ear collects these sound waves and sends them into the tube.

Next, the sound waves reach the middle ear.

Here, the waves make the *eardrum* move to and fro. This is the thin "skin" across the entrance of the middle ear. The moving eardrum sets tiny bones vibrating in the middle ear.

The vibrations travel on into the inner ear. Here they make liquid in the *cochlea* move. The cochlea looks like a snail's shell. The nerves inside it turn vibrations into messages that travel to your brain. The inner ear also has three hollow loops containing liquid. These loops send signals to the brain to help you keep your balance.

Ears are delicate and easily damaged. Hitting or poking into an ear can cause injury and may lead to DEAFNESS.

> If you spin around quickly and stop suddenly, the liquid in the hollow loops in your inner ear keeps on spinning for a while. The nerve cells in your ear send confusing messages to your brain, and you feel dizzy. The dizziness ends when the liquid in the loops stops moving.

◀ *This picture shows the main parts of the outer, middle, and inner ear. The eustachian tube helps to keep air pressure the same on both sides of the eardrum.*

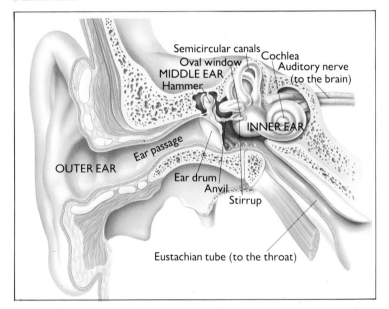

Semicircular canals
Oval window — Cochlea
MIDDLE EAR — Auditory nerve
Hammer — (to the brain)
INNER EAR
Ear passage
OUTER EAR
Ear drum
Anvil
Stirrup
Eustachian tube (to the throat)

Earth

Our Earth is the fifth largest of the PLANETS that move around the SUN. Seen from space, the Earth looks like a giant ball. Land and WATER cover the surface, and AIR surrounds the Earth. (See pages 218–219.)

Earthquake

In some places, buildings sometimes topple over because the ground starts trembling. This trembling is called an earthquake. About half a million earthquakes happen every year. Most are so weak that

Continued on page 220.

> **FAMOUS EARTHQUAKES**
> **Shensi Province, China, 1556:** Over 800,000 people perished—more than in any other earthquake.
> **Lisbon, Portugal, 1755:** About 60,000 people died, and shocks were felt as far away as Norway.
> **San Francisco, 1906:** An earthquake and the fires it caused destroyed the center of the city.
> **Kwanto Plain, Japan, 1923:** Some 570,000 buildings collapsed. This was the costliest earthquake ever when measured by damage to property.
> **Lebu, Chile, 1977:** The strongest earthquake shock ever recorded.

EARTH

As far as we know, the Earth is the only planet that supports life. Our world is a medium-sized planet, orbiting a star (the Sun) along with eight other planets. What makes our Earth unique are its atmosphere and its water. Together, they make possible a rich variety of animal and plant life. Seen from space, Earth can look mostly covered by ocean, wreathed in swirling clouds. Land covers only about one quarter of the planet's surface. Beneath the surface is an intensely hot, dense core.

If the Earth were the size of a basketball, the highest land masses such as the Himalayas would be no higher than a coat of paint on the ball. The deepest ocean trenches would be almost invisible scratches in the paint.

Although the Earth is between 4 and 5 billion years old, no rocks that old have ever been found. It is thought that the Earth's original rocks have all been worn away. Rocks found in the United States have been dated at about 3,800,000,000 years old.

EARTH'S VITAL STATISTICS

Age: about 4.6 billion years
Weight: about 6,000 million million tons.
Diameter: from Pole to Pole through the Earth's center: 7,900 miles (12,719 km); across the Equator through the Earth's center: 7,927 miles (12,757 km)
Circumference: around the poles: 24,860 miles (40,007 km); around the Equator: 24,903 miles (40,076 km)
Area of water: about 139,346,000 sq. miles (361 million sq. km) – 71 percent
Area of land: about 57,514,000 sq. miles (149 million sq km) – 29 percent
Volume: 4,440,064 million cu. miles (1,084,000 million cubic km)

INSIDE THE EARTH

Core Mantle Crust

The Earth's **outer core** lies below the mantle and above the inner core. It is 1,400 miles (2,240 km) thick. The outer core is made mainly of metals, under enormous pressure and so hot they are molten (melted). Four-fifths of it may be iron and nickel. The rest is probably silicon.

The **inner core** is a solid ball, about 1,516 miles (2,440 km.) across. Like the outer core, it may be made mainly of iron and nickel. The core temperature is 6,692°F (3,700°C) and the pressure there is 1,900 tons per sq. inch (3,800 tons per sq. cm).

The **mantle** lies beneath the crust and above the outer core. Nearly 1,400 miles (2,900 km) thick, the mantle is made up of hot rocks. Temperature and pressure here are lower than in the core. Even so, much of the mantle rock is semi-molten.

The **crust** is the Earth's solid outer layer. It is up to 20 miles (30 km) beneath mountains, but only 3³⁄₄ miles (6 km) thick under the oceans. Its rocks float on the denser rocks of the mantle.

◄ *The Earth photographed from space. Cloud "swirls" are depressions—areas of low atmospheric pressure where warm tropical air meets cold polar air. Such views help weather experts to plot the paths of hurricanes and so give warning of dangerous storms. Astronauts see the Earth outlined by a black sky.*

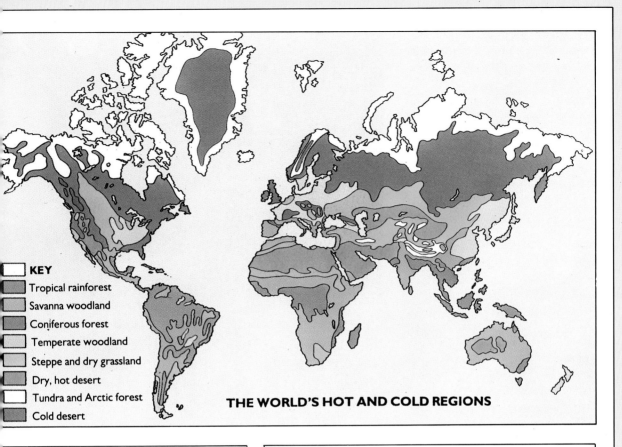

KEY

- Tropical rainforest
- Savanna woodland
- Coniferous forest
- Temperate woodland
- Steppe and dry grassland
- Dry, hot desert
- Tundra and Arctic forest
- Cold desert

THE WORLD'S HOT AND COLD REGIONS

WORLD FACTS AND FIGURES

Highest mountain: Everest (Asia) 29,028 ft. (8,848 m)

Longest river: Nile (Africa) 4,145 miles (6,670 km)

Greatest ocean depth: Marianas Trench (Pacific Ocean) 36,161 ft. (11,022 m)

Largest desert: Sahara (Africa) 3,243,000 sq. miles (8,400,000 sq. km)

Largest ocean: Pacific 69,866,000 sq. miles (181,000,000 sq. km)

Highest navigated lake: Titicaca (South America) 12,500 ft. (3,810 m) above sea level

Largest lake: Caspian Sea (Asia) 169,380 sq. miles (438,695 sq. km)

Highest waterfall: Angel Falls (Venezuela, South America) 3,230 ft. (979 m)

Hottest place: Al'Aziziyah in Libya, where 136°F (58°C) was recorded in 1922

Coldest place: Vostock, Antarctica, where -128.6°F (-89.2°C) was recorded in 1983

Wettest place: Mt. Waialeale, Hawaii, with 460 inches (11,680 mm) of rainfall a year

Driest place: Atacama Desert, Chile, with an average rainfall of only 0.76 mm a year

HOW MOUNTAINS ARE FORMED

Fold mountains (below right) are thrown up when huge forces buckle rock layers into giant wrinkles. The Rocky Mountains and the Andes were formed in this way when the Earth's crustal plates collided. Some rocks were folded over onto others, and over millions of years, a new mountain range was born. Other kinds of mountains are formed when faults (breaks) in the Earth's crust take place.

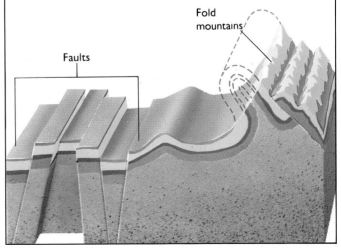

Fold mountains

Faults

For more information turn to these articles: CONTINENTS; DESERT; GEOGRAPHY; GEOLOGY; ISLAND; LAKE; MOUNTAIN; OCEAN; RIVER; SOLAR SYSTEM; VOLCANO; WEATHER.

EARTHWORM

▶ *A devasting earthquake in Alaska in 1964 was followed by a tsunami (tidal wave) that was almost as destructive.*

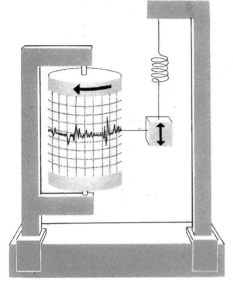

▲ *A seismograph shows earth tremors as wriggles in a line traced on a turning drum. A tremor vibrates the weight that holds the tracer.*

only special instruments called *seismographs* show that they have happened. Only one earthquake in 500 does any damage. But some earthquakes can cause terrible damage and suffering. Three-quarters of a million people are thought to have died when an earthquake hit the northeastern Chinese city of Tangshan in 1976.

Small tremors can happen when VOLCANOES erupt, when there is a landslide, or when the roof of an underground cave falls in. The largest earthquakes occur when one huge piece of the Earth's crust slips suddenly and crashes against another piece. This slipping may take place deep underground. But the shock travels up through the crust and sets the surface quaking.

A seabed earthquake may set off a huge ocean wave called a *tsunami*. These can rise higher than a house and travel faster than the fastest train. They occur most often in the Pacific Ocean.

Earthworm *See* Worm

Easter

Easter is the day when Christians remember the resurrection of JESUS. Most Christians celebrate Easter on the Sunday following the first full moon that occurs after the first day of spring in the northern half of the world.

We have eggs at Easter because they tell us of the new life that returns in nature at about this time. People have been exchanging eggs at Easter since ancient times. The Egyptians and Persians dyed eggs and gave them to their friends. The Persians believed that the Earth had hatched from a giant egg.

Echo

An echo is a SOUND bounced back from a wall or some other object. Sound travels at a known, fixed speed, so we can use echoes to find how far away some objects are. A ship's SONAR uses echoes to find the depth of the sea. Echoes help BATS to fly in the dark. RADAR depends on echoes from radio signals.

▲ *When you hear an echo, you hear the sound twice, or more. This is because the sound waves that reach your ears also bounce off nearby cliffs or walls. These waves reach your ears a second or two later, and you hear an echo.*

Eclipse

An eclipse happens when the shadow of one planet or moon falls on another. If the shadow hides all of the planet or moon, there is a total eclipse. If the shadow hides only a part, there is a partial eclipse.

The only eclipses you can easily see without a telescope take place when the Sun, Moon, and Earth are in line. When the Earth lies between the Sun and the Moon, the Earth's shadow falls on the Moon. This is an eclipse of the Moon. When the Moon lies between the Earth and the Sun, the Moon's shadow falls on a part of the Earth. An eclipse of the Sun, or solar eclipse, can be seen from that part.

The center of the shadow of a solar eclipse is called the *umbra*. It is a dark circle only about 170 miles (270 km) across. Inside the umbra, the eclipse is complete—the Moon completely hides the Sun. Around the umbra is a lighter shadow about 1,865 miles (3,000 km) across, in which part of the Sun can be seen.

▼ *A solar eclipse is caused as the Moon's shadow falls on the Earth, and a lunar eclipse as the Earth's shadow falls on the Moon. Only the umbra—the dark middle part of the Moon's shadow—is shown for a solar eclipse.*

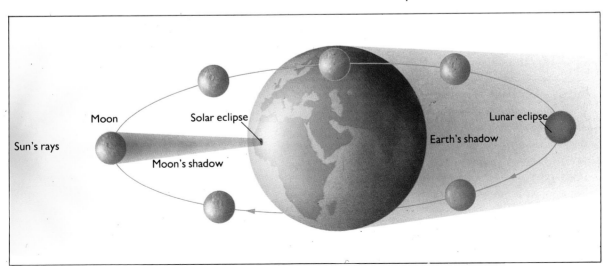

Sun's rays — Moon — Solar eclipse — Moon's shadow — Earth's shadow — Lunar eclipse

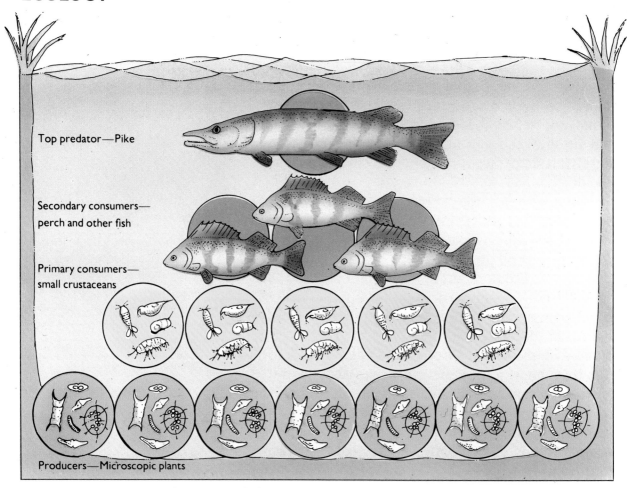

Top predator—Pike

Secondary consumers—
perch and other fish

Primary consumers—
small crustaceans

Producers—Microscopic plants

▲ *The food pyramid above gives some idea of just how much food it takes to keep the creatures in a pond alive and healthy. About 2,200 lbs. (1,000 kg) of plant life is needed to feed the animals that feed the fish that in turn feed just 2 lb. (1 kg) of pike.*

The introduction of animals from foreign lands can have harmful effects on the balanced ecology of a place. In 1850, three pairs of European rabbits were turned loose in Australia. With no natural enemies, the rabbits multiplied so quickly that they became a plague to farmers. Only the introduction of a disease that was fatal to rabbits halted the plague.

Ecology

Ecology is the study of living things and their surroundings. Scientists called ecologists try to find out how living things and their surroundings affect each other. Ecology shows us that most plants and animals can live only in a special set of surroundings such as a pond, field, forest, or desert. Within each place live plants that are suited to a certain soil, temperature, and so on. All the animals living there eat the plants, or each other. So the plants and animals are linked in what ecologists call a food web. If some kinds die out, those that eat them lose their food and may die too.

Everything in the world changes. Human inventions and discoveries are causing rapid changes. Sometimes the air is being filled with poisons; waterways are being polluted. Ecologists can help us to use the inventions and discoveries without making the world sick.

Economics

Economics is the study of people's needs, such as food, clothes, and housing, and the ways in which people fill these needs. Economists study trade and money, and the ways in which a community's needs can be met. No country has enough resources to supply all the things that its people want. It has to decide the best way of using the resources that it has. Many economists believe that deciding how to economize (spend less) is the most important decision nations must make.

Ecuador

Ecuador is a country slightly bigger than Colorado, but fewer than ten million people live there. It is in northwestern South America and lies on the equator. Its name is Spanish for *equator*. More than half of the people live in the high mountain valleys where sheep and llamas graze. The chief products are bananas, oil, coffee, rice, and sugar. The Galapagos Islands, 600 miles (960 km) off the Pacific coast of South America, belong to Ecuador.

Ecuador has been torn by many rebellions in its history and has been ruled by civilian and military dictatorships. Since 1979, the country has been governed by a democratic civilian government.

▲ Business as usual on the Tokyo stock exchange. The buying and selling of shares is a basic part of the capitalist economic system.

ECUADOR

Government: Republic
Capital: Quito
Area: 109,483 sq. miles (283,561 sq. km)
Population: 9,400,000
Language: Spanish
Currency: Sucre

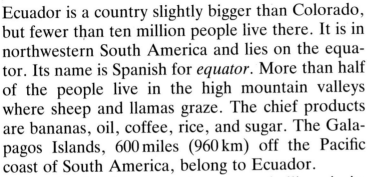

◄ A woman sells leeks and plantains in a market in Ecuador. Indians and mestizos (of mixed Indian and European ancestry) make up about 80 percent of the population.

▲ *In 1877, Edison produced a hand operated "phonograph" that made recordings on tinfoil cylinders.*

▶ *Edward VIII and Mrs. Simpson, the American divorcee for whom he abdicated (gave up the throne).*

▲ *Two English kings named Edward: Edward the Confessor ruled from 1042 to 1066, before the Norman conquest. Edward VII was the eldest son of Queen Victoria.*

Edison, Thomas

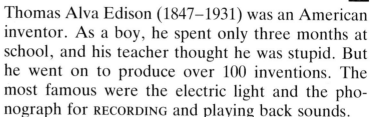

Thomas Alva Edison (1847–1931) was an American inventor. As a boy, he spent only three months at school, and his teacher thought he was stupid. But he went on to produce over 100 inventions. The most famous were the electric light and the phonograph for RECORDING and playing back sounds.

Edwards (Kings)

Nine kings of England were named Edward. Edward "The Confessor" (about 1002–1066) founded Westminster Abbey. Edward I (1239–1307) brought Wales under English rule. Edward II (1248–1327) was the first English Prince of Wales. Edward III (1312–1337) began the Hundred Years' War. Edward IV (1442–1483) took the crown from Henry VI in the Wars of the Roses. Edward V (1470–1483) was murdered in the Tower of London. Edward VI (1537–1553) reigned as a boy for only six years. Edward VII (1841–1910) was Prince of Wales for 60 years. Edward VIII (1894–1972) gave up the throne to marry Mrs. Simpson, a divorced American.

Eel

Eels are long, slim fish with fins like narrow ribbons. Some eels have tiny scales. Some are covered with slime. European and American freshwater eels swim thousands of miles to spawn far out in the

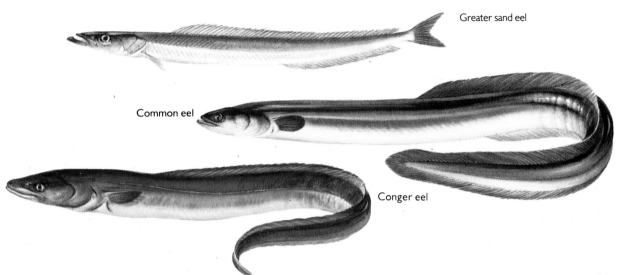

Greater sand eel

Common eel

Conger eel

Atlantic Ocean. Then they die. The tiny, transparent young that hatch look nothing like their parents. These babies find their way all the way back to their parents' homes in America and Europe. There, they travel up rivers and streams. The young eels grow up in fresh water and stay there until they are ready for their long journey back across the Atlantic.

▲ *Eels look like snakes, but are actually fish. The common eel lives in lakes and rivers, but returns to the sea to breed. The conger eel and the greater sand eel both live in the sea.*

Egg

An egg is a female CELL that will grow into a new young plant or animal. Most eggs grow only if they are joined with, or fertilized by, male cells. In most MAMMALS, the fertilized eggs grow inside the mother's body, but birds and most reptiles and fish lay eggs that contain enough food to help the developing young grow inside the egg.

Egg

Egypt

Modern Egypt dates from A.D. 642 when Egypt was conquered by Muslim soldiers from Arabia. Egypt is now a Muslim, mainly Arab, country. It has about 50 million people, more than any other nation in Africa. No other African city is as large as Cairo, Egypt's capital. But Egyptians still depend upon the waters of the River NILE, which made Egypt great.

In 1979, Egypt signed a peace treaty with ISRAEL. This agreement was disliked by other Arab states, leaving Egypt isolated from its Arab neighbors.

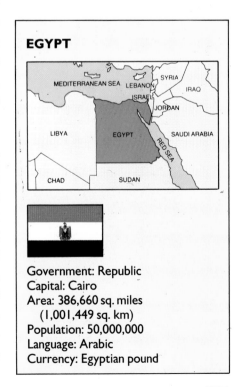

EGYPT

Government: Republic
Capital: Cairo
Area: 386,660 sq. miles
　(1,001,449 sq. km)
Population: 50,000,000
Language: Arabic
Currency: Egyptian pound

Egypt, Ancient

About 5,000 years ago, the ancient Egyptians began to build one of the world's first great civilizations. For the next 2,500 years, ancient Egypt was one of the strongest, richest nations on Earth.

The people who made Egypt great were short, slim, dark-skinned men and women with dark hair. They probably numbered no more than six million. Scarcely any of them lived in the hot sand and rock deserts that cover most of Egypt. Almost all the people settled by the River NILE, which runs from south to north across the land.

Each year, the river overflowed and left rich mud on nearby fields. Farmers learned to dig and plow the fields. They could grow two crops a year in the

▼ *A scene showing how the ancient Egyptians farmed by the Nile. They grew flax to make linen and grain for food. They also caught birds and fish, raised chickens, and grew produce in their gardens. In the picture, men are threshing wheat. In the foreground women are winnowing. Part of all produce was paid to the government as tax.*

warm, fertile soil. The farmers grew more than enough grain, fruit, and vegetables to feed themselves. The rest of the food helped to feed Egyptian craftsmen, miners, merchants, priests, noble families, and the PHARAOHS who ruled over the entire land.

Most Egyptians were poor and lived in mud-brick huts with palm-leaf roofs. Rich Egyptians lived in large, well-furnished houses and had meat and cakes to eat. They wore fine clothes and jewels.

The most splendid buildings in the land were tombs and temples. Thousands of workers toiled for years to build the mighty PYRAMIDS. In each such tomb, Egyptians would the place the mummy (preserved body) of a pharaoh. They believed the dead went on living, so they buried food and furniture beside each mummy. Thieves later emptied almost all the tombs. But the boy pharaoh TUTANKHAMUN'S tomb shows us what royal burials were like.

The dry Egyptian air has preserved HIERO-GLYPHICS written on fragile paper made from the papyrus plant. Paintings and hieroglyphics tell us a great deal about how the ancient Egyptians lived. They also left many fine statues.

In time, foreign armies using iron weapons defeated the Egyptians. Their land fell under foreign rule after 525 B.C.

▲ *The sphinx is an imaginary creature found in the folk tales of many ancient peoples. Egyptian sphinxes combined the body of a beast—usually a lion—with the head of the ruling pharaoh. The most famous sphinx is the one shown above. It guards the great pyramid of Khafre at Giza, 6 miles (10 km) from Cairo. It is 240 ft. (73 m) long and about 66 ft. (20 m) high. Unfortunately, the sphinx's nose is missing. It was used by soldiers for target practice.*

> Several times during the Twentieth Egyptian Dynasty, the workmen building a tomb for the pharaoh were not paid their food and other goods on time. The men went on strike. They marched to the temple where supplies were kept and sat down outside calling for bread. They soon got what they wanted, because it was unthinkable that the pharaoh's tomb should not be finished on time.

DWIGHT D. EISENHOWER

Thirty-fourth President 1953–1961
Born: Denison, Texas
Education: U.S. Military Academy,
    West Point, New York
Occupation: Army officer
Political Party: Republican
Buried: Eisenhower Center Chapel,
    Abilene, Kansas

SEE IT YOURSELF

Air has elasticity, too. It can be squeezed into a container, and the energy stored in it can be used to drive machines such as pneumatic drills and hammers. You can feel the elasticity of air by putting your thumb over the end of a bicycle pump and pushing the pump handle.

Einstein, Albert

Albert Einstein (1879–1955) was a great scientist who was born in Germany. His theory of relativity was a new way of looking at time, space, matter, and ENERGY. Einstein showed that a small amount of matter could be changed into a vast amount of energy. This made it possible for people to use NUCLEAR ENERGY.

Eisenhower, Dwight David

Dwight D. Eisenhower (1890–1969) was the 34th president of the United States. He served from 1953 to 1961. He was also a successful soldier. He was the commander of the Allied forces in WORLD WAR II. His most important job was the D-DAY invasion in 1944, when American and British soldiers landed in France to defeat the Germans. Later, he was head of NATO, a military union between the Western powers against the Soviet Union. As president, his biggest problems were with the Soviet Union. This was the Cold War, when the United States and the Soviet Union were fierce opponents. He had fewer problems at home. All through his presidency, the country prospered.

Elasticity

When you pull a rubber band, it stretches. When you let it go, it springs back to its original size. It is elastic—it has elasticity. If you drop a rubber ball, the part of the ball that hits the ground is flattened. Then the ball springs back into its original round shape. As this happens, the ball pushes on the ground and it jumps up—it bounces. The ball has elasticity.

Elasticity happens because the molecules that make up the elastic material like to stay at a certain distance from each other. If they are squeezed more tightly together, they immediately push apart. If they are pulled apart, they want to get together again. All solids and liquids have some elasticity. Even a steel ball bounces a little when it hits a concrete floor.

Electricity

Electricity is the kind of ENERGY that powers electric trains, vacuum cleaners, radios, television sets, and many more devices.

The electricity that we use flows through wires as electric CURRENT. Current flows when tiny particles called electrons jump between the ATOMS that make up the metal in the wire. Current can flow only if a wire makes a complete loop called a circuit. If a gap is made in the circuit, the current stops flowing. Switches are simply devices that open and close gaps in circuits.

BATTERIES produce electric current that can be used to start cars, light flashlight bulbs, and work radios. But most of the electricity we use is produced in POWER PLANTS. In a power plant GENERATOR, coils of wire are made to rotate between powerful magnets. This makes electric current flow through the coils of wire. This current then flows through other long wires to our homes.

In 1752, the American scientist and statesman Benjamin Franklin wondered whether lightning and thunder were caused by electricity. During a thunderstorm, he flew a kite with a metal tip joined to à silk string. He attached a key to the string at a point near the ground. In a few seconds, Franklin had the answer to his question. When he touched the key, there was a spark. He could *feel* the electricity. But don't try this; it is very dangerous!

▼ Electricity travels from a power station through a network of high-voltage power lines. It passes through transformers and substations, where the current is changed to the lower voltage used in homes and factories.

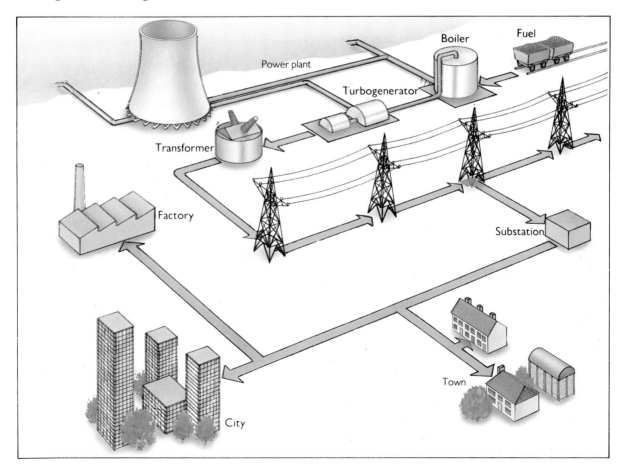

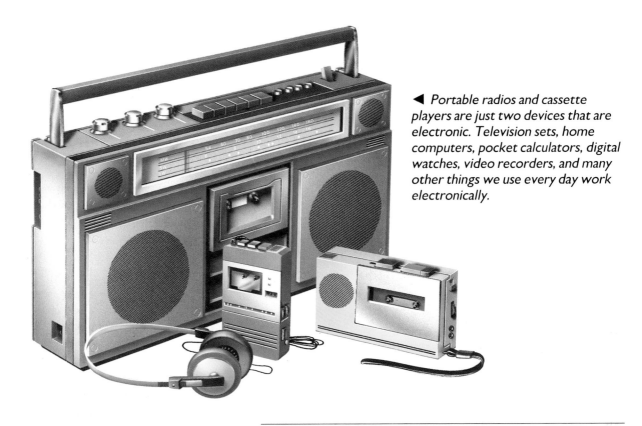

◄ *Portable radios and cassette players are just two devices that are electronic. Television sets, home computers, pocket calculators, digital watches, video recorders, and many other things we use every day work electronically.*

Electronics

Electronics is an important part of the study of ELECTRICITY. It deals with the way in which tiny particles called electrons flow through certain CRYSTALS, GASES, or a VACUUM. Electronic devices like TRANSISTORS and SILICON CHIPS are used in such things as COMPUTERS, RADAR, television sets, and radios. Electronics help us to see the smallest living things, to guide planes, and to do difficult sums instantly. Without electronics, space travel would be impossible.

▼ *This pellet of the element plutonium shines from the glow of its own radioactivity. Plutonium (Pu) does not occur in nature except in tiny quantities from the decay of Uranium-238.*

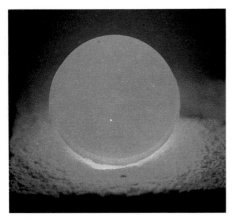

Element

Your own body and everything you see around you is composed (made up) of chemical ingredients called elements. In each element, all the ATOMS are of the same kind. You can join different elements to make more complicated substances called COMPOUNDS, but you cannot break an element into a simpler kind of substance.

Chemists have found more than 100 different

elements. Ninety-two of these occur naturally. Scientists have produced other elements in laboratories. At ordinary temperatures, some elements are *gases*, some are *liquids*, and some are *solids*.

OXYGEN is the most plentiful element on Earth. Half of the Earth's crust and most of your body is made of oxygen.

Elephant

Asiatic elephant

African elephant

Elephants are the largest living land animals. A big bull (male) elephant may stand twice as high as a man and weigh as much as seven family cars. An elephant has larger ears, thicker legs, a longer nose, and longer teeth than any other creature. Its skin is nearly as thick as the heel of a man's shoe.

Baby elephants stand no taller than big dogs. Elephants are fully grown after 20 years. They live almost as long as people.

Indian elephants can be trained to move heavy loads. African elephants are harder to tame. Many thousands have been killed just for the IVORY of their tusks. Today, most are protected by law.

▲ The African elephant has larger ears and tusks than the Indian, or Asiatic, elephant. It also has a different-shaped back.

▼ The African elephant protects the herd with an aggressive display—ears forward and trunk raised.

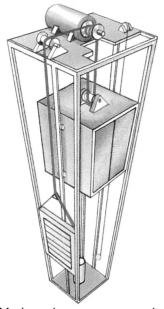

▲ *Modern elevators are complex machines, often controlled by computers. But all elevators have the basic parts shown in the diagram. The car is wound up and down by an electric motor. A counterweight at the other end of the steel cable balances the weight of the car. A safety rope connected to the car operates a governor. Should the car fall, the governor throws a switch which causes the car to grip the guide rails and stop.*

▼ *Escalators can move as fast as 13 ft. (4 m) a second. The steps are joined to a continuous, moving chain. At the end, the steps go underneath the escalator and back to the beginning.*

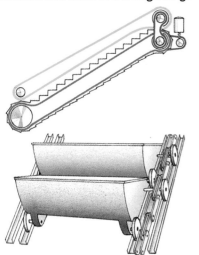

Elevators and escalators

Elevators and escalators are machines for transporting people or goods upstairs—or downstairs.

Elevators are metal cars like boxes that travel vertically in shafts. Their doors open and close automatically. They are used in many office and apartment buildings. Some elevators can travel at more than 500 ft. (150 m) per minute, There are many different types of elevator, but most are powered by electricity. All have important safety features in case of accident. The first elevators were invented in the 1800s. They were powered by steam, but were not very reliable. Electric elevators were introduced in the 1890s. The first completely automatic elevators were invented in the 1950s.

Escalators are moving stairways. As they reach the top or bottom, the steps flatten to let people on or off. They are used in department stores and malls, at airports, and at subway stations. The first escalator was installed in 1900. Today, they are used throughout the world.

El Greco

El Greco (1541–1614) was a Greek painter who was born on the island of Crete during the RENAISSANCE. His real name was Domenikos Theotokopoulos—El Greco simply means "the Greek." He soon left Crete and went to Venice. Later, he lived in Spain, in a town called Toledo. His paintings have strange, swirling compositions and bright colors.

Eliot, Thomas Stearns

T.S. Eliot (1888–1965) was a poet, playwright, and critic. Some say he was the most important poet of the 20th century. Though he was born in the United States, he spent most of his life in England. In 1927 he became a British citizen.

His most famous poem is called *The Waste Land.* In it, Eliot wrote of the need for people to have strong moral and religious beliefs. The poem is complex and combines references to myths, history, and literature, as well as scenes of modern life.

Elizabeth I

Elizabeth I (1533–1603) was a famous English queen. She never married, but she reigned for 45 years with the help of wise advisers. She worked for peace between quarreling religious groups, but had her rival, MARY QUEEN OF SCOTS, put to death. Elizabeth's seamen crushed the Spanish Armada and made England powerful at sea. Great English playwrights, poets, and scholars lived in her reign. People often call it "the Elizabethan Age."

▲ Elizabeth I reviews her troops at Tilbury before the arrival of the Spanish Armada. With the defeat of the Armada, England gained in wealth and confidence.

Elizabeth II

Elizabeth II (1926–   ) is Queen of the United Kingdom of Great Britain and Northern Ireland and head of the COMMONWEALTH. Her husband is the Duke of Edinburgh. Her eldest son is Charles, Prince of Wales.

EL SALVADOR

Government: Republic
Capital: San Salvador
Area: 8,122 sq. miles (21,041 sq. km)
Population: 5,000,000
Language: Spanish
Currency: Colon

▶ *Despite their political troubles, the people of El Salvador still enjoy their festivals.*

▼ *This photograph of Ralph Waldo Emerson was taken in 1876.*

El Salvador

El Salvador is Central America's smallest country, but it has more people per square mile than any other country in Central America. Most of the people are *mestizos* (of mixed Indian and European descent). Their main occupation is farming. Leading crops are coffee, cotton, corn, and sugar. The capital is San Salvador.

El Salvador has had several clashes with its neighbor Honduras, and there is a continuing struggle in El Salvador between government forces and left-wing guerrillas.

Emerson, Ralph Waldo

Ralph Waldo Emerson (1803–1882) was a critic and writer whose work was important for the development of many American thinkers and writers in the 1800s. He also wrote many poems.

He was born in Boston in a poor family. His father died when he was young, and two of his brothers also died young. Another was mad.

Emerson took his ideas from many sources, but he always wanted to show that men must be strong and not afraid to do what they believed in.

Emu

The ostrich is the only bird that is larger than this big Australian bird. An emu is as tall as a man, but not as heavy. Emu feathers are thick and dark. Its wings are small, and an emu cannot fly. But it can run as fast as a horse on its long, strong legs.

Emus eat leaves and insects. Big herds of emus sometimes attack farm crops.

Each female lays up to 10 green eggs on the ground. The male sits on the eggs and later guards the chicks.

Energy

Having energy means being able to do work. Mus-CLES and machines have mechanical energy—they can move loads. Energy exists in several forms. There are two main kinds—*potential energy* and *kinetic energy*. Potential energy is the energy of position—stored energy. For example, the water in a high dam has potential energy. Then, when the water falls through pipes and works turbines to make electricity, it has kinetic energy—energy of movement. Other forms of energy are electrical, heat, chemical, sound, radiant, and nuclear. These forms can be changed into each other. For example, the chemical energy of gasoline is turned into kinetic energy as it moves a car's pistons; to electri-cal energy in the car's generator to work the head-

▲ Emus are now rare in their native Australia, though they are being bred successfully in captivity.

▼ When an archer draws back a bow, he or she gives it a store of potential energy. As the arrow is released, the potential energy is turned into kinetic (moving) energy.

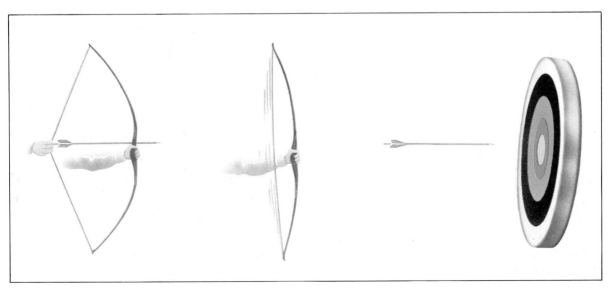

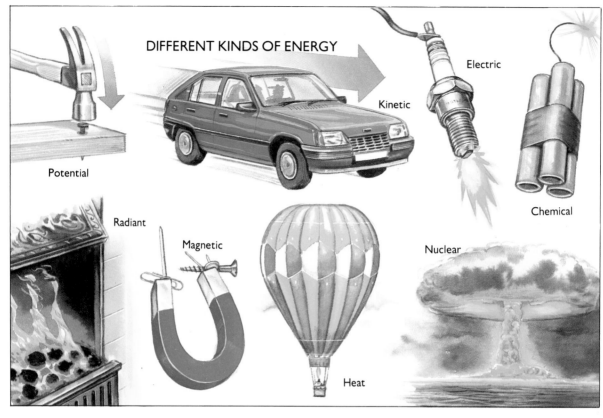

DIFFERENT KINDS OF ENERGY

Potential

Kinetic

Electric

Chemical

Radiant

Magnetic

Nuclear

Heat

▲ *Energy can exist in many forms. All forms of energy can do work.*

▼ *Stephenson's Rocket (1829) was the first locomotive to use steam power successfully as a means of fast travel.*

lights and sound the car's horn, and so on. At every stage, some energy is turned into heat.

Radiant energy from the Sun gives us most of our energy on Earth. Coal, oil, and natural gas—the fossil fuels—were formed from plants and animals that depended for their life on the Sun's light and warmth.

Engine

Engines are devices that change potential (stored) energy into useful energy that does work. People have used simple engines such as windmills and water wheels for hundreds of years.

In the 1700s, the STEAM ENGINE took over to drive everything from ships, trains, and cars to all kinds of factory machinery. Steam still drives many machines—such as the steam turbines in nuclear power plants.

INTERNAL COMBUSTION ENGINES—gasoline engines and DIESEL ENGINES—are easier to handle than steam engines and light enough to be fitted in aircraft. After them came JET and ROCKET engines.

Engineering

Engineers do a great many different types of jobs. Mining engineers find useful MINERALS and take them from the ground. Metallurgical engineers separate METALS from unwanted substances and make them usable. Chemical engineers use chemicals to make such things as explosives, paint, plastics, and soap. Civil engineers build bridges, tunnels, roads, railroads, ports, airports, and so on. Mechanical engineers make and use machines. They design JET ENGINES and factory machinery. Electrical engineers work with devices that produce and use electricity. Some specialize in building a particular type of GENERATOR. Others, such as those who design and build computers, are known as electronic engineers. Electronic engineers form the newest branch of electrical engineering. Power engineers maintain machinery in power plants. Most kinds of engineering fall into one or other of these groups.

▼ *Engineers design big machines such as this excavator to save time, labor, and cost. One such machine can do more work in an hour than a hundred men using hard tools could do in a day.*

The ancient Egyptians were the first real engineers. When the pyramids were being built about 2500 B.C., Egyptian workmen were already using tools such as the lathe. They smelted and cast metals. Their quarrying and stoneworking techniques were so advanced that they could fit blocks of stone weighing 2½ tons so closely together that a hair couldn't be passed between them.

▲ *As an island nation, the English have had a long association with the sea. This is a small fishing village in Yorkshire.*

England

England is the largest country in the UNITED KINGDOM of Great Britain and Northern Ireland. If Great Britain were divided into five equal parts, England would fill three of them. England's neighbors are Scotland and Wales, but most of England is surrounded by sea. Green fields spread over the plains and low hills that cover most of the country. In the north and west, there are mountains with moors and forests. Most English people live and work in big cities like London, Birmingham, Liverpool, and Manchester.

England gets its name from the Angles, a Germanic people who, like the Saxons, sailed to the island and settled there about 1,500 years ago.

English Language

More people speak English than any other language except Chinese. English is the main language spoken in the United Kingdom, Ireland, Australia, New Zealand, Canada, the United States, and some other countries. Altogether, more than 450 million people speak English as their everyday language. Another 100 million or more speak at least some English. Most English words come from old Anglo-Saxon, French, or Latin words.

ENGLAND

Area: 50,858 sq. miles
(131,722 sq. km)
Population: 49,000,000
Highest point: Scafell Pike 3,224 ft.
(982 m)
Greatest width: 322 miles (518 km)
North to south: 356 miles (570 km)
Longest rivers: Thames 216 miles
(348 km) Severn 211 miles
(338 km)
Largest lake: Windermere

Equator

The equator is an imaginary line around the world, halfway between the NORTH POLE and the SOUTH POLE. A journey around the equator covers 24,903 miles (40,076 km). The word "equator" comes from an old Latin word meaning "equalizer." The equator divides the world into two equal halves. The half north of the equator is called the Northern Hemisphere. The half south of the equator is the Southern Hemisphere. Distances north and south of the equator are measured in degrees of latitude. The equator has a latitude of 0 degrees.

On the equator, nights are always as long as days. At noon, the sun always shines from directly or almost directly overhead. So all places on the equator are warm all through the year.

Equatorial Guinea

Equatorial Guinea is a small country on the west African coast. The largest territory is on the mainland, and there are several offshore islands. The largest island is Bioko, which has the country's capital. Most of the people speak Spanish, for the country was a Spanish possession until 1968.

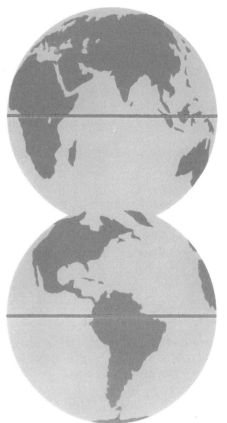

▲ Europe and North America both lie north of the equator; Australasia and much of South America lie south.

Ericson, Leif

Lief Ericson (11th century) was a Norse sailor who led what was probably the first European expedition to North America. According to old Norse stories, Leif first went ashore at a place where grapes were growing. He named it Vinland (Wineland). Some people think that Vinland was in northern Newfoundland.

Eskimo

Eskimos are hardy people who live in the cold, ARCTIC lands of Greenland, North America, and northeast Asia. They have slanting eyes, a wide flat face, and a short, thick body with short arms and legs. This shape helps to keep them warm in the cold, Arctic climate.

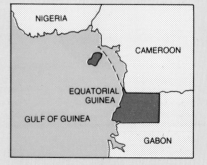

EQUATORIAL GUINEA

NIGERIA
CAMEROON
EQUATORIAL GUINEA
GULF OF GUINEA
GABON

Government: Republic
Capital: Malabo
Area: 10,832 sq. miles (28,055 sq. km)
Population: 350,000
Language: Spanish
Currency: Ekuele

Eskimos once wore only fur clothes. Some lived in tents in summer and built snow homes called igloos for the winter. They made bows and arrows and harpoons, and hunted seals, whales, fish, seabirds, and deer. Eskimos paddled skin BOATS and canoes called kayaks. Many Eskimos no longer lead this kind of life. They now live and work in towns. Eskimos call themselves by words that mean "people"—*Inuit* or *Yuit*.

► *Nomads in Eritrea, in northeastern Ethiopia. One of the poorest of Ethiopia's provinces, Eritrea has been torn by civil war and famine since the 1960s.*

ETHIOPIA

Government: Military
Capital: Addis Ababa
Area: 471,776 sq. miles
(1,221,900 sq. km)
Population: 43,000,000
Language: Amharic
Currency: Ethiopian dollar

Ethiopia

Ethiopia covers a huge area of the northeastern part of AFRICA. It was formerly called Abyssinia. Much of Ethiopia consists of high, cool tablelands. Here, Ethiopian farmers grow grain and coffee. Herdsmen wander over the hot deserts of the north and south. The RED SEA coast in the north is one of the hottest places on Earth. Among Africa's countries, only Egypt and Nigeria have more people. Most Ethiopians are Christian.

For years, Ethiopia has suffered from CIVIL WAR and drought. Famine is widespread, and there has been a worldwide campaign to raise money for relief and aid.

Europe

Europe is a peninsula sticking out from the western end of Asia. Some small peninsulas jut from the main one, and there are many offshore islands. Australia is the only continent smaller than Europe, but Europe holds more people than any continent except Asia.

European people have settled in the Americas, Australia, New Zealand, South Africa, and Siberia. European ideas and inventions helped shape the way of life of many people all around the world.

Mountains cross the countries of southern Europe. From west to east, there are the Pyrenees, Alps, Apennines, Balkans, Carpathians, Caucasus, and other ranges. The Caucasus has Mount Elbrus, Europe's highest peak.

In northern Europe, low mountains cover much of Iceland, Ireland, Scotland, Wales, Norway, and Sweden. Between the mountains of the north and south lies a great plain. Here flow Europe's longest rivers. The Volga, in the U.S.S.R., is the longest of them all.

All of Europe lies north of the hot tropics, and most of it lies south of the cold Arctic. So most of Europe does not have extremes of temperature. But Mediterranean lands have hot summers, and countries in the north and east have long, cold winters.

Shrubs and flowering plants grow in the far north. Next come the great northern forests of CONIFERS. Farther south lie most of Europe's farms and cities.

▲ Europe has more advantages for people than any other continent. It has scarcely any desert, and a greater proportion of the land can be farmed than in any other continent. It is rich in coal and iron, essential for industry. Its climate is seldom either too hot or too cold.

▼ Like much of Mediterranean Europe, Italy's coast has wide bays and rocky headlands. Behind lie volcanic mountains, and the hills cut into terraces for vineyards and olive groves.

EUROPE

ARCTIC OCEAN

Murmansk

Narvik

NORWEGIAN SEA

Arkhangelsk

KJØLEN MOUNTAINS

Trondheim

SWEDEN

FINLAND

L. Onega

FAROE IS.

Tampere

Vyborg

L. Ladoga

SHETLAND IS.

NORWAY

Sundsvall

Helsinki

Leningrad

Bergen

Oslo

Stockholm

Novgorod

Yaroslavl

ORKNEY IS.

Stavanger

Vänern

Riga

Aberdeen

Vättern

Moscow

Glasgow

Edinburgh

NORTH SEA

Gothenburg

BALTIC SEA

Smolensk

Belfast

UNITED

DENMARK

Dvina

Minsk

UNION OF SOVIE

IRELAND

KINGDOM

Copenhagen

Malmö

Kaliningrad

SOCIALIST REPUBL

Dublin

Manchester

Hamburg

Gdansk

Vistula

Warsaw

Cork

Birmingham

NETHER-

Poznan

Kharkov

Cardiff

London

LANDS

Elbe

E. Berlin

POLAND

Kiev

Thames

Amster-

GERMANY

Dnepr

English Channel

Rhine

Brussels

Bonn

Dnepropetrovsk

Le Havre

BELGIUM

W. Frankfurt

Prague

CZECHOSLOVAKIA

Dnestr

Brest

Paris

LUX-

GERMANY

Stuttgart

Vienna

CARPATHIANS

Prut

Odessa

Nantes

EMBOURG

Seine

Munich

AUSTRIA

Budapest

Loire

Saône

Bern

HUNGARY

ROMANIA

La Coruña

FRANCE

ALPS

Zurich

Geneva

SWITZ-

LIECHTENSTEIN

Bucharest

BLACK SEA

Santander

Bordeaux

Lyons

ERLAND

Zagreb

Bilbao

Rhône

Turin

Po

Milan

Venice

Trieste

Belgrade

Oporto

Toulouse

MONACO

SAN MARINO

YUGOSLAVIA

Danube

BULGARIA

Valladolid

PYRENEES

Nice

Dubrovnik

Lisbon

Madrid

ANDORRA

Marseille

Florence

Sofia

Douro

Tagus

Barcelona

Corsica

ITALY

ADRIATIC SEA

ALBANIA

Istanbul

Seville

Guidiana

Valencia

Ajaccio

Rome

Bari

Tirana

TURKEY

SPAIN

BALEARIC IS.

Sardinia

Naples

Taranto

Thessaloniki

Cadiz

Malaga

Cagliari

GREECE

GIBRALTAR

Palermo

Messina

Athens

Sicily

MALTA

Crete

MEDITERRANEAN SEA

PORTUGAL

ATLANTIC OCEAN

NORWAY

Ebro

Guadiana

■ Capital Cities

0   100   200   300   400 miles

0   200   400   600 kilometers

242

Much of Europe's wealth comes from its factories, farms, and mines. Europe's richest nations include West Germany and Switzerland. The largest European country is the U.S.S.R. The smallest European country is the Vatican, in Rome. There are 34 countries in Europe.

▲ *This valley along the Moselle River in the Rhineland in Germany is one of the chief wine-producing regions in Europe. Vineyards can be seen on the hillside in the foreground.*

European Community

This is a group of western European nations that work together to help goods, people, and money travel between countries in the Community. Its members are Belgium, Denmark, France, Ireland, Italy, Great Britain, Greece, Luxembourg, the Netherlands, Portugal, Spain, and West Germany. People also call the Community the European Common Market.

Everest, Mount

Mount Everest is the world's highest peak. It rises 29,028 ft. (8,848 m) above sea level. The mountain stands in the HIMALAYAS on the borders of Nepal and Tibet. Gales and falling masses of rock and snow sweep the steep, cold slopes. Many climbers tried to reach the top before two finally succeeded in 1953. They were the New Zealander Edmund Hillary and Tenzing Norgay, a Nepalese Sherpa.

EUROPE
Area: 4,066,263 sq. miles (10,531,623 sq. km) 7 percent of the world's land area
Population: 680,000,000 (14 percent of world total)
Highest point: Mount Elbrus, 18,481 ft. (5,633 m)
Lowest point: Caspian Sea, 92 ft. (28 m) below sea level
Longest river: Volga, 2,300 miles (3,700 km) long
Biggest lake: Lake Ladoga in the Soviet Union, 7,100 sq. miles (18,388 sq. km)
Northernmost point: North Cape, Norway
Southernmost point: Cape Tarifa, Spain
Westernmost point: Dunmore Head, Ireland
Easternmost point: Ural Mountains
Largest city: Greater Paris has 10,073,000 people

▲ *The modern horse evolved from an animal no bigger than a dog, with four toes on its front feet and three on its hind feet.*

Evolution

The theory of evolution states that today's plants and animals are descended from other forms that lived long ago. This slow process of change has been going on for millions and millions of years—ever since life first appeared on earth—and is still happening. Much of the evidence for evolution comes from FOSSILS. Rocks contain the remains of extinct plants and animals and so help to build up a family tree for species now living.

The theory of evolution says that plants and animals must adapt to their surroundings if they are to survive. Those which adapt best are most likely to survive.

Charles DARWIN, an English naturalist, first put forward the theory of evolution in 1859, in a book entitled *On the Origin of Species*.

Exercise

Exercise usually means activities that strengthen the muscles and improve health. Nearly all sports are good ways to exercise, but it is better to take regular mild exercise than to take strenuous exercise only once in a while. Brisk walking is one of the best exercises.

Exercise helps the blood to circulate through our bodies, cleaning out waste and supplying plenty of oxygen. When people want to lose weight, they should take exercise as well as dieting.

▲ *Jogging is a good form of exercise. It keeps the heart and lungs fit.*

On April 30, 1978, Neomi Uemura, a Japanese explorer, became the first person to reach the North Pole alone. During his 54-day dogsled trek over the ice, Uemura survived several attacks by a polar bear.

Explorer

Explorers are people who travel to find out about unknown places. There have always been explorers. The Stone Age men and women who wandered across continents were, in a way, explorers. Phoenician seamen sailed the Mediterranean about 2,600 years ago. ALEXANDER THE GREAT, in the 300s B.C., explored and conquered all of the Middle East as far as India. In the Middle Ages, MARCO POLO reached China from Europe.

But the great age of exploration began in the 1400s. Sailors like Vasco da GAMA, Christopher

Continued on page 246

Millions of Years

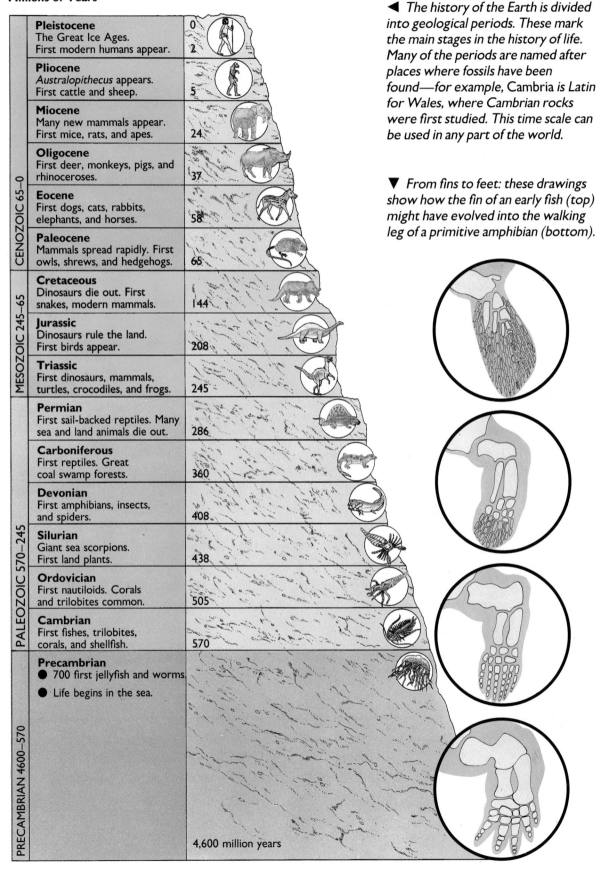

CENOZOIC 65–0	**Pleistocene** The Great Ice Ages. First modern humans appear.	0 / 2
	Pliocene *Australopithecus* appears. First cattle and sheep.	5
	Miocene Many new mammals appear. First mice, rats, and apes.	24
	Oligocene First deer, monkeys, pigs, and rhinoceroses.	37
	Eocene First dogs, cats, rabbits, elephants, and horses.	58
	Paleocene Mammals spread rapidly. First owls, shrews, and hedgehogs.	65
MESOZOIC 245–65	**Cretaceous** Dinosaurs die out. First snakes, modern mammals.	144
	Jurassic Dinosaurs rule the land. First birds appear.	208
	Triassic First dinosaurs, mammals, turtles, crocodiles, and frogs.	245
PALEOZOIC 570–245	**Permian** First sail-backed reptiles. Many sea and land animals die out.	286
	Carboniferous First reptiles. Great coal swamp forests.	360
	Devonian First amphibians, insects, and spiders.	408
	Silurian Giant sea scorpions. First land plants.	438
	Ordovician First nautiloids. Corals and trilobites common.	505
	Cambrian First fishes, trilobites, corals, and shellfish.	570
PRECAMBRIAN 4600–570	**Precambrian** ● 700 first jellyfish and worms. ● Life begins in the sea.	

4,600 million years

◄ The history of the Earth is divided into geological periods. These mark the main stages in the history of life. Many of the periods are named after places where fossils have been found—for example, Cambria is Latin for Wales, where Cambrian rocks were first studied. This time scale can be used in any part of the world.

▼ From fins to feet: these drawings show how the fin of an early fish (top) might have evolved into the walking leg of a primitive amphibian (bottom).

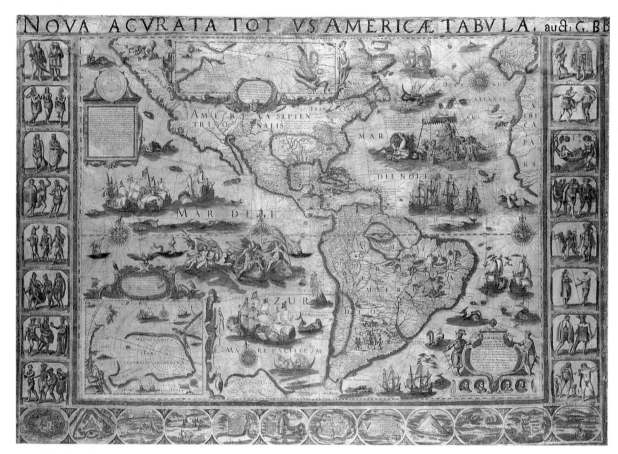

▲ *This Dutch map of newly-explored America was originally drawn in 1608 and updated in 1655.*

▲ *Robert Peary, the American naval officer who reached the North Pole in 1909.*

COLUMBUS, Ferdinand MAGELLAN, and James COOK discovered the shape, size, and position of continents and oceans. Later, David Livingstone, Roald AMUNDSEN, and others explored wild, untamed continents. The world's highest peak, Mount Everest, was climbed by Edmund Hillary and Tenzing Norgay in 1953. SPACE EXPLORATION now takes people beyond the Earth, and the explorations of the next century will probably make all past discoveries seem minor by comparison.

Explosive

Explosions happen when people heat or strike certain solid or liquid substances. These suddenly turn into hot GASES. The gases fill more space than the solids or liquids, so they rush violently outward. High explosives like dynamite explode faster and do more damage than low explosives like gunpowder. Engineers use explosives to break up rocks and old buildings. Armies use explosives to destroy vehicles and cities.

Eye

Our eyes show us the size, shape, and color of objects in the world around us. Our eyes can see something as small and near as a tiny insect crawling on this page, or as far off and large as the Moon or stars.

A human eye is much larger than the part you can see. The eye is a ball bigger than a marble. It works much like a camera. Both bend LIGHT rays to form a picture of the object that the rays are reflected from.

Light rays enter the eye through a layer of transparent skin called the *conjunctiva*. The rays pass through a hard, transparent layer called the *cornea*. This bends the rays. The LENS brings them into focus on the *retina* at the back of the eye. But you do not "see" the picture formed there until light-sensitive nerve endings on the retina send the brain a message along the *optic nerve*.

To see properly, all the parts of the eye have to work correctly. For example, the *iris* (the eye's colored part) can open and close to let more or less light through the *pupil*.

Human eyes have a better sense of color than those of any other animal. We can distinguish 250 different pure colors, from red to violet, and about 17,000 mixed colors. We are also able to distinguish about 300 shades of gray between black and white.

The animal with the largest eye is the giant squid. One big specimen has eyes nearly 16 in. (40 cm) in diameter. The biggest whales have eyes about 4 in. (10 cm) across.

▼ Inside the eye, the image on the retina is upside down, but the brain turns it over so that we see things the right way up.

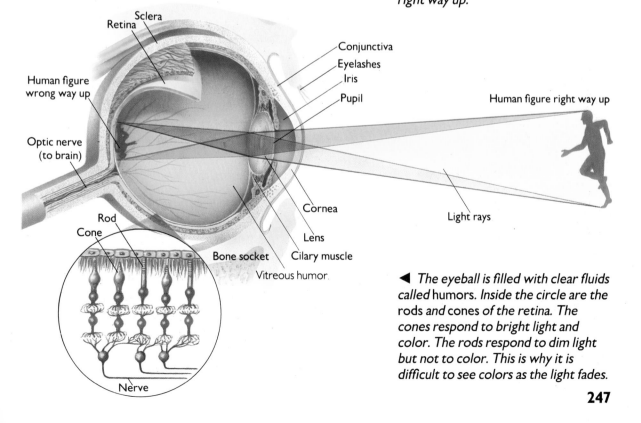

Sclera
Retina
Conjunctiva
Eyelashes
Iris
Pupil
Human figure wrong way up
Human figure right way up
Optic nerve (to brain)
Cornea
Light rays
Rod
Cone
Lens
Bone socket   Cilary muscle
Vitreous humor
Nerve

◄ The eyeball is filled with clear fluids called humors. Inside the circle are the rods and cones of the retina. The cones respond to bright light and color. The rods respond to dim light but not to color. This is why it is difficult to see colors as the light fades.

Fable

Fables are short tales in which the main characters are usually animals that can speak and act like human beings. Fables always teach a lesson. Some of the most famous are those of AESOP, an ancient Greek storyteller. His fables of the fox and the crow, and of the grasshopper and the ant, are told to this day.

Falcon

Falcons are a group of birds of prey that are found all over the world. They can be recognized by the dark markings around their eyes and by their pointed wings. Falcons use their large, hooked beaks for tearing flesh, but they kill their prey with their sharp claws. Falcons swoop down on their victims from above, hitting them with their claws. This act is called "stooping." It is used to kill smaller birds in mid-flight and also to take RODENTS and other small animals on the ground.

The biggest of all falcons is the gyrfalcon of the Arctic. It may reach over 24 inches (60 cm) in size. The American kestrel is the smallest and most common North American falcon. It is about 8 inches (20 cm) long.

▲ *The merlin is one of the smallest of the falcons. It flies low and fast as it chases smaller birds.*

Falkland Islands

This group of cold, windy islands form a British colony in the stormy South Atlantic Ocean. They lie about 480 miles (770 km) northeast of the tip of South America. Sheep farming is the main occupation.

Argentina claims the islands, although 97 percent of the inhabitants are of British origin. In 1982, Argentine troops invaded the Falklands, but they were defeated by British forces.

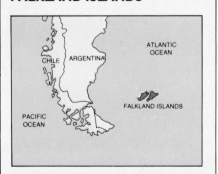

FALKLAND ISLANDS

Area: 4,633 sq. miles (12,000 sq. km)
Capital: Stanley
Population: 1,800
Average temperature: 6°C

Famine Relief

Sometimes, a country does not have enough food to feed the people who live there. People may even starve to death. This is famine. Many of the

developing countries of Africa and Asia are subject to famine, often because there has not been enough rain to grow enough food for an increasing population. This is when famine relief is needed. Richer countries organize a supply of food for the starving people, but getting the food to the places where it is needed most is seldom easy. There are usually transportation problems and in some cases civil war. To prevent future famines, help with irrigation and farming methods is needed.

▲ Ethiopian children receive food during one of the terrible droughts of the 1980s, when thousands of people died of starvation and disease.

Faraday, Michael

Michael Faraday (1791–1867) was a brilliant English scientist. His studies of chemistry and physics made him world famous. Faraday is best known for his experiments with ELECTRICITY. He showed that it could be made to flow in a wire when the wire was passed between the poles of a magnet. Today this is how most electricity is produced in big generators.

Farming

Farming is the world's most important human activity. More people work at it than at any other job. (See pages 250-251.)

▲ For many years, Michael Faraday gave science lectures for children. One of the best-known lectures is called "The Chemical History of a Candle."

FARMING

Farming began somewhere in the Middle East about 9,000 years ago. Today, about half the world's people are farmers. Many are *subsistence* farmers, growing just enough to feed themselves. Others grow *cash crops* to sell.

Farming has become more and more scientific. In the 1600s, turnips and clover were introduced to feed farm animals in winter. Before, they had always been killed as winter approached. So, breeders could keep good stock longer and develop larger, fatter breeds of cattle, sheep, and pigs. New World plants, such as potatoes and tomatoes, became widespread. In the 1800s, steam engines and motor tractors replaced horses and oxen.

Today, most farms in developed countries are mechanized. Few people are needed to work on them. Poultry and calves are often raised indoors, as if in a factory. The rich countries produce more food than they need. But despite the success of the "green revolution," which has brought new crops and new farm methods to the Third World, many people in poor countries still starve. In Africa, Asia, and South America, most farms are small, and the work is done mainly by hand.

THE HISTORY OF FARMING

7000 B.C. Farming begins when people discover how to grow grain and raise domestic animals.

4000 B.C. Irrigation of crops in Mesopotamia and Egypt.

500 B.C. Iron tools and heavy ox-drawn plows in use.

A.D. 600 Open-field system common in northern Europe. Peasants share fields, growing crops in narrow strips.

1400s Enclosure (fencing or hedging) of open fields. Sheep-rearing important.

1500s New plants introduced to Europe from America.

1600s Improved breeds of farm animals developed in Europe.

1700s New machinery, such as Eli Whitney's cotton gin (1793).

1800s Steam power, threshing, and reaping machines, new fertilizers; North America and Australia become important farming regions.

1900s Wide use of chemicals as fertilizers and insecticides; new strains of plants able to resist disease; factory farming and the "green revolution" improve food production.

STRIP FARMING

In Saxon times, people shared fields. They each had a narrow strip. The strips were plowed up and down the slope of the field, seldom across. Thus the strips of one group ran in one direction, those of a neighboring group in another.

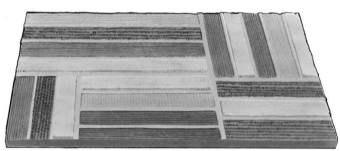

CROP ROTATION

In the 17th century, it was found that fodder crops put goodness back into the soil. In the four-course method of farming, cereals such as wheat and barley alternate with clover and root crops such as turnips.

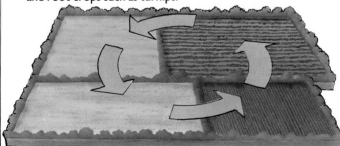

IMPORTANT FARM CROPS

Bananas grow in the tropics. Plantains (cooking bananas) are eaten in Asia, Africa, and the Americas.

Barley is an important cereal grown in temperate climates.

Cassava is a tropical root crop.

Maize (corn) grows well in warm, moist conditions.

Oats are grown in North America, Europe, and the U.S.S.R.

Potatoes are an important crop in Europe.

Rice is the main food of half the world's people. It grows best in warm, wet areas.

Sorghum is grown for food by people in Asia and Africa.

Sugar comes either from sugarbeet, grown in cool climates, or from sugarcane grown in the tropics.

Vegetable oils come from coconuts, cotton seed, peanuts, sunflowers, soybeans, olives, and maize.

Wheat is a cereal grown worldwide in areas with moist, mild winters and warm, dry summers.

Plowing with oxen

Winnowing rice

cking tea

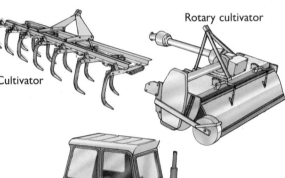

Cultivator

Rotary cultivator

Tractor

Plow

Potato planter

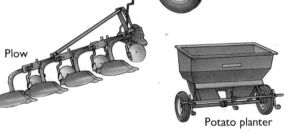

▲ In some parts of the world, old farming methods are still used. Modern machinery is slowly taking over.

▲ In battery farming, poultry are reared to produce more eggs in less time and at a low cost.

▲ Combine harvesters at work on a prairie wheatfield in the Midwest.

For more information turn to these articles: BEANS; CEREAL; COFFEE; COTTON; COW; FERTILIZER; FOOD; GOAT; HORSE; IRRIGATION; OLIVE; PIG; POTATO; POULTRY; RICE; SHEEP; SUGAR; TEA; VEGETABLE; WHEAT.

▶ *The Fascist followers of the Italian dictator Mussolini adopted black shirts as an official uniform.*

The *fasces*, an ancient Roman symbol of unity, became the Fascists' symbol.

SOURCES AND USES OF FATS
Animal fats

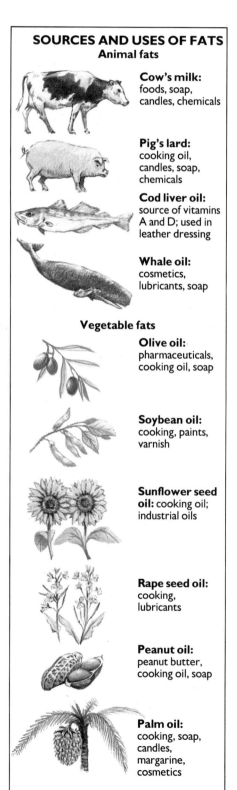

Cow's milk: foods, soap, candles, chemicals

Pig's lard: cooking oil, candles, soap, chemicals

Cod liver oil: source of vitamins A and D; used in leather dressing

Whale oil: cosmetics, lubricants, soap

Vegetable fats

Olive oil: pharmaceuticals, cooking oil, soap

Soybean oil: cooking, paints, varnish

Sunflower seed oil: cooking oil; industrial oils

Rape seed oil: cooking, lubricants

Peanut oil: peanut butter, cooking oil, soap

Palm oil: cooking, soap, candles, margarine, cosmetics

Fascism

Fascism is a political belief. It was founded in Italy in the 1920s by Benito MUSSOLINI. Mussolini seized power in 1922 as DICTATOR of Italy and head of the Italian Fascist Party. Fascism takes its name from the Roman *fasces*, the bundle of rods and the ax that were the symbol of authority in ancient Rome.

Fascist political ideas include the belief that the government of a country should be all-powerful. Its citizens must work hard and obey the government for the good of the nation. Fascists believe in strict discipline and training for all people, including children, and in the wearing of military-style uniforms.

Anybody opposed to a Fascist government is made an outlaw. In Fascist Italy, many people were jailed, exiled, or put to death because they did not agree with the Fascists. All the other political parties were made illegal.

Fat

Fat is an important food for both animals and plants. The tissue of these living things contains fat. Fat in a pure state can take the form of a liquid, such as vegetable oil, or a solid such as butter or lard.

Fat is a store of ENERGY. A unit of fat contains twice as much energy as the same amount of PROTEIN or STARCH. Fats play an important part in our diet. Vitamin A, which is necessary for growth, and Vitamin D are both contained in most fats.

We get most vegetable fats from the seeds and fruits of plants, where it is stored. In animals and human beings, fat is stored in tiny "droplets" in a layer under the skin and in the CELLS of the body. Pigs and cattle are our main sources of animal fats.

Some people do not use up all the fat they eat, so they gain too much weight. Some fats cause cholesterol to build up in the bloodstream. Both conditions can be unhealthy.

Fathers of the Confederation

The Fathers of the Confederation were a group of Canadian politicans in the mid-1800s who wanted to bring together all the separate parts of what is now Canada into one country. Until then, Canada was a group of separate colonies, each part of the British Empire.

The Fathers of the Confederation first met in 1864. They agreed that, like the United States, Canada should be a "federation" of states, or provinces. They wanted it to become a self-governing nation, but they also wanted it to stay a part of the British Empire, with the British king or queen as its head.

The British government supported them. It thought that a united Canada would be easier to defend from attacks from overseas and that trade between Canada and other countries could increase. In 1867, the British Parliament passed the British North America Act, and Canada was born.

Feather

The only animals with an outer layer of feathers are BIRDS. Feathers protect birds and keep them warm. They give their bodies a smooth, streamlined shape. Feathers also form the broad surface area of the wings that allows birds to fly.

Feathers are replaced once or twice a year. This process is called molting. Old feathers that are worn and broken fall out. New ones grow in their place.

▲ *A close-up of part of a feather, showing the thread-like barbs which are "glued" together by smaller hooked fibers called barbules.*

SEE IT YOURSELF

Collect feathers in the woods and look at them with a magnifying glass to see how they are made. "Unzip" part of the flat vane to see the tiny hooked branches that fit neatly together to form it. Mount your feathers in a notebook, and label them with the birds' names if you know them.

▲ *Fencers wear wire mesh masks, thick jackets, and padded gloves for protection.*

Fencing

Fencing can be described as the sport of "friendly dueling." Fencers wear a special glove, pads, and face masks. They fight with blunted swords. The winner is the one who scores the most points by touching his opponent with his sword.

Today, fencing is a popular sport and an OLYMPIC GAMES event, but in the past it was a form of sword practice for real duels.

Fermentation

Milk goes sour, bread dough rises, grape juice turns into wine. All these are examples of fermentation. Fermentation is caused by the work of very tiny living BACTERIA, YEASTS, and MOLD. These tiny things break up substances into simpler forms. People have been using fermentation since the earliest times to make bread, beer, wine and cheese. But it was not until the 1800s that the French scientist Louis PASTEUR found out how fermentation really works.

Fermi, Enrico

Enrico Fermi (1901–1954) was a great Italian scientist. His studies of the ATOM were rewarded by the NOBEL PRIZE in 1938.

In 1942, during World War II, Fermi built the first atomic reactor. He constructed it in an empty squash court under a football stadium in Chicago. Here he set off the first manmade nuclear chain reaction. Later, Fermi helped to develop the atom bomb.

▼ *The comon polypody grows on rocks and walls in damp woodlands. The small adder's tongue looks more like a leaf than a fern. Its spores develop on the slender spike.*

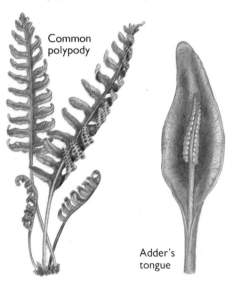

Common polypody

Adder's tongue

Fern

The primitive ferns were some of the earliest land plants. Today their delicate, feathery leaves look much the same as they did millions of years ago.

About 10,000 different kinds of ferns live on the Earth today. They are found all over the world, usually in damp shady places. In the tropics, giant tree-ferns grow to over 50 ft. (15 m) high.

Ferns do not have FLOWERS or SEEDS. Instead, they form spores from which new ferns develop.

Fertilizer

Fertilizers are chemicals. They are dug into the SOIL to nourish it. In this way, fertilizers help plants to grow bigger and healthier by giving them the chemical nutrients, or "foods," they need to grow. The most important fertilizers are calcium, phosphorus, potassium, and SULFUR.

Fertilizers are usually added to soils that do not contain enough natural nutrients. This can happen if the same crops have been planted in the soil year after year, or if the rain has washed out all the nutrients.

Under the fern frond are many spore cases called sporangia. These contain several hundred spores.

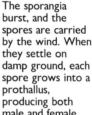

The sporangia burst, and the spores are carried by the wind. When they settle on damp ground, each spore grows into a prothallus, producing both male and female organs.

Fiber Optics

An optical fiber is a flexible glass strand thinner than a human hair. Along this fine fiber, a beam of light can travel very easily. The light can be used to carry telephone conversations and television pictures, or allow doctors to see inside our bodies. The fibers are made of especially pure glass designed to reflect the light in toward the center of the strand. Using LASER light, signals can be sent for more than 30 miles

The young fern develops from these organs, feeding on the prothallus. The leaves unroll as the plant grows.

▲ *Ferns reproduce themselves from spores rather than seeds. It can take several years before a fern is able to produce spores.*

◀ *A bundle of optical fibers. Each is much thinner than a human hair.*

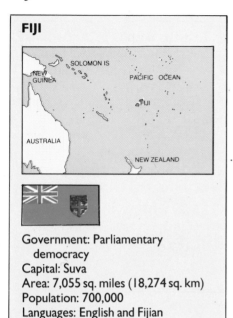

FIJI

Government: Parliamentary
    democracy
Capital: Suva
Area: 7,055 sq. miles (18,274 sq. km)
Population: 700,000
Languages: English and Fijian
Currency: Fiji dollar

► *Ceremonial dancers on the little island of Taveuni, now a Fijian national park.*

MILLARD FILLMORE

Thirteenth President 1850–1853
Born: Cayuga County, N.Y.
Education: Rural schools
Occupation: Lawyer
Political Party: Whig
Buried: Buffalo, New York

(50 km) before they have to be amplified. This means that optical fibers are much more efficient than copper cables and much thinner and lighter. A pair of fibers can carry hundreds of telephone conversations at the same time.

Fiji

Fiji is a country made up of hundreds of islands in the Pacific Ocean. The biggest island is Viti Levu, on which is the capital, Suva. Fiji became a British possession in 1874, but gained its independence in 1970. The main product of the islands is sugar. In 1879, peasants from India were brought to the islands to work on the sugar plantations. The offspring of these Indians now outnumber the original Fijians, and tension between the two groups led to an army takeover of government in 1987.

Fillmore, Millard

Millard Fillmore (1800–1874) was the 13th president of the United States. He came from a poor family and was a clothmaker's apprentice. He became vice president in 1848 and president after the death of the then president, Zachary TAYLOR. Though he was in office for less than three years, Fillmore played an important part in the argument about slavery. Though he opposed slavery, he knew that to outlaw it, as many in the North wanted to do, would bring war. This realistic view cost him the support of many people in the North.

Fingerprint

Fingerprints are marks we leave behind whenever we touch something. You can see them by pressing your fingertips into an ink pad and then onto a sheet of white paper. Everybody has patterns of lines and swirls on their fingers. But each person's fingerprints are different from everybody else's. Because of this, police officers use fingerprints to help identify criminals. They keep files of thousands of different prints. By comparing those on file with

In many hospitals, the footprints of babies are taken shortly after birth. Footprints, like fingerprints, never change, so the person will always be known by these prints. The owners of valuable dogs sometimes have nose prints made of their animals in case they should stray.

SEE IT YOURSELF

Press your fingertips gently but firmly onto an ink pad. The ridges on the skin of your fingertips will be covered with ink.
Transfer your fingerprints onto a clean piece of white paper and examine them through a magnifying glass. Can you tell which fingerprint group you belong to?

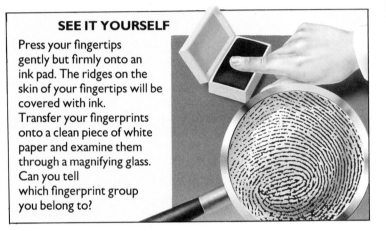

▶ All fingerprints can be divided into four main types – the arch, the whorl, the loop, and the composite.

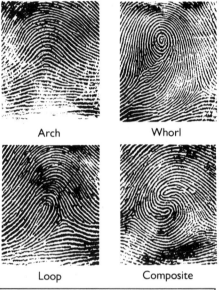

Arch Whorl

Loop Composite

those found at the scene of a crime, they can often trace the guilty person. Computers can now hold details of the fingerprints of half a million people. In a few seconds, the computer will match any of these prints with those of a suspect.

Finland

Finland is a country in northen EUROPE tucked between Scandinavia and the U.S.S.R.

The thousands of lakes and rivers that dot the Finnish landscape form a great inland waterway. About 75 percent of the land is covered by thick forests of spruce, pine, and larch trees. The main industries of Finland are logging and the making of wood products, such as paper.

Russia controlled the country from 1809 until 1917, when Finland became independent.

FINLAND

Government: Constitutional republic
Capital: Helsinki
Area: 130,120 sq. miles
  (337,009 sq. km)
Population: 4,900,000
Languages: Finnish and Swedish
Currency: Markka

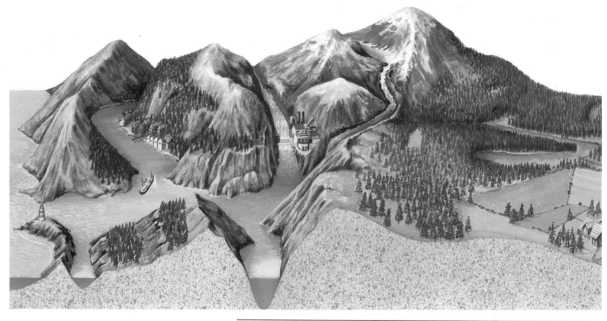

▲ The coast of Norway is broken by hundreds of fiords, some with steep, rocky sides several hundred feet high.

Fiord (Fjord)

Along the coasts of NORWAY and GREENLAND are a series of steep-sided valleys called fiords. Here the sea has invaded the land. Narrow tongues of water wind inland in narrow mountain gorges.

Fiords were formed when the great glaciers of the ICE AGES gouged out valleys as they flowed to the sea. When the ice melted, the sea flooded the valleys. Fiords are very deep and make perfect shelters for large ocean-going ships.

▼ In ancient times, people found that two flints struck sharply together produced a spark. Later, a flint was struck against a piece of steel to make a spark which could be used to light an easily-burned material called tinder.

Fire

The ability to make and use fire is one of the great advantages people have over animals. Primitive people found fire frightening, just as animals do. But once they learned to make and control fire, it became a necessary part of life. It kept out the cold, lit up the dark, cooked food, kept people warm, and scared away animals. But even today, fires that get out of control cause terrible damage and suffering.

Fireworks

Fireworks are devices that produce spectacular displays of lights, colors, smoke, and noise in the night sky. They were invented in China centuries ago, and only became known in Europe in the 1300s.

Fireworks are often launched in ROCKETS. They are shot in the air and made to explode by a black powder called *gunpowder*. The brilliant colors of fireworks come from burning different chemicals.

Fir Tree *See* Conifer

Fish

There are more fish than all the other backboned animals put together. The fish shown on pages 260–261 are just a few of more than 30,000 different kinds.

Fishing

Fishing is one of the world's most important activities. In one year, about 60 million tons of fish are taken from the seas, rivers, and lakes.

Although fish are a good source of food, much of the catch ends up as animal feed or FERTILIZER. Oil

Continued on page 262

In 1749, George Frideric Handel wrote his *Fireworks Music* for a display in London's Green Park. A report written at the time says: "Although Signor Servandoni's display of fireworks was not a complete success, Mr. Handel's music was enthusiastically received."

▼ *Some of the ways in which fish are caught. From left to right: fish such as cod and haddock are caught by their gills in gill nets; in long-line fishing, a series of baited hooks are attached to a long main line; in purse seine fishing, a net is drawn around a shoal of fish; lobsters are caught in traps; the otter trawl net has boards or buoys which keep the net open as it is dragged over the seabed, trapping bottom fish. The diagram also shows some important food fishes.*

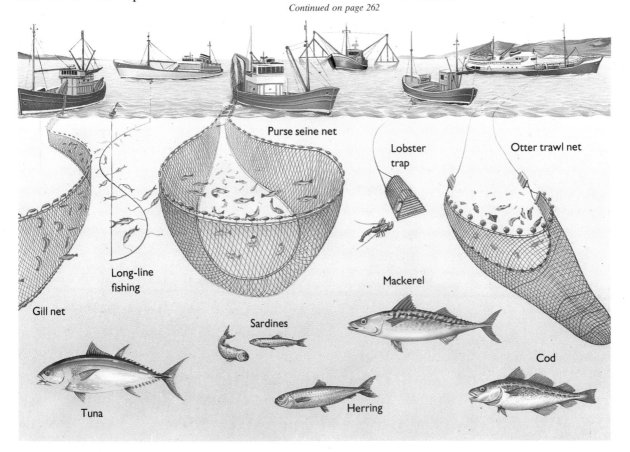

FISH

Fish were the first animals with backbones (vertebrates) to develop on Earth. They are the animals best adapted to life in water. They breathe by means of gills, and they swim by using their fins and tails. Fish are found in salt and fresh water, from the cold polar seas to the warm tropics.

Scientists divide fish into three groups. The *cartilaginous* fish have gristly, rather than bony, skeletons, and leathery skins, not scales. They include the sharks and rays. The *bony* fish make up the next, and largest, group. All these fish have bony scales covering their body. The third, and smallest, group are the *lungfish*, which are unusual in being able to come out on land and breathe air.

People have eaten fish since earliest times. Today, the world's fishing fleets catch millions of tons of fish every year.

▲ *A catch is sorted on a trawler. Trawlers fish in waters as far away as Greenland and the Arctic Ocean. Some stay at sea for weeks at a time, storing their catches in deep freezers on board.*

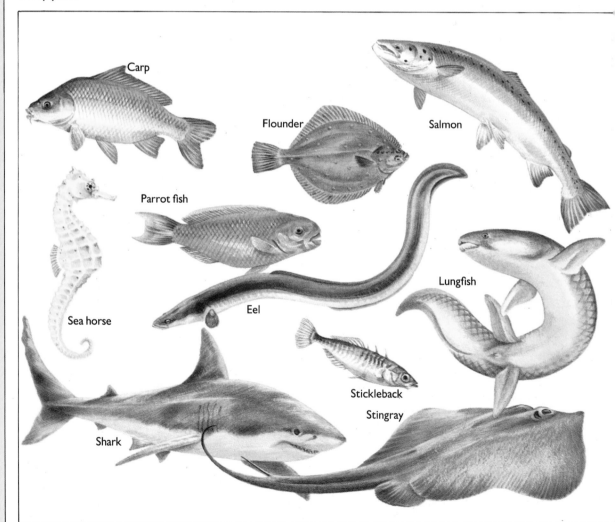

Carp

Flounder

Salmon

Parrot fish

Sea horse

Eel

Lungfish

Stickleback

Stingray

Shark

WHAT IS A FISH'S SIXTH SENSE?

Fish have an organ called the lateral line, found in no other animal. It detects vibrations in the water through sensors beneath the fish's scales. Using this sixth sense, a fish can detect another fish before it comes into view.

HOW DOES A FISH BREATHE?

A fish breathes by means of gills on each side of its head. It takes in water through its mouth and, as the water passes over the gills, the gills extract oxygen from the water. The oxygen enters the fish's bloodstream. Fish are cold-blooded.

HOW DOES A FISH SWIM?

Most fishes swim by beating their tails from side to side. They use their fins for steering and balance.

WHY CAN'T SEA FISH LIVE IN FRESH WATER?

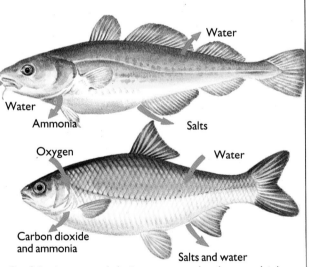

Water

Water

Ammonia

Salts

Oxygen

Water

Carbon dioxide and ammonia

Salts and water

Sea fish are constantly losing water, so they have to drink a lot. Unwanted salt is excreted in their urine. Freshwater fish take in water through their skin. They excrete large volumes of water. Regulation of the amount of salt in a fish's body is also carried out by the gills and the kidneys.

SOME INTERESTING AND UNUSUAL FISHES

Archer Fish This river fish catches insects by squirting water at them.

Catfish, like other bottom-dwelling fish, have feelers or "barbels" to help them find food.

Cleaner fish remove parasites and food scraps from the jaws of fierce barracuda.

Eels have an amazing life cycle, migrating from Europe and America to the Sargasso Sea to breed.

Flatfish A baby flounder swims upright. But as it grows, one eye travels across its head, and its body twists until the fish is lying on its side.

Flying Fish glide, using their long stiffened fins as wings. They take to the air to escape pursuing enemies.

Mudskippers use their leg-like fins to crawl over the mud to find food.

Pilot Fish often swim with sharks. They feed on the sharks' leftovers.

Porcupine Fish have prickly skins and blow themselves up like balloons to baffle a hungry enemy.

Salmon swim upriver to breed, often returning to the spot where they were born.

Scorpion Fish This fish is one to keep away from, for it has poisonous spines.

Sea Horse This curious-looking fish carries its young in a pouch.

For more information turn to these articles: EEL; FISHING; GOLDFISH; LAKE; OCEAN; RIVER; SALMON; TROPICAL FISH; TUNA.

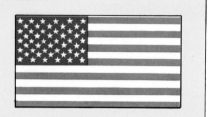

The United States flag, or "Stars and Stripes," has had the same basic design since 1777, during the Revolutionary War. It has 13 horizontal stripes which represent the original 13 colonies that rebelled against British rule. Fifty white five-pointed stars, representing the 50 states of the Union, appear on a dark blue field in the *canton*, the rectangular area in the top corner near the staff, or pole.

▼ *International signal flags used by ships at sea include a flag for each letter of the alphabet as well as for the numerals one to ten, shown below. On the right, the basic patterns in flag design are shown. The* canton *design is seen in the United States flag above. The* quarterly *is used on the flag of Panama; the* triangle *is seen in the flags of Guyana and Jordan. The* serration *appears in Qatar's flag, the* border *in Grenada's.*

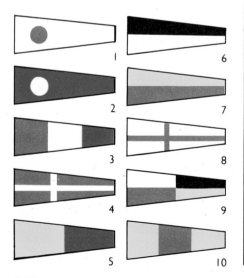

from fish is used to make SOAPS or for tanning—turning animal skins into leather.

Often the catch is made far from the home port. The fish must be preserved, or they will quickly spoil. In the past, fish were often dried, smoked, or salted, because there were no refrigerators. Today they are packed in ice or frozen. Some fishing fleets include large factory ships. They take fresh fish straight from the other ships and can them or package them on the spot.

The best places to fish at sea are where the sloping sea bottom is no more than 600 ft. (180 m) deep. Here, fish can be found feeding in huge numbers. The Grand Banks off the coast of Newfoundland is one such region. It has been fished for hundreds of years.

Flag

Flags are pieces of colored cloth, often decorated with bold markings. They have special fastenings so that they can be flown from masts and poles. Flags are used by countries, armies, and groups such as marching bands and sports teams.

Flags have been used as emblems since the time of the ancient Egyptians. Their flags were flown on long poles as battle standards, held by "standard-bearers." Flying high in the air, flags helped soldiers to find their companions as they plunged into

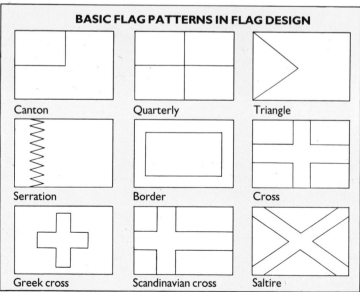

BASIC FLAG PATTERNS IN FLAG DESIGN

Canton · Quarterly · Triangle

Serration · Border · Cross

Greek cross · Scandinavian cross · Saltire

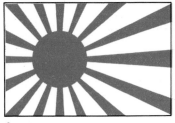

1   2   3   4

battle. And they showed which soldiers belonged to which king or general.

Today, national flags are flown as a symbol of a country's history, its power, and its importance, or *prestige*.

Flags are also used for signaling. Since 1857, there has been an international code for flag signals. It is used by ships. A yellow flag, for example, means that a ship is in quarantine because of illness on board. For thousands of years, flags have been important as a way of identifying ships at sea.

Other well known signals are a white flag—a sign of truce—and a flag raised to half-mast—a sign that people are mourning someone's death.

▲ *The World Scout flag (1) and the flag of the Red Cross (4) both represent organizations. The Japanese naval ensign (2), flown from the stern of a ship, is a recognized flag of nationality. The personal standard of Britain's Queen Elizabeth II (3) is just one of the royal standards.*

Flame

When something is heated enough to make it burn, it will also often burst into flames. These flames are gases that are given off during burning. Bright flames that give off plenty of light, such as those of candles, wood, or coal, have tiny CARBON particles in them that glow brightly. Flames are not all equally hot. Wood fires burn at about 1,800°F (1,000°C). The flames of acetylene WELDING torches are about 5,400°F (3,000°C).

Flamingo

Flamingos are tropical birds found in huge flocks in many parts of the world. The bright color of their feathers ranges from pale to deep pink. Flamingos live in marshes and shallow lakes, wading on their stilt-like legs. A flock of thousands of these splendid birds is a wonderful sight.

The flamingo's body is not much bigger than that of a goose, but its long legs and neck can make it up

▼ *Flamingos are timid birds and usually live together in large colonies on the edges of lakes and marshes.*

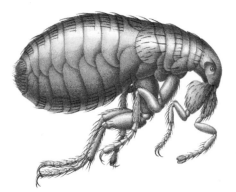

▲ *This greatly magnified body of a flea shows the large abdomen where blood is stored.*

▲ *Sir Alexander Fleming, the British bacteriologist who discovered penicillin.*

▼ *A pointed flint tool and a tool for scraping, both made by Neanderthal people about 50,000 years ago.*

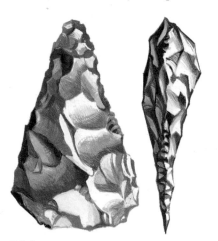

to 6 ft. (1.8 m) tall. These elegant birds feed on tiny plants and animals that are found in shallow waters. When feeding, they tuck their heads right under the water and use their broad, hooked beaks like strainers to filter their food from the water and mud.

Flea

Fleas are tiny wingless insects less than ⅛ in. (3 mm) long. They live on the bodies of birds, animals, and human beings. Fleas are PARASITES, and they feed on their hosts by biting through the skin and sucking the blood. Fleas can carry germs from one host to another. Rat fleas, for example, can give bubonic plague to people.

Fleming, Alexander

Sir Alexander Fleming (1881–1955) was a British doctor who discovered the antibiotic drug penicillin. It is one of the most important drugs known. Penicillin fights infections caused by many kinds of germs and BACTERIA. Although the drug fights the infection, it does not usually harm the body. Penicillin has saved thousands of lives.

Fleming discovered the drug by accident in 1928. He found an unknown kind of mold growing in his laboratory. From it, he was able to make pencillin. For his work, Fleming shared the 1945 Nobel Prize in medicine with Howard W. Florey and Ernst B. Chain, the doctors who found a way to produce penicillin in large quantities.

Flint

Flint is a glassy MINERAL that is a form of QUARTZ. It is found in beds of chalk and limestone. A lump of flint is dull white on the outside and shiny gray to black on the inside.

Flint is very hard, but it can be easily chipped into sharp-edged flakes. Stone Age people made tools and weapons out of flint. Because it will give off a spark when struck against iron, it can be used to start a FIRE. A spark from a flint also ignited the powder in a flintlock GUN.

Flood

There are two main kinds of floods: those caused by rivers overflowing their banks, and ocean floods caused by high tides and strong winds blowing from the ocean toward the land. Rivers usually flood in the spring, when spring rains add to water produced by melting snow and ice. The water overflows, causing much destruction in the area of the river.

Throughout history, three great rivers have flooded regularly—the Nile in Egypt, the Yellow River in China, and the Mississippi.

▼ *Below left: Florida's seaquarium in Miami was the first center of its type in the world when it was built in 1938. Below: Palms and slash pines at the Lower Keys Wildlife Refuge, off the Florida coast.*

Florida

Florida is the most southerly state. It is located on the east coast, and juts out into the sea, with the Atlantic Ocean to the east and the Gulf of Mexico to the west. It has more coastline than any state other than Alaska. Tourism is the most important industry. Miami Beach and Walt Disney World are just two of the major attractions. Florida's warm climate attracts visitors all year round, and many retired people live here, too. The sunny weather also encourages agriculture, and many kinds of fruit and vegetable are grown.

Florida was discovered by the Spanish as early as 1513. In 1763 the British captured it, but it returned to Spain soon afterward. In 1821 it passed to the United States.

FLORIDA

Capital: Tallahassee
Population: 11,670,000
Area: 58,560 sq. mi. (151,658 sq. km)
State flower: Orange Blossom
State bird: Mockingbird
State tree: Palmetto Palm
Statehood: March 3, 1845
    27th state

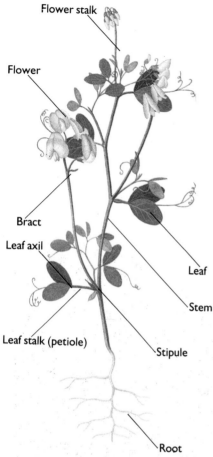

Flower stalk

Flower

Bract

Leaf axil

Leaf

Stem

Leaf stalk (petiole)

Stipule

Root

▲ *The parts of a flowering plant.*
▶ *A flower cut away to show its parts. Fertilization occurs when pollen from the anther unites with an ovule in the ovary. The ovule becomes a seed from which a new plant will eventually grow.*

▼ *Houseflies lay their eggs in decaying matter. The life cycle can be complete in a week in warm weather. The sponge-like mouth is drawn in the circle.*

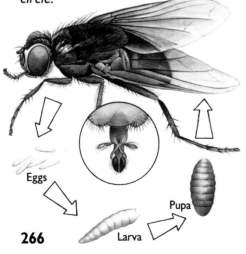

Eggs

Larva

Pupa

Flower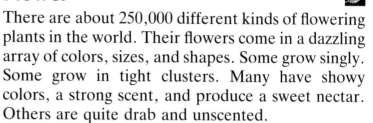

There are about 250,000 different kinds of flowering plants in the world. Their flowers come in a dazzling array of colors, sizes, and shapes. Some grow singly. Some grow in tight clusters. Many have showy colors, a strong scent, and produce a sweet nectar. Others are quite drab and unscented.

Whatever they look like, flowers all have the same part to play in the life of the plant. Flowers help plants to reproduce themselves. Inside a flower are male parts, called *stamens*, and female parts

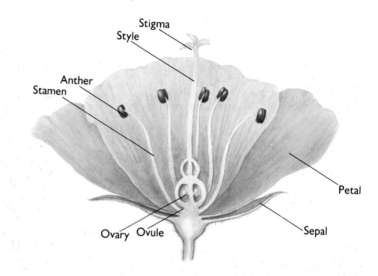

Stigma

Style

Anther

Stamen

Petal

Ovary   Ovule

Sepal

known as *pistils*. The stamens contain hundreds of powdery grains of pollen. These fertilize the pistil. Then a FRUIT begins to form and grow. Inside the fruit are the SEEDS for a new generation of plants. The seeds are scattered in different ways. They may be blown by the wind, or carried off by birds and animals. From them, new plants will grow.

Fly

Flies are winged insects. They are one of the largest groups of insects in the world. There are more than 750,000 different kinds of flies. They have two pairs of wings, one pair for flying and a smaller set behind the main pair to help them to balance in flight.

Many flies are dangerous. They spread deadly diseases such as cholera and dysentery. They pick up germs from manure and rotting food and carry them into homes, where they leave them on our food.

Some flies bite and feed on the blood of animals. Horseflies and gadflies attack cattle and horses in great swarms. Tsetse flies, which live in the tropics, spread sleeping sickness among domestic animals and humans. Blowflies lay their eggs in open wounds on the skin of animals. The maggots that hatch from the eggs eat into the flesh and cause great harm.

Fog

What we call fog is simply a low-lying bank of CLOUD. Fog forms when warm, moist air comes into contact with cold ground. As the air cools, the moisture it contains forms the tiny droplets that make up any cloud.

Fog may form when warm air currents blow across chilled water or land. This kind is common around the coast. Another kind occurs on still, clear winter nights, when the cold ground chills the air above it and there is no wind to blow the resulting fog away.

Food

Anything that people eat can be called food. But it makes more sense to talk of it as being only those plant and animal products people enjoy eating.

Primitive and ancient peoples often ate insects and animals raw, or only very lightly cooked.

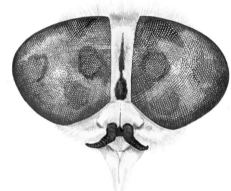

▲ A fly has two huge compound eyes made up of thousands of six-sided lenses.

The famous "London fogs" of Sherlock Holmes's day are now a thing of the past. They were not really fogs, but smogs. Smog is caused by drops of water condensing on smoke particles or the exhaust gases of cars or factories. Air pollution is a serious problem in many large cities.

Monday				
Tuesday				
Wednesday				
Thursday				
Friday				
Saturday				
Sunday				

SEE IT YOURSELF
You can find out whether you are eating enough healthy foods by making a chart like the one on the left. Draw pictures at the top to show the four main food groups—fruit, meat or fish, bread or rice, and vegetables. Every day, check the box under each group when you have eaten something in that group. After a few days, look to see how you have done. If you have at least one check in each box, you are probably eating a healthy diet.

You can judge a country's standard of living (how rich or poor people are) by the amount of cereals that people eat. (Cereals are wheat, rye, barley, oats, corn, and rice.) In rich countries such as the United States, cereals provide only about a third of all foods eaten. In parts of Europe, cereals provide about half of the food eaten. In most of Asia, three-fourths of the people's food is rice.

Today, food may be very skillfully prepared, decorated, and cooked before being eaten. Much of our food is prepared in factories. It is bottled, canned, frozen, or dried before it is sold to us.

Food is essential for life. It gives us the energy to move around and stay warm, and keeps our bodies healthy. A "balanced diet" is necessary for good health. The three main kinds of food are carbohydrates, PROTEINS, and FATS. We also need certain MINERALS and VITAMINS.

Food Chain

When you eat a piece of fish, such as bass, you are taking part in a food chain that began somewhere in the sea. There, the tiny floating plants and animals called plankton were eaten by tiny fish. The tiny fish were eaten by bigger fish, and these bigger fish were eaten by even bigger fish such as your bass.

▶ In this diagram, arrows show how food energy is passed along a typical food chain. Here, there are two possible chains—one from plants to crustaceans to perch to pike, and the other taking a different route—plants to crustaceans to stickleback to pike. There are many other possible food chains.

At each stage in any food chain, energy is lost. This is why food chains seldom extend beyond four or five links. In overpopulated countries, people often increase the total food supply by cutting out a step in the food chain. Instead of eating cows that eat plants, the people themselves eat the plants. Because the food chain is made shorter, the total amount of energy available to the people is increased.

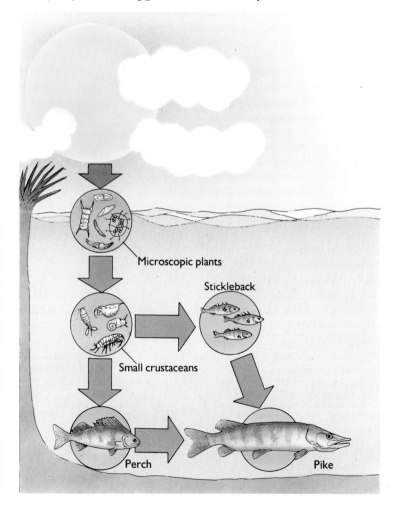

Microscopic plants

Stickleback

Small crustaceans

Perch

Pike

Every living thing has its place in one or many food chains. The chain begins with green plants. They make their own food from water, chemicals in the soil, and air and sunlight. Animals cannot make their own food as plants can. Instead, they eat plants or other animals. When animals or plants die, tiny BACTERIA that live in the soil break down the animal or plant tissues. The chemicals that make up the animals or plants are released into the soil. These chemicals act as FERTILIZERS to enrich the soil and help the green plants to grow. And so the food chain begins all over again.

▲ *In football, the players carry or throw the ball much more than they kick it.*

Football

This American sport is played in schools, colleges, and by professional teams. Unlike BASKETBALL and BASEBALL, which are played in other parts of the world, football, until recently, has been uniquely American.

The game is played on a field 100 yards (91 m) long from goal line to goal line, by 160 feet (49 m) wide. End zones extend 10 yards (9 m) behind each goal line. The field is marked with white lines every 5 yards (4.5 m) along its length.

A football game lasts 60 minutes, and is divided into four 15-minute quarters. The team kicking off kicks the ball from its 35-yard line in professional football. The receiver on the opposing team tries to run up the field without being tackled. He is *downed* if he is touched by an opponent while any part of his body other than his feet and one hand is in contact with the ground. The teams then take up positions facing each other on the line of *scrimmage* where the ball carrier has been downed.

In four downs the team must advance the ball at least 10 yards. If they succeed they have a *first down*, and can try for another 10 yards. If they fail, the defending team gains possession of the ball. Points are scored either by carrying the ball over the opponent's goal line (a *touchdown*), or by kicking the ball over the goalpost from any part of the field (a *field goal*). A touchdown is worth 6 points; a field goal 3 points. After a touchdown, the scoring team tries for a *conversion* point.

▼ *In this diagram of a football field, only the 10-yard lines are shown.*

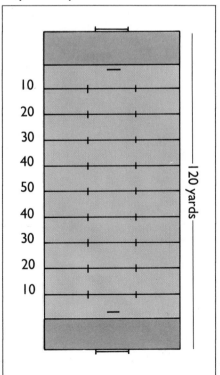

GERALD R. FORD

Thirty-eighth President 1974–1977
Born: Omaha, Nebraska
Education: Michigan University
Occupation: Lawyer
Political Party: Republican

Force

Force is a motion or an action that affects an object, causing it to move or to change shape. If you push something so that it moves, you have applied force to it. How much force you need to move an object depends on how big it is and how much it weighs. There are many kinds of force, and many complicated rules controlling them. These rules govern the way objects behave throughout the universe.

Ford, Gerald Rudolph

Gerald Ford (1913–) was the 38th president, and the only president to come to office after the resignation of a president. He was a Michigan Republican who was elected to the House of Representatives 13 straight times. Ford became president in 1974 when Richard NIXON resigned. Nixon was unpopular because of the Watergate scandal. Many people welcomed Ford because they thought he would be a reliable president. Though he brought stability to the government, he also faced problems with the economy and the Vietnam War.

Ford, Henry

Henry Ford (1863–1947) was a pioneer automobile maker. He was the first to use assembly lines. By building his cars from standard parts, he was able to turn out hundreds a day. His cars were so cheap that many people could afford to buy them. Ford's biggest success was the Model T. His Detroit factories turned out 15 million Model T's during the 19 years it was in production.

▲ *The Ford family of automobiles spans nearly a century, from the production of the first Model T to the cars of today.*

Forest

Forests are large areas of tree-covered land. Tropical rain forests are found near the EQUATOR. In this hot and steamy climate, many kinds of trees and plants grow very quickly. In some places, the trees grow so close together that the sunlight cannot reach the dark, bare forest floor.

Coniferous forests are nearly always found in cold

northern lands. These forests are made up mainly of one kind of tree, such as spruce, fir, or pine. Few other plants grow there. In temperate lands like the U.S., Europe, and the cooler parts of Africa, there are deciduous forests with trees like oak and beech which shed their leaves. Most Australian forest trees are eucalyptus.

Fossil

Fossils are the hardened remains or impressions of animals and plants that lived a very long time ago. A fossil may be a shell, a bone, a tooth, a leaf, a skeleton, or even sometimes an entire animal.

Most fossils have been found in areas that were once in or near the sea. When the plant or creature died, its body sank to the seabed. The soft parts rotted away, but the hard skeleton became buried in the mud. Over millions of years, more and more mud settled on top of the skeleton. Eventually, these layers of mud hardened into rock, and the skeleton became part of that rock. Water seeping through the rock slowly dissolved away the original skeleton. It was replaced by stony MINERALS which formed exactly the same shape.

These fossils lay buried until movements in the Earth's crust pushed up the seabed and made it dry land. In time, water, ice, and wind wear away the rock, and the fossil is exposed. The oldest known fossil is over three billion years old.

▼ *Five layers can be seen in a tropical forest. At ground level, fungi, moss, and ferns grow in the rich leaf litter. Then comes a layer of tree ferns, shrubs, and lianas. Above this is a layer of young tree crowns and then the thick canopy, the crowns of mature trees. The topmost layer consists of the few trees that stand above the canopy.*

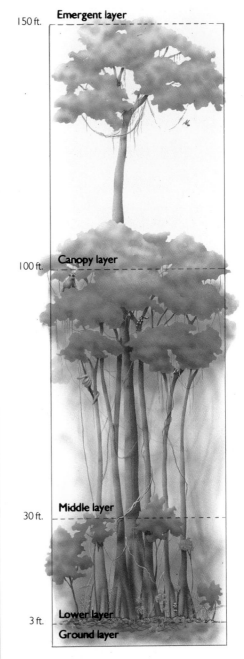

Emergent layer
150 ft.
Canopy layer
100 ft.
Middle layer
30 ft.
Lower layer
3 ft.
Ground layer

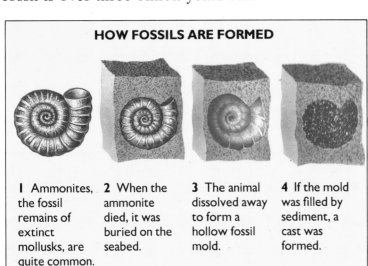

HOW FOSSILS ARE FORMED

1 Ammonites, the fossil remains of extinct mollusks, are quite common.

2 When the ammonite died, it was buried on the seabed.

3 The animal dissolved away to form a hollow fossil mold.

4 If the mold was filled by sediment, a cast was formed.

FOX

▼ *The red fox is about 3 ft. (1 m) long, from its nose to the tip of its tail. It stands about 12 to 16 in. (30 to 40 cm) high. Its back is reddish-brown and the underside white.*

▼ *The fennec fox (below) is the smallest of the foxes. The bat-eared fox (bottom) looks more like a jackal than a fox. Both these animals have very large ears because they live in open desert country and their ears help to get rid of excess heat from their bodies. Their big ears also give them acute hearing.*

Fox

Foxes belong to the same animal family as dogs. The most common kind is the red fox, which is found in Europe, North Africa, North America, and parts of Asia. It eats small birds, animals, and insects, and occasionally poultry or lambs.

Foxes live in holes called "earths," which they either dig themselves or take over from rabbits or badgers. Recently, more and more foxes have been found in cities. They live under the floors of buildings or in any hidden place they can find. They eat scraps from trash cans.

Foxes are very cunning animals. Sometimes they catch rabbits and other prey by chasing their own tails very fast. This fascinates the rabbit, who watches without realizing that the fox is gradually getting nearer and nearer. When the fox gets close enough, it suddenly straightens out and grabs its dinner.

Fraction

If you cut a cake into equal parts, each part is a fraction of the whole cake. We can write this as a number, too. If the cake is cut into two, each half can be written like this: $^1/_2$. If the cake is cut into four, each quarter is written $^1/_4$. The number above the dividing line in a fraction is called the *numerator*. The number below is called the *denominator*.

Until fractions were invented, people had to manage with just *whole* numbers. It was not possible to express a length or weight between two whole numbers.

Fractions help us to divide things. They can be used to mean a part of one: a half of one is a half ($^1/_2 \times 1 = ^1/_2$). They can also be used to divide numbers greater than one. A box of eggs has 12 eggs in it. Half the box has 6 eggs ($^1/_2 \times 12 = 6$).

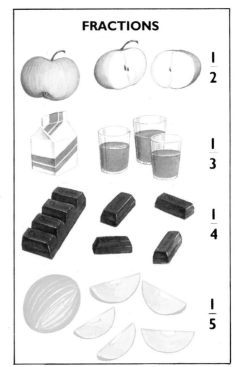

FRACTIONS

$\frac{1}{2}$

$\frac{1}{3}$

$\frac{1}{4}$

$\frac{1}{5}$

France

France is the largest country in western EUROPE. It has a population of 55,000,000. In ancient times, France was inhabited by CELTS, but Julius CAESAR conquered it, and for 500 years it was part of the Roman Empire. The Franks, from whom the country got its name, invaded in the A.D. 400s. France was once divided into hundreds of small parts. There was no standard language until the founding of the French Academy in the 1630s.

France is a very varied and beautiful country. It has a temperate climate and is very fertile. Farmland covers about half the country, and many of the people are employed in farming, fishing, or forestry. France produces a lot of grain, fruit, and vegetables, and it is famous for its WINES.

The history of France is long and turbulent. For centuries, the French and English were enemies and fought many wars. The French people suffered under the rule of greedy kings and nobles. Then in 1789, the people started the FRENCH REVOLUTION. They overthrew their king and made France a republic.

But the country was soon taken over by NAPO-

FRANCE

Government: Republic
Capital: Paris
Area: 211,207 sq. miles
   (547,026 sq. km)
Population: 55,000,000
Language: French
Currency: French franc

▶ *The Tour de France, an annual bicycle race around France, is an internationally popular event.*

▼ *Three well-known French monuments—from top to bottom, the Eiffel Tower, Sacré Coeur, and the Arc de Triomphe. The Arc de Triomphe, in Paris, was built by Napoleon. The white-domed church of Sacré Coeur is a landmark on Montmartre, the tallest hill in Paris. The Eiffel Tower was erected for the Paris Exhibition of 1889.*

LEON, who made himself emperor. He went to war and conquered most of Europe before he was finally defeated at Waterloo in 1815. Later, France became a republic once again.

Today, France is one of the wealthiest nations in Europe. It was one of the first members of the EUROPEAN COMMUNITY. The capital city is PARIS, on the River Seine.

Francis of Assisi

St. Francis (1182–1226) was born in Assisi in central Italy. When he was 22, he suffered a severe illness. Afterward, he decided to devote his life to the service of God. He lived in poverty and gathered around him a band of monks who became known as the Franciscans. St. Francis was very fond of birds and animals, whom he called his brothers and sisters.

Franklin, Benjamin

Benjamin Franklin (1706–1790) was a gifted American politician and scientist. He was born in Boston, the youngest of 17 children. Franklin became a printer and then began to publish a yearly almanac, which made him his fortune.

He became involved in the REVOLUTIONARY WAR, which brought the United States freedom from British rule. He was one of the men who signed the

DECLARATION OF INDEPENDENCE and helped draw up the peace treaty at the end of the war.

His scientific inventions include bifocal eyeglasses and the lightning conductor, a rod that protects buildings from lightning.

French and Indian Wars

The French and Indian Wars were fought in the 1600s and 1700s between Britain and France for control of North America. They ended in 1763 with victory for Britain and the American colonies. Before that, France had controlled large areas of Canada and along the Mississippi. There were four separate wars, but the most important was the last, fought between 1754 and 1763. After it, France lost almost all her huge North American empire.

▲ By flying a kite in a thunderstorm, Benjamin Franklin proved that lightning was electricity.

French Revolution

In the 1700s, the poor people of FRANCE suffered under the rule of their kings and nobles. Rich people built themselves lavish palaces and mansions

▼ On July 14, 1789, a Paris mob stormed the Bastille, a prison, and sparked off the French Revolution.

while many others starved in misery. French kings forced the peasants and shopkeepers to pay taxes to support their extravagant way of life and to finance the wars they were always fighting.

There was no parliament to stop the king from treating his subjects badly, and eventually, in 1789, the French people's anger exploded into revolution. King LOUIS XVI was imprisoned, but tried to escape. Violent leaders like Danton, Robespierre, and Marat directed the Revolution, and the king and queen and many nobles were beheaded.

Then followed the "Reign of Terror," when the revolutionary leaders began to quarrel among themselves, and many of them were beheaded, too. The people grew tired of bloodshed, and in 1795, they set up a government called "The Directory." But it ruled the country badly, and in 1799, it was overthrown by NAPOLEON

Freud, Sigmund

Sigmund Freud (1856–1939) was an Austrian doctor who made a great contribution to our understanding of the human mind.

Freud received a degree in medicine from the University of Vienna in 1881 and began to devote himself to the study of mental illness. He taught that the *subconscious*—the thoughts and memories we are not aware of—held the key to a person's mental state. To open up the subconscious, he developed the system of *psychoanalysis*, a kind of clinical examination of the mind. Freud published several books on this and other subjects.

Friction

When two things rub together, it causes friction. Friction makes it hard to move something across a surface. Smooth objects cause much less friction than rough objects, so when things need to go fast, we try to reduce friction. This is why the wheels of a train and the rails of the track are smooth. When we want things to slow down, we add friction; for example, putting on the brakes in our cars. If two things rub together at great speed, the friction

▲ *Sigmund Freud, whose theories did much to advance the study of nervous diseases.*

Without friction, the world would be a strange place. We could not walk because our shoes would not grip the ground. Cars would stand still no matter how fast their wheels turned. Nails and screws would not hold.

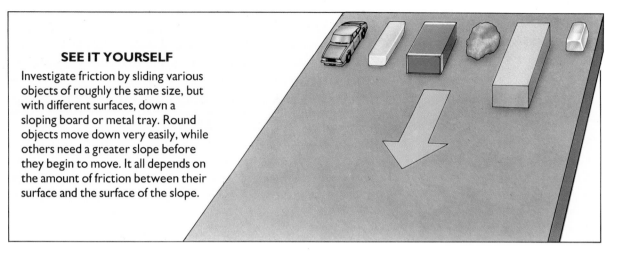

SEE IT YOURSELF

Investigate friction by sliding various objects of roughly the same size, but with different surfaces, down a sloping board or metal tray. Round objects move down very easily, while others need a greater slope before they begin to move. It all depends on the amount of friction between their surface and the surface of the slope.

produces HEAT. If you rub your hand hard against your leg, you can feel the heat made by the friction.

Frog and Toad

Frogs and toads are amphibians. This means that they can live both on land and in water. Frogs and toads are found all over the world, except in very cold lands that are always frozen. There are hundreds of different kinds. The biggest is the Goliath frog of Central Africa. This frog can be over 12 in (30 cm) long and weigh over 6½ lbs. (3 kg). The smallest is a tree frog native to the U.S., which is less than ³/₄ inch (2 cm) long.

Frogs and toads breathe through their skins as well as their LUNGS. It is important that they keep their skins wet, because if the skin became too dry, they could not breathe and would die. This is why you will never find a frog very far away from water.

Common frogs feed on insects, grubs, and slugs. They catch their food with a long sticky tongue

▼ *These are just a few of the world's 2,500 different species of frogs and toads. The brightly-colored arrow-poison frogs of South America are among the most poisonous of all. Indians of the Amazon basin use their poison to tip hunting arrows. Tree frogs have pads on their fingers and toes which help them to climb trees. Gliding frogs have webs on their feet which they use as "wings."*

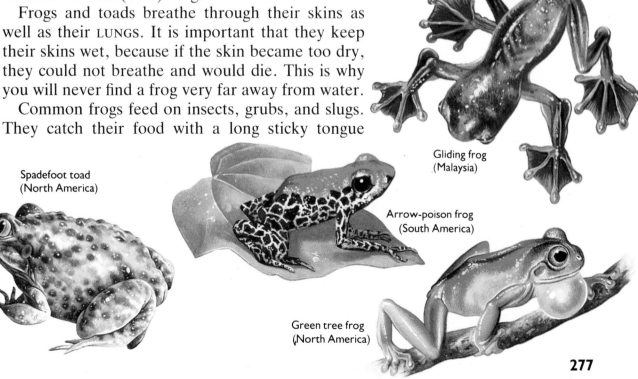

Gliding frog
(Malaysia)

Spadefoot toad
(North America)

Arrow-poison frog
(South America)

Green tree frog
(North America)

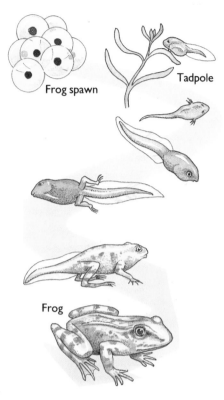

which is attached to the front of the mouth. A frog can flick its tongue in and out in a fraction of a second. Really big frogs eat snakes, small animals, and other frogs, as well as insects.

Toads' skins are rough, dry, and lumpy. They can live in drier places than frogs can.

Frost

Frost is a covering of tiny CRYSTALS of ice that form on cold surfaces. There are three kinds of frost. Hoarfrost forms when tiny drops of water in the air freeze as they touch cold objects. Hoarfrost makes lacy patterns on windowpanes. Glazed frost forms when rain falls on a cold road and covers the surface with a glassy coat. Rime frost is white ice that forms when cold fog or drizzle freezes on surfaces such as cold aircraft wings.

Fruit

To most of us "fruit" means juicy foods which grow on certain plants and trees. Apples, oranges, and pears are three examples. These fruits taste good and are important in our diet. They give us mineral salts, sugar, and VITAMINS. The water, skins, and seeds of fruit help our DIGESTION.

To scientists who study plants, fruits are the ripe SEED cases of any flowering plant. The fruits protect the seeds as they develop and help spread them when they are ripe. Some fruits scatter seeds. Others are eaten by birds and animals that spread the seeds.

▲ The life cycle of a frog: The jelly-like eggs, or spawn, are laid in a pond and hatch into tadpoles. The tadpoles gradually develop legs, and their tails shrink. They develop lungs instead of gills. They become adult frogs in about 3 years.

▼ In many plants, the seeds are enclosed in fleshy fruits. Many fruits are good to eat. As the fruits develop from the flowers, the sepals and petals wither and finally drop off.

Tomato

Crab apples

Blackberries

Fuel

Fuels are substances that give off heat when they burn. Fuels provide our world with the ENERGY we use for heating, cooking, powering ships, planes, cars and machines, and producing electricity.

The most important fuels are COAL, OIL, and NATURAL GAS. They were formed underground from the remains of prehistoric plants or animals. People often call them fossil fuels.

Some fuels give out more heat than others. A pound of coal gives nearly three times as much heat as a pound of wood. Oil gives nearly four times as much, and HYDROGEN gas ten times as much. But URANIUM can give more than half a million times as much heat as hydrogen.

As fossil fuels are used up, we shall have to make more use of atomic energy, SOLAR ENERGY, and wind and water power.

Fuel Cell

A fuel cell is a special kind of electric battery that keeps on making electricity as long as fuel is fed into it. The main use for the fuel cell is in spacecraft. Fuel cells supplied electricity in the Apollo spacecraft that flew to the Moon in 1969–72. These cells used oxygen and hydrogen as fuel. Inside the cells, the oxygen and hydrogen combined together to produce electricity and water. The astronauts drank the water.

FUELS

Natural gas is a fuel that is widely used for cooking and heating. It is found deep underground close to oil pools.

Coal is still used to produce most of the world's electricity. For a century and a half, it has been the most important fuel for producing heat to make steam.

Oil, or petroleum, comes from oil wells sunk deep into the Earth. Gasoline, kerosene, and diesel oil are all separated from petroleum.

Nuclear fuel is usually uranium. It is put into nuclear reactors and produces great amounts of energy. Nuclear reactors generate electricity.

Solar energy — energy from the Sun— is radiant energy, energy that travels in waves. It gives us light and heat. It is also the source of most of the energy on Earth.

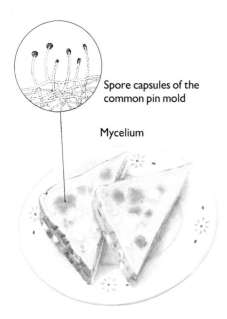

Spore capsules of the common pin mold

Mycelium

▲ *The fungus family includes molds. Uncovered food offers a perfect place for molds to grow. The tiny, thread-like growths (inset) spread quickly.*

▼ *Throughout history, furniture has often been beautiful as well as useful. Below are some very individual pieces of everyday furniture from 4,000 years ago to the 20th century.*

Fulton, Robert

Robert Fulton (1765–1815) was an American inventor who designed and built one of the earliest steamboats, the *Clermont*. It sailed between New York city and Albany. He also designed the first steam-powered warship, which he called *Fulton the First*. Among his other important inventions were a new type of canal boat and a machine for cutting canals. Though it was never a complete success, Fulton also designed a type of submarine.

Fungus

A fungus is a simple PLANT with no true roots, stem, or leaves. Fungi do not have the chlorophyll that helps green plants to make food. So fungi have to find a ready-made supply of food. Some feed as parasites on living plants or animals. Others feed on animal and plant remains.

There are more than 50,000 kinds of fungus. Some have only one CELL. Other fungi are chains of cells. These produce tiny, thread-like growths that spread through the substance they feed on. Many fungi grow a large fruiting body which sheds spores that produce new fungus plants. The MUSHROOMS we eat are the fruiting bodies of a fungus. Some fungi are useful. Pencillin, the ANTIBIOTIC drug, and YEAST are both fungi.

▲ *A highly-decorated queen's bathtub from the early Greek civilization at Knossos, on the island of Crete (1500 B.C.).*

▼ This chair dates from 2690 B.C. and is an example of the fine wooden furniture made by the ancient Egyptians.

▲ A French writing desk from the 1700s. French furniture from this period was often ornate and elaborately decorated.

Furniture

Furniture is used for resting things on and for storing things in. Beds, chairs, and tables all support some kind of load. Chests and closets hold things such as sheets and china. But as well as being useful, furniture can also be beautiful. People have always tried to make furniture attractive to look at as well as useful.

The first pieces of furniture were simple slabs of stone and roughly carved wood. As people became more sophisticated and wealthy, so furniture became more complex. The ancient Egyptians had carefully carved and painted tables and beds as much as 4,000 years ago. The Romans used bronze and marble as well to make furniture. Their furniture was often very skillfully made. After the RENAISSANCE, furniture-making in Europe became a great craft. In the 1700s especially, furniture-makers produced work that many people think has never been surpassed, and many people prize their work highly today. In the 1800s, people began to use new materials to make furniture. Furniture began to be mass produced and less expensive. This meant that more and more people were able to buy at least some pieces of furniture. Today, furniture is made from many different materials in many styles. A lot of modern furniture has clean, simple lines.

Furniture was so scarce in Europe during the Middle Ages that it was quite common for a visitor to bring along his or her bed and other pieces of furniture.

In England until the 17th century, the three-legged stool was still widely used. People thought that a chair should be used only by the lord of the manor.

▼ The sturdy Welsh dresser is a fine example of good country furniture of the 1800s.

▼ An American parlor bed, dating from 1891, which folded away when not in use.

▶ A light and elegant chair designed by Charles Rennie Mackintosh, the Scottish architect and designer.

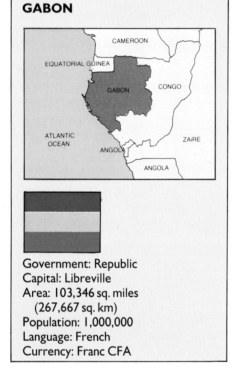

Government: Republic
Capital: Libreville
Area: 103,346 sq. miles
    (267,667 sq. km)
Population: 1,000,000
Language: French
Currency: Franc CFA

Gabon

Gabon is a country on the west coast of Africa. It lies on the equator, so it is hot and rainy there. Gabon is a land of high plateaus, mountains, and dense tropical forests. The country is rich in mineral resources, and trees are cut down for export. Most of Gabon's people are farmers who live in villages along the coast or along the rivers.

Gagarin, Yuri

Yuri Gagarin (1934–1968) was the first human being to travel into space. The Soviet cosmonaut was rocketed upward in *Vostok I* on April 12, 1961. He circled the Earth once in 108 minutes and landed by parachute within 6 miles (10 km) of the planned spot. After his famous flight, Gagarin continued to train as a cosmonaut, but he was killed in a plane crash in March, 1968.

Galaxy

Someone once called galaxies "star islands" in space. A galaxy is made up of a huge group of STARS. Our SUN is just one star of about 100,000 million stars that belong to the Milky Way galaxy. A beam of light would take about 100,000 years to shine from one side of the Milky Way to the other. Yet the Milky Way is only a middle-sized galaxy.

Beyond our galaxy, there may be as many as 10,000 million more. The nearest large galaxy is

▶ Our galaxy belongs to what we call the Local Group—a collection of about 30 galaxies. This diagram of the Local Group shows the galaxies so far discovered. It is drawn to a scale that shows their relative distances apart, although their sizes are not shown in scale.

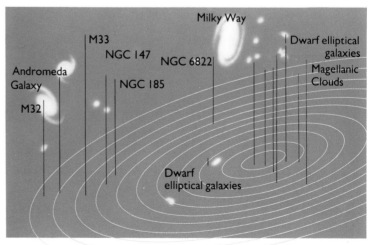

called Andromeda. The light we see it by took more than two million years to reach us.

Some galaxies have no special shape. Others have spiral arms made up of many millions of stars. The Milky Way and Andromeda galaxies both look like this. There are also galaxies that look like saucers or balls. Astronomers used to think that these changed into galaxies with spiral arms. Now some astronomers believe that the spiral galaxies shrink into the other kind instead.

RADIO ASTRONOMY has shown that radio waves are sent out from many galaxies. Strong radio waves also come from strange starlike objects known as QUASARS. Quasars are very powerful energy sources. Some people think that a quasar may be the beginning of a new galaxy. Scientists think that galaxies may form where GRAVITY pulls huge clouds of gas together.

▲ Edge on, our Milky Way galaxy looks like a flat disk with a swollen middle—the nucleus. From above, it looks like a whirlpool of stars. The position of our solar system is marked by the red arrows.

Galileo

Galileo Galilei (1564–1642) was an Italian mathematics teacher and one of the first true scientists. Instead of believing old ideas about the way the world worked, Galileo made careful experiments to find out for himself. He learned that a PENDULUM took the same time to make a long swing as it did to make a short one. He showed that light objects fell as fast as heavy ones when pulled toward the Earth

▲ Galileo was a mathematician, astronomer, and physicist, and one of the first true scientists.

283

by what we know as GRAVITY. He built a TELESCOPE and became the first man to use this tool for studying the Moon and PLANETS. What he saw made Galileo believe COPERNICUS's idea that the Earth was not the center of the UNIVERSE. The Church punished him for his belief in this idea. But later scientists like Isaac NEWTON built new knowledge on Galileo's discoveries.

Galleon

This kind of heavy, wooden sailing ship was used for carrying fighting men and cargoes over oceans in the 1500s. A galleon was four times as long as it was wide. It had a special deck to carry cannons. There were square sails on its two front masts and three-cornered *lateen* sails on its one or two rear masts. Lateen sails helped galleons to sail against the wind. Galleons were faster and easier to manage than some other ships, but some Spanish galleons were clumsy and top-heavy.

▲ A galleon sets sail. A gang of seamen unfurl the mainsail, and others in the main top adjust the running rigging.

INSIDE A GALLEON

1 Forecastle	6 Stone	11 Sail locker
2 Gun deck	ballast	12 Hold
3 Orlop	7 Cookhouse	13 Rudder
4 Bitts	8 Pump	14 Tiller
5 Anchor	9 Cannonball	15 Whipstaff
cable	store	16 Captain's
locker	10 Capstan	cabin

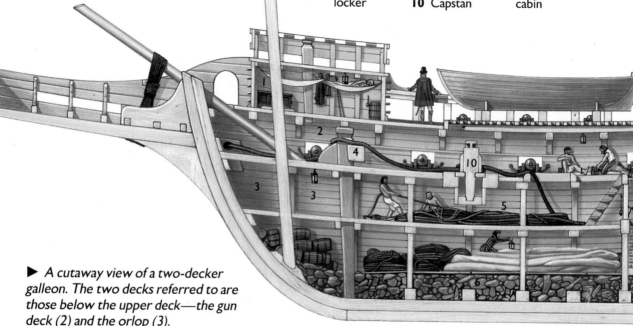

► A cutaway view of a two-decker galleon. The two decks referred to are those below the upper deck—the gun deck (2) and the orlop (3).

Gama, Vasco da

Vasco da Gama (about 1469–1524) discovered how to sail by sea from Europe to India by way of southern Africa. This Portuguese navigator left Lisbon with four ships in July, 1497. In East Africa, he found a guide who showed him how to sail across the Indian Ocean. Da Gama reached Calicut in southern India in May, 1498. But Arab traders who were jealous of the Portuguese tried to stop him from trading with the Indians. On the journey home, 30 of his 90 crewmen died of scurvy, and only two of the four ships got back to Lisbon.

But da Gama had found a way to reach the spice-rich lands of the East.

Gambia, The

The Gambia is Africa's smallest country. It is on the west coast and is about half the size of Massachusetts. Most Gambians are poor and earn their living as farmers. Peanuts are the main crop. In recent years, tourism has increased. Once a British colony, Gambia became independent in 1965.

THE GAMBIA

Government: Republic
Capital: Banjul
Area: 4,361 sq. miles (11,295 sq. km)
Population: 800,000
Language: English
Currency: Dalasi

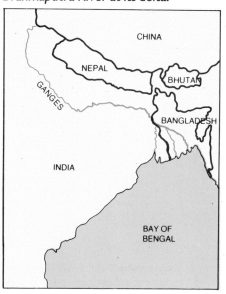

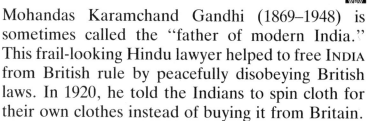

Gandhi

Mohandas Karamchand Gandhi (1869–1948) is sometimes called the "father of modern India." This frail-looking Hindu lawyer helped to free INDIA from British rule by peacefully disobeying British laws. In 1920, he told the Indians to spin cloth for their own clothes instead of buying it from Britain.

People admired Gandhi's beliefs, his kindness, and his simple way of life. He was called the Mahatma, meaning "Great Soul." In 1947, Britain gave India independence. Soon after, one of his fellow HINDUS shot Gandhi for preaching peace between Hindus and Muslims, followers of ISLAM.

▲ *Gandhi was called the* Mahatma *by his followers, which means "Great Soul."*

Gandhi, Indira

Indira Gandhi (1917–1984) was prime minister of India from 1966 until 1977 and from 1980 until her death. Her father, Jawaharlal Nehru, supported GANDHI and became India's first prime minister after independence. In 1942, Indira married a lawyer, Feroze Gandhi. For years, she helped her father. Then she went into politics herself. In power, Mrs. Gandhi fought for economic progress, social reforms, and national unity. In 1984, she was killed by two Sikhs, members of an Indian religious group, some of whom want their own state. Her son Rajiv succeeded her as India's prime minister.

▼ *The Ganges rises in the Himalayas and flows southeast to join the Brahmaputra River at its delta.*

Ganges River

The Ganges is the greatest river in INDIA. It flows for about 1,560 miles (2,500 km) and drains an area three times the size of Spain. The river rises in the HIMALAYAS and winds across northern India and BANGLADESH, then through a DELTA to the Bay of Bengal. Rich farmlands and great cities line its banks. HINDUS believe the river is sacred.

Garden

Gardens are pieces of land kept especially for growing lawns, flowering plants, fruits, vegetables, and other attractive shrubs and trees.

Rich people in ancient Egypt had gardens 4,500 years ago. The city of Babylon was later famous for hanging gardens. In the MIDDLE AGES, many monasteries also had gardens. New types of gardens with fountains, pools, terraces, steps, and pathways were developed during the RENAISSANCE in Italy. In the 1600s and 1700s, the French developed this type of garden, making it larger and more formal. In England, people preferred gardens that seemed more natural looking, with large lawns and trees around big houses. In the 1800s, cities laid out gardens where anyone could walk. Today, many houses have some sort of garden or yard.

JAMES A. GARFIELD

Twentieth President Mar.–Sept. 1881
Born: Orange, Ohio
Education: Williams College, Mass.
Occupation: Teacher
Political Party: Republican
Buried: Cleveland, Ohio

Garfield, James Abram

James Garfield (1831–1881) was the 20th president of the United States. But he served less than one year of his term in office. In July 1881, he was shot at the Washington train station and he died 80 days later. He was the second president to have been "assassinated," or killed. The man who killed him was protesting because he had not been given a job by the new president. In those days, many government jobs were given to supporters of the president. Many thought this was a bad way to run the government. After Garfield's death, reforms helped to end this system.

Garfield was a college professor and a soldier before he became a politican. He served bravely in the CIVIL WAR for the North and was made a general when he was only 31.

Garibaldi, Giuseppe

Giuseppe Garibaldi (1807–1882) was an Italian patriot who helped to turn Italy from a collection of small states into a united and independent country. After two periods of exile in America, Garibaldi led his followers, known as Redshirts, against the Austrians, who then controlled Italy. In 1860, he gained control of Sicily and southern Italy. Then he invaded mainland Italy and captured the important city of Naples. This victory helped make possible the uniting of Italy under King Victor Emmanuel.

▲ Giuseppe Garibaldi, who helped to create the modern state of Italy, began his career as cabin boy on a ship.

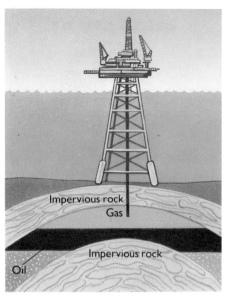

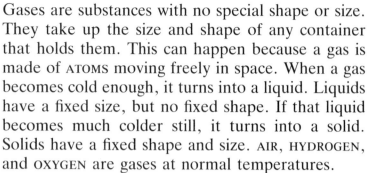

Gas

Gases are substances with no special shape or size. They take up the size and shape of any container that holds them. This can happen because a gas is made of ATOMS moving freely in space. When a gas becomes cold enough, it turns into a liquid. Liquids have a fixed size, but no fixed shape. If that liquid becomes much colder still, it turns into a solid. Solids have a fixed shape and size. AIR, HYDROGEN, and OXYGEN are gases at normal temperatures.

The gas some people use to cook and heat homes with is called NATURAL GAS. This gas is found beneath the Earth's surface in many parts of the world.

▲ *Oil and natural gas collect in porous rocks (rocks that allow liquids to soak through). They are trapped between impervious rocks (which will not allow liquids to pass through).*

Gasoline

Gasoline is made from an oil called petroleum, and is used to power cars and trucks. It is one of the most important fuels. It is made by "refining" the elements that make up petroleum. Though it is so important, gasoline also pollutes the air when it is burned. Its use has to be controlled carefully.

Gear

A gear is a wheel with teeth along its rim. These teeth can fit into the teeth of other gear wheels. Metal rods, or *axles*, are fitted into the center of each gear. If one axle is turned, its gear turns and makes the second gear turn. This makes the second axle turn, too.

Gears are used to increase or decrease the *speed* at which wheels turn. They are also used to increase or decrease the *turning power* of wheels.

In the picture on the left, the large gear wheel has twice as many teeth as the small wheel. If the small wheel is turned by an engine, the big wheel will turn at only half the speed of the small wheel, and the big wheel will turn in the opposite direction to the small wheel. But the big wheel will have twice the turning power of the small wheel. When a car is in low gear, this is what happens. The car goes quite slowly, but it has plenty of power for starting or going up hills.

▼ *Gear wheels turn at different speeds in proportion to the number of teeth they possess. The small wheel turns twice as fast as the large one if it has half the number of teeth.*

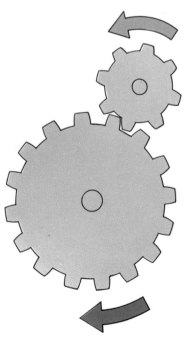

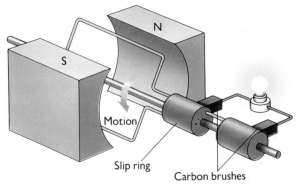

ALTERNATING CURRENT

Inside an AC generator, a coil of wire is turned between the poles of a magnet. Halfway through each turn, the coil becomes positioned for an instant at a right angle to the magnet. This causes the direction of the current to change.

Motion

Slip ring

Carbon brushes

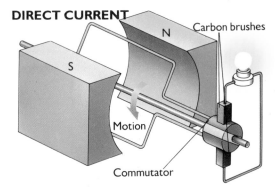

DIRECT CURRENT

Carbon brushes

N

S

Motion

Commutator

Direct current, such as that from a battery, can be obtained from a generator by using a device called a commutator. This makes the current flow continuously in the same direction.

Generator

Generators produce electric CURRENT. Huge generators in POWER PLANTS provide ELECTRICITY for homes and factories. The largest generators can light 20 million 100-watt electric lights. But there are tiny generators, too. A bicycle dynamo is a generator you can hold in one hand.

If a loop of wire is turned between the ends of a horseshoe-shaped magnet, an electric current flows in the wire. Generators work like this. They change the ENERGY of motion into electrical energy. The energy to work a generator's moving parts can come from wind, flowing water, or steam produced by heat from FUELS such as oil or coal. Big generators have thousands of coils of wire which are made to turn very quickly between powerful magnets.

Genetics

Each animal or plant passes on certain characteristics to its offspring. For example, we say that someone has "his father's eyes" or "her mother's hair." The science of genetics explains why living things look and behave as they do.

Heredity works in an amazing way. Each individ-

▲ An AC and a DC generator. Each has a wire coil held between the poles of a magnet.

▼ Albino animals such as this hedgehog are born white, with no coloring matter in their skin or hair. They have pink eyes. Albinos inherit their colorless condition from their ancestors' genes. An albino parent may produce normal young, and the young may later produce albinos.

The chances of a baby being a girl or boy are about the same. But one in 16 families with four children is likely to have four boys, while another such family will have four girls. Much longer strings of boys or girls have been recorded. One French family had nothing but girls—72 of them—in three generations.

▶ *Each of us has two genes for a characteristic such as eye color, one from each parent. If the two genes are different, one may have a stronger influence than the other. It is called the* dominant *gene. If someone inherits one brown eye gene and one blue eye gene, they will have brown eyes because the brown eye gene is dominant. The blue eye gene is called the* recessive *gene. If someone inherits two blue eye genes, one from each parent, he or she can only have blue eyes.*

▼ *At its height, the Mongol empire under Genghis Khan stretched from China in the east right across Asia.*

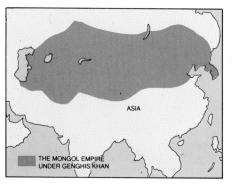

THE MONGOL EMPIRE
UNDER GENGHIS KHAN

ual produces sex cells. If a male and female cell join, the female cell grows into a new individual. Inside every cell there are tiny chromosomes, largely made of a chemical called DNA. Different parts of each chromosome carry different coded messages. Each of these parts is called a *gene*. The genes carry all the information needed to make a new plant or animal look and behave as it does. They decide its sex and also every other characteristic it inherits from its parents.

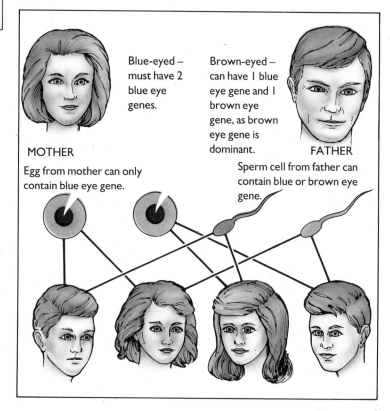

Blue-eyed — must have 2 blue eye genes.

Brown-eyed — can have 1 blue eye gene and 1 brown eye gene, as brown eye gene is dominant.

MOTHER

FATHER

Egg from mother can only contain blue eye gene.

Sperm cell from father can contain blue or brown eye gene.

Genghis Khan

Genghis Khan (1167–1227) was a Mongol chief who cruelly attacked many Asian peoples and won a mighty empire. His real name was Temujin ("iron-smith").

At 13, he took his dead father's place as chief of a small Mongol tribe of nomads. He soon won power over nearby tribes as well. In 1206, he became known as Genghis Khan, "Very Mighty King." Genghis Khan formed a huge army of tough, hard-riding nomads on the great grasslands of central Asia. Then he set off to conquer the lands around

him. His troops pushed southeast to Beijing in China, and south into Tibet and what are now Pakistan and Afghanistan. In the southwest, they invaded Persia (Iran) and southern Russia.

After he died, other Mongol rulers won more land and made the empire even larger.

▲ *Genghis Khan put together a huge, organized army. Each man had five ponies, ridden in turn so that they would not get tired. When the Mongols besieged a city, most of the inhabitants were killed, and the land around was laid waste.*

Geography

Geography is the subject we study when we want to learn about the surface of the Earth. Geographers study everything on the Earth—the land, sea, air, plants, animals, and people. They explain where different things are found, how they got there, and how they affect one another.

There are many different areas, or branches, of geography. For instance, physical geography describes things liks mountains, valleys, lakes, and rivers. Meteorology describes weather. Economic geography deals with farming, mining, manufacturing, and trade. Human geography divides the peoples of the world into *cultures*.

MAPS AND CHARTS are the geographer's most useful tools.

> **Ptolemy of Alexandria was the most famous ancient geographer—he lived about A.D.150. Ptolemy drew a map of the then-known world that is remarkably accurate, considering what was known about the Earth in those days. His eight-volume *Guide to Geography* consisted of a list of all known places, each with its latitude and longitude, a system Ptolemy devised.**

GEOLOGY

► *Geologists study rocks, which tell them about the Earth's structure. There are three kinds of rock:* igneous, *formed when molten rock is pushed up from deep inside the Earth;* sedimentary, *which is hardened layers of sediment; and* metamorphic, *which is igneous or sedimentary rock that has been changed by heat and pressure inside the Earth. Of the rocks shown here, obsidian (1) and granite (2) are igneous rocks, marble (3) and slate (4) are metamorphic rocks, and coal (5), limestone (6), and sandstone (7) are sedimentary rocks. Conglomerate (8) is made up of stone stuck together in a sedimentary "concrete."*

For a long time, people have tried to work out the age of the Earth. In the 1600s, an Irish archbishop named Ussher decided from reading the Scriptures that the world was created in 4004 B.C. It was not long, however, before geologists realized by examining the rocks that this date was very wrong. We now know that the Earth was formed about $4\frac{1}{2}$ billion years ago.

In geometry, we learn that the three angles of any triangle add up to 180 degrees—a straight line. You can prove this by cutting out a triangle from a piece of paper. Tear off the three angles and rearrange them so that the sides, angles and corners are together. They make a straight angle of 180°.

Geology

Geology is the study of the Earth itself. Geologists discover what things the Earth is made of, where they are found, and how they got there. Geologists study the chemicals in ROCKS and MINERALS. They also try to find out how rocks are formed, and how they are changed by movements beneath the surface of the Earth. VOLCANOES and EARTHQUAKES give us useful clues about movements deep down underground.

Geologists also study the history of the Earth. They have found rock 3.8 billion years old and FOSSILS showing that EVOLUTION began over 3.4 billion years ago.

Geologists help engineers to choose where to build a road or tunnel. They help miners to find coal, oil, or gas beneath the ground. By studying rocks brought back by astronauts, they were able to tell us what the Moon is made of.

Geometry

Geometry is a branch of MATHEMATICS. It can help you to find out the shape, size, and position of an object, or how much a container holds. People draw lines and measure ANGLES to help them solve geometric problems.

Georgia

Georgia is a southern state, and one of the 13 original states. Farming is important to it, but many modern "service" industries help to make Georgia prosperous today. Some people think Georgia one of the most beautiful states. Its lush vegetation, especially its pine trees and magnolias, are famous.

Georgia was named in 1732 for George II of England. But the first Europeans to visit it were Spaniards, in 1540. Later, Frenchmen settled here, too. But by the mid-1700s, Georgia was an English colony. There was fierce fighting here in the Revolutionary War before the British were driven out.

In the 1800s, Georgia's prosperity was based on cotton and slaves. It was one of the first states to leave the Union before the Civil War. Union troops destroyed huge areas of the state and burned the capital, Atlanta. For many years afterward, Georgia was one of the poorest states.

Germ See Bacteria; Virus

Germany

Germany used to be one great nation. After WORLD WAR II, the land was divided into two countries: West Germany and East Germany. Both lie in the middle of EUROPE, and their peoples speak the same language, German.

West Germany is a little smaller than the state

GEORGIA

Capital: Atlanta
Population: 5,970,000
Area: 58,876 sq.mi. (152,488 sq.km)
State flower: Cherokee Rose
State bird: Brown Thrasher
State tree: Live Oak
Statehood: January 2, 1788
4th state

▲ *The Okefenokee National Wildlife Refuge at Folkston, Georgia.*

◀ *The city of Dresden in East Germany was almost totally rebuilt after being heavily bombed in World War II.*

▶ *Traditional buildings line this street in Lohr-am-Main in West Germany.*

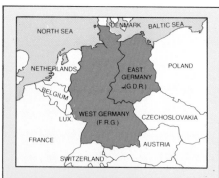

WEST GERMANY (FEDERAL REPUBLIC OF GERMANY)

Government: Federal republic
Capital: Bonn
Area: 95,976 sq. miles (248,577 sq. km)
Population: 60,000,000
Language: German
Currency: Mark

EAST GERMANY (GERMAN DEMOCRATIC REPUBLIC)

Government: Communist
Capital: East Berlin
Area: 41,768 sq. miles (108,178 sq. km)
Population: 16,700,000
Language: German
Currency: DDR Mark

of Wyoming and has more people than any other nation in Western Europe. Farms and cities stand on the low plain in the north and in the valley of the River Rhine. The south has low, wooded mountains and sharp tall peaks belonging to the ALPS.

West Germany's farms produce more pigs and barley than any other western European nation. No other western European country produces so much coal or steel, or so many cars and television sets. West Germany's mines and factories make it the richest nation in Europe. The capital is Bonn.

East Germany is less than half the size of West Germany. There is only one East German for roughly every three West Germans. Like West Germany, East Germany has low, flat land in the north and forested mountains in the south. The rivers Elbe and Oder flow north toward the Baltic Sea. East Germany, too, has factories and mines. It is a communist country, but in 1989 its people secured a more democratic form of government.

Gershwin, George and Ira

George (1898–1937) and his brother Ira (1896–1983) were two of the most important American songwriters of the 20th century. George wrote the music, Ira wrote the words. Their most famous works includes the opera *Porgy and Bess* and songs such as *I Got Rhythm*. George also wrote many orchestral works. The best known and most influential is *Rhapsody in Blue*.

Geyser

Geysers are hot springs that now and then squirt out steam and scalding water. They work like this. Water fills a deep crack in the ground, often near VOLCANOES. Hot rock heats the water deep underground, but the weight of the water above it stops the hot water from boiling until it is much hotter still. Then it turns to steam, which forces the water upward, emptying the crack. The next eruption happens when the crack is full again.

There are many geysers in some parts of Iceland, the United States, and New Zealand. The tallest geyser ever known was the Waimangu Geyser in New Zealand. In 1904, it squirted steam and water nearly 1,520 ft. (460 m) into the sky.

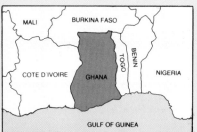

Geyser

Hot rock

Super-heated water

▲ *A geyser seems to work in a similar way to a pressure cooker. The higher the pressure, the hotter the water has to be to boil. The super-heated steam and water is pushed out as a powerful jet. When enough water has seeped back and heated up, the process starts again.*

Ghana

Ghana is a nation in West AFRICA. It is a little smaller than Oregon. The country is hot, with plenty of rain in the south where Ghana meets the Atlantic Ocean. The land here is low, with tropical

▼ *Women sell pineapples in a market in Ghana. Two-thirds of Ghana's people live in the southern third of the country.*

GHANA

Government: Authoritarian
Capital: Accra
Area: 92,100 sq. miles (238,537 sq. km)
Population: 13,000,000
Language: English
Currency: Cedi

295

▼ *A giraffe's long neck and legs enable it to eat the leaves from branches that are far above the reach of other browsing animals.*

forests and farms. The north is drier and grassy.

Most of Ghana's 13 million people are farmers. They grow cocoa and mine diamonds and gold. Lake Volta provides water power to make electricity. This manmade lake covers a greater area than any other manmade lake in the world.

Giraffe

Giraffes are the tallest animals. An adult male may stand three times taller than a tall man. They have long legs and a long neck. Yet this neck has only seven bones, the same as any other MAMMAL. Giraffes live in the hot grasslands of Africa and feed on leaves from shrubs and trees.

Glacier

Glaciers are rivers of ice. Most form high up in mountains where snow falls and never melts. As snow piles up, the lower layers are crushed and turn to ice. This begins to flow very slowly downhill through valleys. Most glaciers take a year to flow as far as you can walk in five minutes. The rocks they

▼ *Glaciers move faster at the center than at the sides. This creates huge gaps, or crevasses.*

The ice in glaciers moves very slowly—usually only a few inches a day. However, sometimes things speed up. In 1936, the Black Rapids Glacier in Alaska advanced by more than 200 feet (60 m) a day.

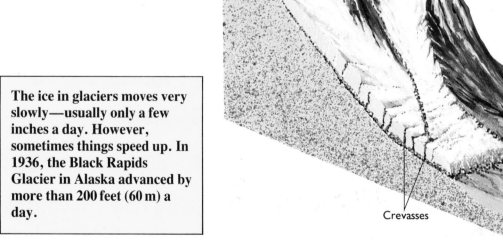

Crevasses

carry grind against the sides and floor of each valley until they make it deep and wide.

During ICE AGES, glaciers spread beyond the mountains. When the weather warms up, they melt, leaving a valley behind. Many valleys in the ALPS and ROCKY MOUNTAINS once held glaciers.

Gladiator

Gladiators were men trained to fight to the death in shows to entertain crowds in ancient Rome. Many gladiators were criminals, prisoners of war, or slaves. Some fought with a sword and shield. Others had a three-pronged spear and a net. Most fights ended when one gladiator killed the other.

▲ *Successful gladiators became famous in Rome. They were carefully fed and received medical care.*

Gland

Glands are organs that produce special substances needed by the body. There are two kinds—*endocrine* and *exocrine* glands. Endocrine glands send their substances, called *hormones*, directly into the bloodstream. One main endocrine gland is the *thyroid*. Its hormone controls the rate at which the body uses energy.

Exocrine glands release their substances through tubes, either into the intestines or onto the skin. Sweat, tears, and saliva come from exocrine glands.

▼ *Endocrine glands produce hormones that control such things as growth and reproduction.*

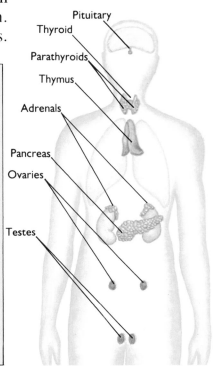

THE ENDOCRINE GLANDS	
Pituitary gland	The small "master gland" that produces at least nine hormones, including those that control growth and reproduction
Thyroid gland	Controls the rate at which food is converted into energy. The tiny **parathyroids** regulate the amount of calcium in your bones and blood
Ovaries	Produce estrogen and progesterone, which control female characteristics. Also produce the ova, or egg cells
Testes	Produce testosterone, which controls the production of sperm cells and male characteristics
Pancreas	Produces insulin, which controls the level of glucose, a source of energy
Adrenal glands	Produce adrenaline, the "emergency" hormone that speeds up heartbeat and breathing rate when danger threatens.

▲ *Hang gliding is a popular sport. The glider's design was the result of NASA research into spacecraft re-entry as part of the U.S. space program.*

Glass

People use glass in windows, eyeglasses, mirrors, tumblers, bottles, electric light bulbs, and many other objects. (See pages 300–301.)

Glenn, John Herschel, Jr.

John Glenn was the third American to go into space and the first to orbit the Earth. His flight was in 1962. It lasted less than five hours but it reassured America that it was keeping pace with the Soviet Union in the space race. Afterward, he became a politician, and in 1975 was elected a senator.

Gliding

Gliding is flying without using engine power. Gliding AIRCRAFT called sailplanes have long narrow wings. This gives them extra *lift*. The glider is launched by a winch or a towing aircraft. Once it is aloft, it loses height very gradually, kept up by rising air currents.

In 1853, the first glider to carry a man flew just across a valley. Modern sailplanes can do much more than that. In 1986, one sailplane reached a

To become a glider pilot in the U.S., a person must be 14 or older, and to get a private glider pilot's license he or she must be at least 16.

height of 37,730 feet (11,500 m) over California.

Hang gliding is a sport in which the pilot is suspended from the glider by a harness and a trapeze-like bar. The wing is light—usually 48 to 100 lbs. (22 to 44 kg) in weight—so that it can be carried and launched by one person. Take-off is from a hill, cliff, or mountain steep enough to achieve flight. While in the air, pilots use their body weight to control the glider.

Goat

Goats are taller, thinner, and more agile animals than their close relatives, the SHEEP. Goats have hoofs and hollow horns; the male has a beard.

Wild goats, found in the mountains of central Asia and the Middle East, live in herds and eat grass and leaves. Domestic goats are kept in many lands. They provide milk, meat, hair, and skins. Two kinds, Angora and Cashmere goats, are famous for their silky wool, which is woven into fine cloth.

Gold

This is a yellow metal that never gets rusty. It is so soft that you can beat it into thin sheets, or pull it out into a wire.

Continued on page 302

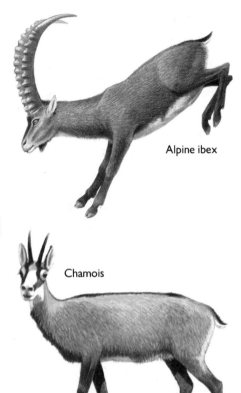

Alpine ibex

Chamois

▲ *The Alpine ibex is a wild goat that lives above the treeline in Alpine meadows and hillsides. It was hunted almost to extinction and is now protected by law. The chamois is a small mountain goat known for its leaps. Its soft hide is used for polishing.*

◀ *These gold bars in a Swiss bank are checked for purity with a machine that can "look" inside them by using sound.*

> **The biggest gold nugget ever found weighed about 471 lbs. (214 kg). It was discovered in New South Wales, Australia, in 1872. When refined, it yielded about 187 lbs. (85 kg) of pure gold.**

GLASS

Glass is one of our most useful materials. It is easy to shape and cheap to make. It is also transparent, so you can see through it. Glass can be made as flat sheets, thick castings, or delicate wafers. It can be made into curved lenses for cameras, microscopes, and other optical instruments. It can be blown into bottles, or drawn out into tubes, wires, and very thin fibers.

Glass is made from mixing and heating sand, limestone, and soda ash. When these ingredients melt, they become glass. Special ingredients can be added to make glass that is heat-proof, extra-tough, or colored. Although glass looks like a solid, it is really a "supercooled" liquid. Glass is a good electrical insulator as it does not conduct current easily. It also resists common chemicals and nuclear radiation.

METHODS OF MAKING GLASS

Blowing Once done only by hand, glass-blowing is now also done by machines to make such things as bottles and light bulbs.

Pressing This is done by pushing partly melted glass into a mold, then cooling it. Ovenware and insulators are made by this method.

Drawing To pull out glass into tubes or wires, molten glass is drawn over a series of pulleys while air is blown through or around it. Drawn glass makes fluorescent tubes and pipes.

Casting This is done by pouring hot, molten glass into molds. The big optical telescopes used by astronomers have cast-glass lens disks.

Rolling A series of rollers squeeze molten glass into flat sheets (like rolling out pastry).

Floating This is a method of making sheet glass by floating the molten glass across a bath of molten tin.

STAINED GLASS

Some of the most magnificent decorative stained glass was made in Europe during the Middle Ages. You can see examples in many churches and cathedrals, especially in Britain, France, Germany, and Italy.
The art of making stained glass flourished from the 1100s. By this time, glassmakers were able to make glass in many colors, and windows could be made much larger than before. Artists fitted pieces of colored glass together with lead to make beautiful designs for windows. Often medieval stained glass illustrates a Bible story, illuminated by the light streaming through the glass. Modern stained glass artists continue the craft, using similar techniques.

▼ *Sparkling crystal glassware has been made in England and Ireland since the 1700s. Lead is used instead of limestone to give crystal its shine.*

BOTTLE GLASS PRODUCTION

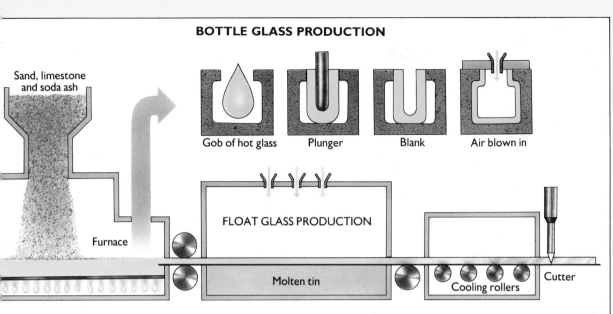

Sand, limestone and soda ash

Gob of hot glass | Plunger | Blank | Air blown in

Furnace

FLOAT GLASS PRODUCTION

Molten tin

Cooling rollers

Cutter

In glass manufacture, sand, soda ash, and limestone are loaded into the furnace, [alo]ng with "cullet"—old pieces of glass. Molten glass from the furnace may either be [mo]lded and blown into hollow shapes (above), or shaped into flat sheets by the "float [gla]ss" method (below). In the float glass process, molten glass is floated on a "bath" of [m]olten tin and then cooled and cut into lengths.

The edges of float glass are automatically trimmed as it moves over rollers. Glass-[bl]owing (inset) is the traditional way of making glass objects. "Gobs" of molten glass are [pl]aced on the end of a long tube. Blowing down the tube produces a bubble that can be [sh]aped before it cools.

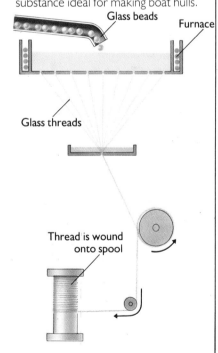

GLASS FIBER

Glass can be drawn out into long threads by pouring red-hot molten glass through the bottom of a furnace. One important use for this thread is in fiberglass. For this, it is combined with plastic to give an easily molded, light and strong substance ideal for making boat hulls.

Glass beads — Furnace

Glass threads

Thread is wound onto spool

For more information turn to these articles: ARCHITECTURE; BUILDING; CATHEDRAL; LENS; LIGHT; TELESCOPE.

▲ *The gold used for crowning teeth is normally at least 20 carats—nearly pure gold.*

▶ *The common aquarium goldfish may be red, gold, yellow, or white. The comet is one of the "fancy" varieties of goldfish.*

▼ *Under Mikhail Gorbachev's leadership, the U.S.S.R. has become a more open society.*

People find thin veins of gold in cracks in certain rocks. It was formed long ago by hot gases and liquids rising from deep underground. If water washes the gold out, lumps called nuggets may collect in the beds of streams and rivers. Half of the world's gold is mined in just one part of South Africa.

Because gold is beautiful and scarce, it is also very valuable. Most of the world's gold is kept in brick-shaped bars (called ingots) in BANKS. People make jewelry from gold mixed with other substances to make it harder. But gold is useful, too. Dentists sometimes put gold fillings in people's teeth.

Goldfish

Goldfish are a type of carp that are usually gold, gold and black, or gold and white in color. They are easy to keep as pets in tanks or ponds. Goldfish came originally from China. They can grow up to 12 in. (30 cm) long and may live for 20 years or more.

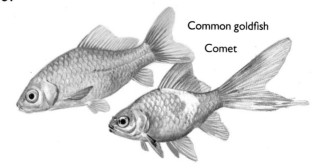

Common goldfish

Comet

Gorbachev, Mikhail

Mikhail Gorbachev is general secretary of the Soviet Communist Party and president of the Soviet Union. He has been in power since 1985. He has attempted many reforms of the Soviet Union to make it a more prosperous and democratic country. The most famous is called "perestroika." It means reconstruction. "Glasnost," or openness, is also an important part of his plan to make the Soviet Union more free. Gorbachev has also taken steps to reduce the number of the Soviet Union's nuclear weapons. He signed an "arms reduction treaty" with President Reagan in 1987, and held important arms and trade talks with President Bush.

Gorilla

Gorillas are the largest of the APES. A big male may be as tall as a man. Gorillas live in family groups in the warm forests of central Africa. They eat fruit, roots, tree bark, and leaves. Every night, they make beds of twigs in the low branches of trees.

▲ Gorillas live in family groups. The leading male defends the group if danger threatens and takes charge of nest building.

Government

When people live and work together, they need some kind of government. Governments are needed to make laws, control trade and finance, and look after relations with other countries. Most modern governments are either *democratic*, *bureaucratic*, or *totalitarian*. DEMOCRACY is a system in which the people vote for their leaders and remove them from power if they think the leaders have failed. Bureaucratic forms of government are run by officials who are usually appointed and who can be removed only by other officials. Totalitarianism is a system in which one person or group has complete control over the people and can't be voted out of office. If one person controls a country, that country is a dictatorship. Hitler and Mussolini were dictators.

There are different kinds of democracies. Great Britain is a democratic monarchy with a king or queen as head of state. The country is, however,

Gorillas in zoos are normally heavier than those in their natural surroundings. It is not unusual for male gorillas in captivity to weigh as much as 570 lbs. (260 kg), four times the weight of a man. They can reach a height of 6 ft. (1.8 m). Females are shorter and weigh about half as much as the males.

▲ *The Palace of Westminster in London is the seat of government where both houses of the parliament of the United Kingdom meet.*

FORMS OF GOVERNMENT

System	Ruled by
Anarchy	No rule of law
Aristocracy	Privileged people
Autocracy	One person, absolutely
Bureaucracy	Officials
Democracy	The people
Matriarchy	A mother, or mothers
Meritocracy	The most able
Monarchy	A hereditary king or queen
Patriarchy	A male head of family
Plutocracy	The wealthy

governed by PARLIAMENT. The United States is a republic with a president as head of state. The U.S. government is divided into three branches. Congress makes the laws. The executive, with the president in charge, proposes and enforces the laws. The judicial branch decides which laws are constitutional (agree with the Constitution).

Grammar

Words must be arranged in special ways to make sentences that are understood. Grammar is the study of the ways in which words are formed and arranged to make sentences.

Words are usually classified as *parts of speech*, according to what they do in a sentence. There are four main kinds of words: VERBS (action words). NOUNS and pronouns (naming words), ADJECTIVES (describing words for nouns or pronouns), and adverbs (describing words for verbs and adjectives). Words can change from one part of speech to another. "Clean" can be a verb or an adjective. "Can" can be a noun or a verb.

If someone says "I see the cat," he or she is speaking of something happening now. If they say "I saw the cat," it happened in the past. The word "see," changes to "saw." Changes like this are called *inflections*.

The order of words in a sentence is very important. "The dog bites the girl" means something quite different from "The girl bites the dog," but exactly the same words are used. It is usual in English for the subject of a sentence—"dog" in the first example, "girl" in the second—to come before the verb—"bites." Exceptions to this rule are called *idioms*—"There goes the boy."

▶ *Every sentence can be broken down into its parts of speech. To be a sentence, it must have a subject (noun) and a verb.*

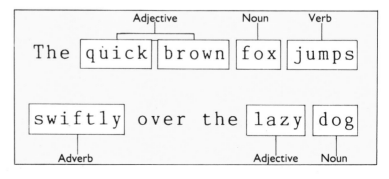

304

Grand Canyon

The Colorado River carved this deep gash in the Earth's surface. The canyon crosses a desert in Arizona. The canyon is about 220 miles (350 km) long. It is up to 12½ miles (20 km) across, and as much as 1¼ miles (2 km) deep. This is the deepest gorge anywhere on land.

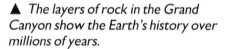

▲ The layers of rock in the Grand Canyon show the Earth's history over millions of years.

▼ Granite quarried in Scotland was used to build this castle near Fort William. Large blocks of granite for building are often blasted with gunpowder instead of dynamite, as it causes less of an explosion.

Granite

Granite is a hard rock made largely of CRYSTALS OF QUARTZ and feldspar. Quartz is transparent, like glass. Feldspar is pink, white, or gray. Granite also has specks of dark MINERALS in it.

Granite was once a mass of hot, melted rock underground. As the rock cooled, it hardened. Then movements of the Earth's crust forced it up to the surface. The weather very slowly breaks down granite into sand and clay.

Builders use granite when they need a hard, strong stone. People also use granite to make polished stone monuments, because they last longer than those made of limestone.

ULYSSES S. GRANT

Eighteenth President 1869–1877
Born: Point Pleasant, Ohio
Education: U.S. Military Academy,
    West Point, New York
Occupation: Army officer
Political Party: Republican
Buried: Grant's Tomb, Riverside
    Drive, New York City

Grant, Ulysses Simpson

Ulysses S. Grant (1822–1885) was the 18th president of the United States, in office from 1869 to 1877. Before that, he was the commander of the victorious Union forces during the last years of the Civil War. To many people, Grant is better known as a soldier than as a politician. He secured many important victories for the Union forces in the war. The commander of the Confederate forces, Robert E. LEE, surrendered personally to him in 1865 to end the war. Grant's presidency was not always successful. Though he helped greatly in the "reconstruction" of the South after the war, and was popular there, many scandals involving corruption of high officials affected his time in office.

Grass

Grasses are flowering plants with long, thin leaves growing from hollow stems. BAMBOO is as tall as a tree, but most grasses are short. Sheep and cattle eat grass. We eat the seeds of cultivated CEREAL grasses like WHEAT and RICE.

Grasshopper

These insects have feelers, wings, and long back legs. A grasshopper can jump 20 times its own length. Grasshoppers eat leaves, and those called LOCUSTS damage crops. Many males "sing" by rubbing their back legs on their wings.

Gravity

Gravity is the pull that tries to tug everything toward the middle of the EARTH. It is gravity that makes objects tend to fall, stops us from flying off into space, and keeps the MOON circling the Earth. When we weigh something, we are measuring the force with which gravity pulls that object down. The more closely packed the substances in an object are, the heavier it seems.

Not just the Earth, but all PLANETS and STARS exert a pulling force. Scientists call this gravitation.

Common reed   False oat   Meadow foxtail

▲ *Three of the more than 10,000 species of grass. The flowers, and later the grains, are contained in scaly spikelets (inset).*

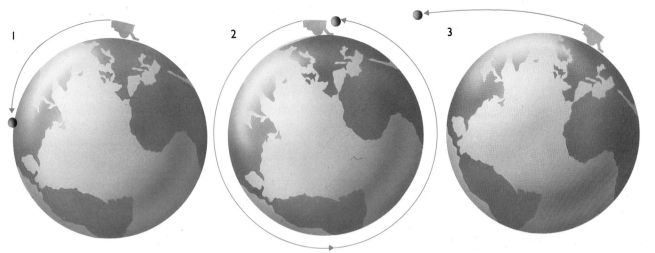

The larger and denser a star or a planet is and the nearer it is to other objects, the more strongly it pulls them toward it. The SUN is far from the planets, but it is so huge that its gravitation keeps the planets circling around it. The Moon is small, and its gravitation is weak. An astronaut on the Moon weighs far less than he weighs on Earth, although his *mass* stays the same.

▲ *A small body, such as the cannonball above, balances its speed against the gravitational pull. The speed in this path is too low, and it falls to the ground (1). When it is fired at a greater speed, it is attracted toward the surface at the same rate as the surface curves away, and it will go into orbit (2). If its speed is too fast, gravity cannot hold it, and it escapes into space (3).*

Great Britain *See* United Kingdom

Great Lakes

This the world's largest group of freshwater lakes. They extend from New York state to Minnesota. Lake Michigan lies in the UNITED STATES. Lakes Superior, Erie, Huron, and Ontario are shared by the United States and CANADA. The largest lake of all is Superior. The lakes were formed when a huge sheet of ice melted 18,000 years ago.

Eight states of the United States touch the Great Lakes. These eight states make more than half of the country's manufactured goods. Two-thirds of Canada's population and most of its factories lie on the Great Lakes or on the St. Lawrence River. A ship can go from the Atlantic up the St. Lawrence River and through the lakes to the western end of Lake Superior, halfway across the continent of North America.

◀ *Lakes Erie and Ontario are on two different levels, linked by the 165 ft. (50 m) Niagara Falls and the Niagara River. Ships avoid this route by using the Welland Canal.*

▲ *The sun-baked buildings of this town on the Greek island of Santorini, also known as Thera, perch on the remains of an exploded volcano.*

Rivers and canals connect the lakes to each other and to the Atlantic Ocean. Ships can reach the sea from lake ports that lie 1,000 miles (1,600 km) inland. Lots of factories are built around the lakes. Most of the goods that the factories produce are taken to other parts of the country by boat.

Great Wall of China

More than 2,000 years ago, the first emperor of CHINA, Shih Huang Ti, built this wall to keep out China's enemies from the north. The Great Wall is the longest wall in the world. It stretches for 1,500 miles (2,400 km) from western China to the Yellow Sea.

The wall is made from earth and stone. Watchtowers were built every 660 feet (200 m) along it. Chinese sentries sent warning signals from the towers if anyone attacked the wall. The signal was smoke by day and a fire at night.

Greece

Greece is a country that lies in southeastern EUROPE. Mountains cover most of the land, and peninsulas poke out into the sea like giant fingers. Greece includes the island of Crete and many smaller islands in the Aegean and Ionian seas. Greek summers are hot and dry. Winters are mild and wet.

Greek farmers produce lemons, grapes, and olives. Millions of tourists visit Greece every year.

GREECE

Government: Presidential parliamentary republic
Capital: Athens
Area: 50,944 sq. miles
    (131,944 sq. km)
Population: 10,000,000
Language: Greek
Currency: Drachma

Greece, Ancient

The first great people in Greece were the Minoans and the Mycenaeans. The Minoans lived in Crete. They had rich cities and farms and led a peaceful life. The Mycenaeans lived on the mainland of Greece. They were warriors and sailors. The heroes of HOMER's poems were probably Mycenaean. Both these civilizations ended in about 1200 B.C.

Around this time, new groups of people began to move into Greece. They came from the north, but spoke Greek. Instead of making Greece one kingdom, they built separate cities. They often fought wars with each other. Sometimes, they joined together to fight foreign enemies, such as the Persians. Two of the strongest cities were Athens and Sparta. In the 400s B.C. Athens was ruled by a DEMOCRACY. It became very powerful.

The Greeks loved the theater, art, and poetry. They had many great thinkers, or *philosophers*, including ARISTOTLE, PLATO, and Socrates. Greek cities had many graceful buildings. They were decorated with beautiful SCULPTURE. The Greeks also started the first OLYMPIC GAMES. In 339 B.C. Greece was conquered by Philip, the father of ALEXANDER THE GREAT.

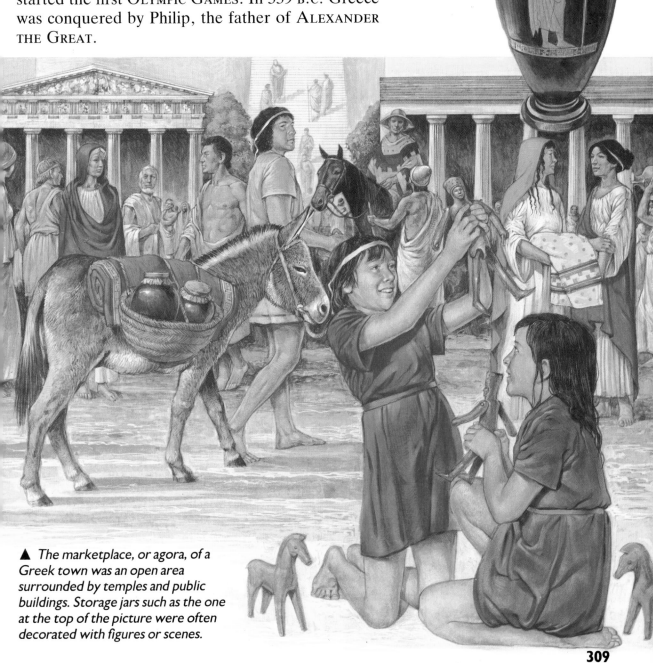

▲ *The marketplace, or agora, of a Greek town was an open area surrounded by temples and public buildings. Storage jars such as the one at the top of the picture were often decorated with figures or scenes.*

GREEK GODS	
God	*Title*
Apollo	God of the Sun
Artemis	Goddess of the Moon and Hunting
Athena	Goddess of Wisdom
Demeter	Goddess of Agriculture
Dionysus	God of Wine
Eros	God of Love
Hades, Pluto	God of the Underworld
Hera	Goddess of Marriage
Hermes	Messenger of the Gods
Hestia	Goddess of the Hearth
Hephaestus	God of Fire
Poseidon	God of the Sea and Waters
Zeus	Leader of the Gods

Greek Mythology

The ancient Greeks, like all peoples who lived thousands of years ago, invented gods and goddesses to explain the world around them. Stories about these *deities* are called *myths*. In Greek mythology, many of the gods lived on Mount Olympus. There they ate a special food called *ambrosia* and drank *nectar* to make them immortal. The greatest god was Zeus. When he was angry, he made thunder. Zeus had many children. One, Athena, was the goddess of wisdom. The city of Athens is named after her. Another, Apollo, was the sun god. He drove the sun's chariot across the sky each day.

▶ *Fishing boats lie at anchor in the coastal town of Jakobshavn in Greenland. Fishing and processing fish are Greenland's chief activities.*

GREENLAND

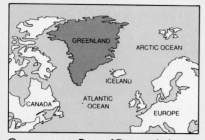

Government: Part of Denmark, but with home rule
Capital: Godthaab (Nuuk)
Area: 839,782 sq. miles (2,175,600 sq. km)
Average ice depth: 4,950 ft. (1,500 m)
Highest point: Gunnbjornsfjaeld, 12,214 ft. (3,700 m)
Official name of Greenland: Kalaallit Nunaat
Population: 53,000

Greenland

Greenland is the world's largest island. VIKINGS discovered it nearly 1,000 years ago. It lies northeast of Canada, but belongs to DENMARK, a small European country. Since 1979, Greenland has enjoyed home rule. It is 50 times the size of Denmark, but it holds no more people than a large town. This is because Greenland is so cold. Most of it lies in the ARCTIC. Thick ice covers seven-eighths of the island. Bare mountains make up much of the rest. The capital is Godthaab.

Most Greenlanders live in villages of wooden houses near the coast. Some are Danes, many are ESKIMOS. A few Eskimos hunt seals, but many Greenlanders are fishermen.

Grenada

Grenada is the smallest nation in the western hemisphere. It is a group of small islands in the south Caribbean Sea. Grenada was a British colony until 1958 and gained full independence within the Commonwealth in 1974. The nation is a leading producer of nutmeg and other spices.

Guam

Guam is the largest of the Marianas Islands in the Pacific Ocean. It has a tropical climate with heavy seasonal rainfall. The country depends largely on income from U.S. military installations. Guam became United States territory after the Spanish-American War. The people have U.S. citizenship, but are self-governing.

Guatemala

More people live in Guatemala than in any other Central American country. Nearly half of them are Indians, descendants of the MAYAS. Guatemala is a land of dense jungles, volcanoes, dry deserts, and sparkling lakes. Most of the people earn their

GRENADA

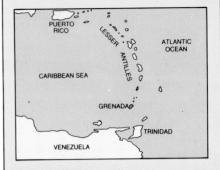

Government: Independent British colony
Capital: St. George's
Area: 133 sq. miles (344 sq. km)
Population: 113,000
Language: English
Currency: East Caribbean dollar

GUAM

Government: Self-governing U.S. territory
Capital: Agana
Area: 209 sq. miles (541 sq. km)
Population: 120,000
Language: English
Currency: Dollar

◄ *This magnificent temple at Tikal in Guatemala was once part of the Mayan Empire, a civilization dating back to the A.D.100s.*

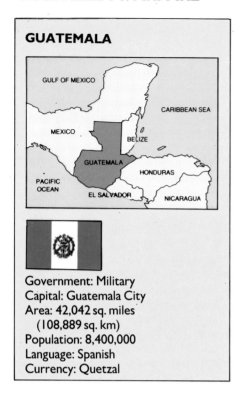

GUATEMALA

Government: Military
Capital: Guatemala City
Area: 42,042 sq. miles
   (108,889 sq. km)
Population: 8,400,000
Language: Spanish
Currency: Quetzal

living by farming—coffee, cotton, and bananas are the main products. The country was conquered by the Spanish in 1524, declared its independence in 1821, and became a republic in 1839.

Guerrilla Warfare

Guerrillas are "hit and run" fighters. Often they do not wear regular uniforms, and they live in the countryside, relying on help from friendly local people. The word "guerrilla" is Spanish for "little war." Guerrilla tactics are most often used by small groups of people who are fighting against a larger and more organized force. Guerrillas usually live in places where they can easily hide, such as forests or mountains. Urban guerrillas operate in cities and towns.

Guided Missile

A guided missile is usually a rocket-powered missile armed with an explosive warhead. The missile is guided to its target by radio or radar commands from Earth or by a device inside the missile. A *ballistic missile* follows a path that is partly outside the Earth's atmosphere. It is guided as it goes up, but

▼ *A radar system may track both the missile and its target. A computer reads the radar signals and controls the missile's guidance system to guide it to the target by radio.*

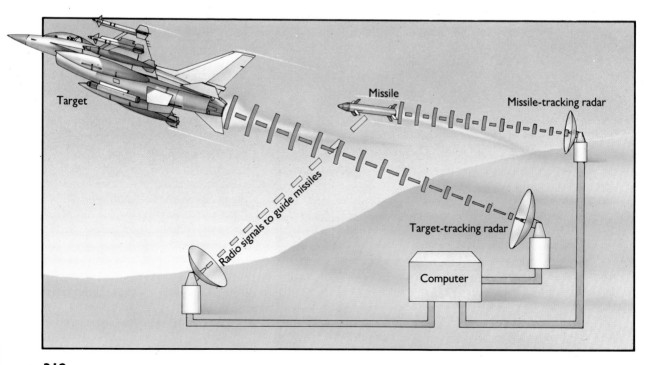

Target

Missile

Missile-tracking radar

Radio signals to guide missiles

Target-tracking radar

Computer

when its rocket engine burns out, it returns to Earth in an unguided path. The only defense against a ballistic missile is to fire another missile at the incoming missile to destroy it before it hits its target. Such defensive missiles are called *anti-ballistic missiles*. However, modern missiles are armed with warheads that split up into several separate nuclear warheads as they descend. This makes defense much more difficult.

Guinea

GUINEA

Guinea is a country on the western coast of Africa. Some of the world's largest deposits of bauxite are in Guinea. Bauxite is the ore from which aluminum is made. Guinea was a colony of France from the late 1800s until 1958, when it became an independent nation.

Government: Republic under military committee
Capital: Conakry
Area: 94,964 sq. miles (245,957 sq. km)
Population: 6,000,000
Language: French
Currency: Syli

Guinea-Bissau

The small country of Guinea-Bissau is on the west coast of Africa. Most of the 900,000 people who live there earn their living by farming. The main crops are peanuts, coconuts, and rice. Guinea-Bissau gained its independence from the Portuguese in 1974.

GUINEA-BISSAU

Government: Republic
Capital: Bissau
Area: 13,948 sq. miles (36,125 sq. km)
Population: 900,000
Language: Portuguese
Currency: Escudo

Guinea Pig and Hamster

The guinea pig is a RODENT, not a pig, and it comes from Peru, not Guinea. It is also called a cavy. Guinea pigs are up to 12 in. (29 cm) long and have no tail. They may be brown, white, black, gray, or a mixture. Some have long, silky hair, or hair that

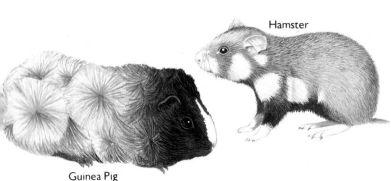

Hamster

Guinea Pig

◀ *The tame guinea pig is descended from the grizzled brown cavy of the Andes. Hamsters' nearest relatives are gerbils and voles.*

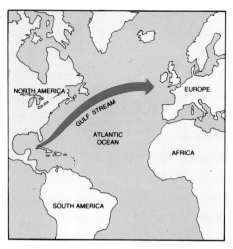

▲ *East of Newfoundland, the Gulf Stream is more correctly known as the North Atlantic Drift.*

forms rosettes. Scientists use guinea pigs in experiments, and many people keep guinea pigs as pets. They eat grass and hay and need a dry cage with clean bedding on the floor.

Hamsters are smaller than guinea pigs and have short tails. They have big pouches in their cheeks where they store food. Most hamsters are light brown on top and white or black underneath.

Gulf Stream

This ocean current is like a giant river flowing through the sea. It carries warm water from the Gulf of Mexico northward along the eastern coast of the United States. The Gulf Stream is up to 38 miles (60 km) wide and 1,970 ft. (600 m) deep. The current separates. One branch crosses the ATLANTIC OCEAN and brings warm water to northwestern Europe. If it were not for the Gulf Stream, winters in countries from France and Britain to Norway would be much more severe.

Gull

Few birds are more graceful than gulls gliding and soaring over the sea. They have webbed feet and swim well, but most do not stray far from land. They can catch fish, but also eat food scraps washed up on the shore.

Gulls breed in noisy crowds called colonies. Their nests are built on the ground. Many gull colonies live on islands. This helps to keep their eggs safe from rats and foxes.

▼ *Despite its name, the common gull is not the most numerous gull. The herring gull and the black-headed gull are often seen inland, but the larger glaucous gull is found only on coasts and in harbors.*

Black-headed gull

Herring gull

Glaucous gull

Common gull

◄ *This breech-loading cannon of the 1400s fired solid balls which could knock down the thickest castle walls.*

▼ *The Gatling gun was the first successful machine gun. Invented in 1861 and first used during the Civil War, it had up to 10 barrels rotated by a hand crank.*

Gun

Guns are weapons that fire bullets or other missiles from a tube which is open at one end.

Guns were probably invented in the 1200s. By the 1300s, guns were firing missiles that could pierce armor and break down castle walls.

Early guns were large weapons, far too heavy for one man to carry. The first gun was a big bucket with a small hole in the bottom. Soldiers put gunpowder into the bucket. Then they piled stones on top. They lit the gunpowder through the hole. When the gunpowder exploded, the stones flew out. The large, long guns called cannons were first used in about 1350. Cannons fired big metal cannonballs. In the 1800s came guns which fired pointed shells that exploded when they hit their target. A spiral groove cut in the gun barrel made the shells spin as they flew through the air. Soldiers could fire such shells farther and hit their targets more often than with cannonballs.

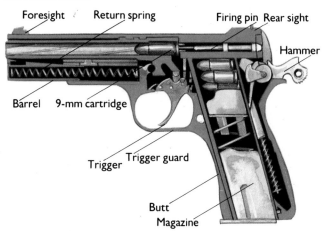

Foresight Return spring Firing pin Rear sight Hammer

Barrel 9-mm cartridge

Trigger Trigger guard

Butt

Magazine

▲ *This modern anti-aircraft gun can destroy attacking aircraft from the ground.*

◄ *This cutaway view of a Browning self-loading pistol of 1968 shows the pistol when loaded.*

▲ *Johann Gutenberg inspects a printed sheet that has just come off his new press. Despite the importance of his achievement, he never made much money from it.*

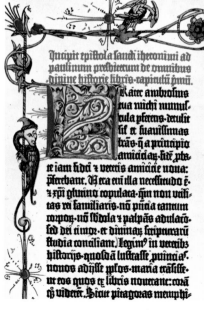

▲ *One of Gutenberg's first books was a Bible printed in Latin in 1455.*

Troops first used small arms in the 1300s. Small arms are guns that one man can carry. Inventors developed short-barreled pistols and revolvers for firing at nearby targets. They developed muskets, rifles, and machine guns for long-distance shooting. In modern guns, a hammer sets off an explosion that drives a shell or bullet from the barrel.

Gutenberg, Johann

Johann Gutenberg (about 1395 to about 1468) was a German goldsmith sometimes called the father of PRINTING. In his day, people slowly copied books by hand or printed them from wooden blocks on which each letter of every page had to be carved separately. About 1440, Gutenberg learned to make metal letters called type. He could pick them up and place them in rows to build pages of type. Each page was held together by a frame. Gutenberg fixed the frame to a press and quickly pressed the inky surface of his type onto sheets of paper. Gutenberg's movable type helped him to make copies of a book faster and more cheaply than ever before.

Guyana

Guyana is a hot, rainy country on the northeastern coast of South America. Most of the people live along the coast in a narrow strip of flat land about 12 miles (20 km) wide. Sugarcane and rice are grown there. Valuable minerals, including gold and diamonds, are found in the hilly region inland. Guyana produces bauxite to make aluminum. A vast forest covers more than three-fourths of the country.

Guyana was once a British colony. It is the only country in South America that has English as its official language. The colony became independent in 1966 and a republic in 1970.

Gymnastics

Gymnastics are exercises that help to make and keep the body fit. The OLYMPIC GAMES have separate gymnastic exercises for men and women. Women perform graceful steps, runs, jumps, turns, and somersaults on a narrow wooden beam. They hang from a high bar and swing to and fro between

GUYANA

Government: Republic
Capital: Georgetown
Area: 86,625 sq. miles
　(214,000 sq. km)
Population: 770,000
Language: English
Currency: Guyanese dollar

▼ *Modern competitive gymnastics.*

Asymmetrical bars

Rings

Parallel bars

Beam

Pommel horse

Floor

Vault

Modern gymnastics grew considerably in popularity because of the performance of tiny Olga Korbut of the Soviet Union in the 1972 Olympics. The widespread television coverage of her dramatic performance increased interest in the sport almost overnight.

it and a lower one. They leap over a vaulting horse. Women also perform floor exercises to music.

Men hang from a high bar and from rings, swinging up and down, to and fro, and over and over in giant circles. Using two parallel bars, they swing, vault, and do handstands. They grip hoops that jut up from a leather-covered pommel "horse" and swing their legs and body. They leap over a vaulting horse. Simpler exercises are done by children and adults in gymnastics classes.

► The traditional, brightly-painted gypsy caravan is now a rarity. Most traveling gypsies live in modern trailers.

Gypsy

Gypsies are an interesting group of people found in Europe and North America. They have dark hair, skin, and eyes. Many speak a language called Romany. Some live in houses; others travel all the time and live in trailers. Gypsies deal in cars and horses and make metalwork or tell people's fortunes. They are famous for their songs and dances.

The name "gypsy" probably comes from the word Egyptian. It was thought gypsies came from Egypt, but they probably came from India 600 years ago.

▼ No matter how much the gyroscope is tilted or twisted, the wheel axle will continue to point in the same direction.

Gyroscope

A gyroscope is a wheel that spins in a special frame. No matter how the frame tilts, the wheel's axle points in the same direction. Even GRAVITY and the Earth's MAGNETISM do not affect the axle.

On a ship or aircraft, a COMPASS made from a gyroscope always points north. Gyroscopes can also keep an aircraft on course without the pilot steering.

Hail *See* Rain and Snow

Hair

Hair grows like living threads from the skins of MAMMALS. It has the same ingredients that make nails, claws, hooves, feathers, and reptiles' scales. Hair helps to keep the body warm and protects the skin. There are several kinds of hair. Cats have plenty of soft, thick fur. Porcupines are protected by sharp, stiff hairs called quills.

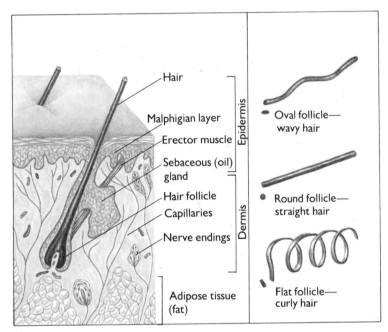

Hair

Malphigian layer

Erector muscle

Sebaceous (oil) gland

Hair follicle

Capillaries

Nerve endings

Epidermis

Dermis

Adipose tissue (fat)

Oval follicle— wavy hair

Round follicle— straight hair

Flat follicle— curly hair

◀ *Each hair root is enclosed in its own follicle, which has a blood supply, a tiny erector muscle, and a gland. The type of hair you have depends partly on the shape of your hair follicles.*

Haiti

Haiti is a small country in the western part of the island of Hispaniola in the West Indies. Much of the country is covered by rugged mountains, but there are fertile valleys and coastal plains where coffee and other crops are grown. Nine-tenths of the people are descended from African slaves. Columbus landed on Haiti in 1492.

A French colony from 1677, Haiti became independent in 1804, following a rebellion. Dr. François Duvalier became president in 1957. Upon his death in 1971, he was succeeded by his son, Jean-Claude. This family dictatorship came to an end in 1986 when Jean-Claude was forced to flee the country.

HAITI

ATLANTIC OCEAN
BAHAMAS
CUBA
DOMINICAN REPUBLIC
JAMAICA
HAITI
PUERTO RICO
CARIBBEAN SEA
COLOMBIA
VENEZUELA

Government: Military
Capital: Port-au-Prince
Area: 10,714 sq. miles (27,750 sq. km)
Population: 5,800,000
Language: French
Currency: Gourde

...Comet passed near ...its center was ... peanut-shaped ...ust, and ice about ...ng. Each return to the Sun leaves the *nucleus with a smaller store of ice and dust, and eventually the comet will "die."*

Edmond Halley was a friend of Isaac Newton, the great scientist. He encouraged Newton and helped him with money to publish his most famous work, *Mathematical Principles of Natural Philosophy*.

▼ *John Hancock was the first to sign the Declaration of Independence because he was then president of the Continental Congress.*

Halley, Edmond

Edmond Halley (1657–1742) was an English astronomer who is best known for his study of comets. In 1676, at the age of 20, he went to the island of St. Helena to catalogue the stars of the Southern Hemisphere, something that had never been done before. He became interested in comets and noticed that the path followed by a comet he had seen in 1682 was very much like those reported in 1607 and 1531. He decided that these sightings must be of the same comet and predicted that it would return in 1758. On Christmas Day, 1758, it did, and Halley's Comet reappears regularly every 76 years.

Hamilton, Alexander

Alexander Hamilton (1755–1804) was a key figure in the development of the United States. He was a supporter of independence, and a close friend of George WASHINGTON. He played an important role in the writing of the U.S. CONSTITUTION. He then became the first Secretary of the Treasury. Hamilton was killed in a duel with a political opponent.

Hancock, John

John Hancock (1737–1793) is famous as the first man to sign the DECLARATION OF INDEPENDENCE. People today still sometimes call a signature a "John Hancock." He was an important figure in the REVOLUTIONARY WAR.

Handel, George Frideric

George Frideric Handel (1685–1759) was a German-born British composer, famous for the oratorio *Messiah* and the orchestral *Fireworks Music* and *Water Music*. He wrote about 21 oratorios.

Hang Gliding *See* Gliding

Hannibal

Hannibal (247–183 B.C.) was a Carthaginian general who invaded Italy. In 218 B.C. he left Spain and marched an army over the Alps into Italy. He fought the Romans for 15 years, but never managed to conquer them. In the end, he killed himself.

▲ *Handel was born in Germany, but made England his home. He became a British subject in 1726.*

Harding, Warren

Warren Gamaliel Harding (1865–1923) became president of the United States after World War I. He grew up in central Ohio, and when he was 19 he bought a bankrupt weekly newspaper and turned it into a prosperous daily newspaper. He was elected to several state offices and then to the U.S. Senate before becoming president.

When Harding became president, he appointed several able men to his cabinet. To other offices, however, he appointed his personal friends. Some of these men used their positions of power to cheat the government. Harding's Secretary of the Interior, Albert B. Fall, was sent to prison for selling government lands to oil companies for large sums of money. The President became aware of this corruption. This may have hastened his death in San Francisco in 1923.

WARREN G. HARDING

Twenty-ninth President (1921–1923)
Born: Corsica, Ohio
Education: Ohio Central College, Iberia, Ohio
Occupation: Newspaper editor
Political Party: Republican
Buried: Marion, Ohio

Hare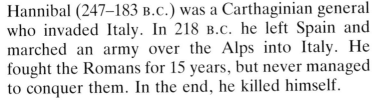

Hares look like large RABBITS with very long ears and long legs. They live in wide open fields and do not burrow. By day, they just crouch in a dip in the ground. At night, they come out to eat grass and other plants.

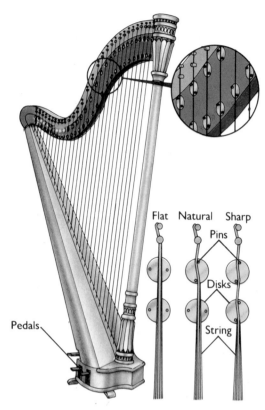

Harp

The harp is the oldest of all stringed instruments. The early harp was little more than a bow with strings of different lengths stretched across it. Harps have been played in Wales and Ireland for many centuries. The modern harp has a wooden frame with strings attached between the hollow sounding board and the top of the instrument. There are seven foot pedals that can change the pitch of the strings. The harpist sits with the sounding board between his or her legs and plucks the strings with fingers and thumbs.

▲ Moving the harp's pedals up and down gives the harpist more notes. The pedals turn small disks at the top of the strings. As the disks turn, pins make the lengths of string that vibrate shorter or longer. This gives sharp or flat notes.

▶ Harpsichords make a rich sound, but it cannot be made loud or soft as easily as the sound from a piano. So when pianos were invented, harpsichords were forgotten for more than a century.

Harpsichord

A harpsichord looks like a HARP laid on its side and put in a box with legs. The first successful harpsichords date from the 1500s. Harpsichords have a keyboard that looks like a PIANO's. When a key is pressed, it lifts a piece of wood called a jack. A quill or piece of leather fixed to the jack plucks a string inside the harpsichord. Harpsichords were popular during the 1700s, but by the 1800s they began to be replaced by pianos.

Harrison, Benjamin

Benjamin Harrison (1833–1901) was the 23rd president of the United States. His grandfather was William Harrison, the 9th president, and his father was a congressman. Benjamin Harrison was a general in the Civil War. In 1881, he became a senator. He became president during a time of great changes. The United States was growing rapidly and becoming a leading industrial power. Six states joined the Union during Harrison's administration. Industry had to be regulated; trade barriers, or tarrifs, had to be controlled; the navy had to be expanded. Farmers faced different sorts of problems when prices fell and they needed government help. Harrison was the first president to say that the Stars and Stripes should fly over government buildings and schools.

BENJAMIN HARRISON

Twenty-third President 1889–1893
Born: North Bend, Ohio
Education: Miami University
Occupation: Lawyer
Political Party: Republican
Buried: Indianapolis, Indiana

Harrison, William Henry

William Harrison (1773–1841) was the 9th president of the United States. His time in office was short; he died only 30 days after becoming president—the first president to die in office.

Harrison was born to a rich Virginia family. After serving in the army, he became secretary of the Northwest Territory. Though he tried hard to protect the Indians living there, he also angered many of them by taking their land for settlement. When the Indians rose against him in 1811, Harrison defeated them at the Battle of Tippecanoe. After the war of 1812, Harrison moved to Ohio, and in 1825 he became a senator.

WILLIAM H. HARRISON

Ninth President March–Apr. 1841
Born: Berkeley, Virginia
Education: Hampden-Sydney College, Virginia
Occupation: Soldier
Political Party: Whig
Buried: North Bend, Ohio

Hawaii

Hawaii is a group of more than 20 islands in the Pacific Ocean. The islands lie more than 2,000 miles (3,000 km) southwest of the United States. They became the 50th state in 1959. The Hawaiian islands were formed as volcanoes built up from the ocean bed. Two volcanoes are still active.

The islands have beautiful beaches and in places there are tropical rain forests filled with unusual flowers. The Hawaiians are descended from the

HAWAII

Capital: Honolulu
Population: 1,060,000
Area: 6450 sq. mi. (16,704 sq. km)
State flower; Hibiscus
State bird: Hawaiian Goose
State tree: Candlenut
Statehood: August 21, 1959
  50th state

▲ The red-shouldered hawk is common in the southeast of the United States. It hunts for rodents, insects, and small birds.

people who have settled on the islands. These include the early Polynesians, and later Americans, Europeans, Filipinos, and Puerto-Ricans. Thousands of tourists flock to Hawaii every year.

The United States entered World War II because Japanese aircraft attacked its base at Pearl Harbor in Hawaii.

Hawk

Hawks are birds of prey in the same family as the VULTURES and all EAGLE species. Hawks are not as large as these relatives. Many look rather like FALCONS, but have broader wings with more rounded ends. Broad wings and a long tail help a hawk to fly fast and nimbly through trees. Hawks hunt birds and small mammals.

Hawthorne, Nathaniel

Nathaniel Hawthorne (1804–1864) was one of the most important American writers of the 1800s. His most famous books are *The Scarlet Letter* and *The House of the Seven Gables*. He wrote many stories for children, too. His best stories can be hard to understand, but all have a strong sense of the world he lived in—the little towns of New England in the 1800s.

▼ The goshawk is widely used in falconry, as it is strong enough to catch game birds and rabbits.

Haydn, Franz Joseph

Franz Joseph Haydn (1732–1809) was an Austrian composer known as the "father of the symphony." For 30 years he wrote music at the court of Prince Esterhazy. He wrote 104 symphonies. Many of them used the ORCHESTRA in a powerful new way. He also wrote fine pieces for the piano, and quartets for four stringed instruments. MOZART and BEETHOVEN both studied Haydn's work. Later, this helped them compose some of their most splendid music.

▲ Haydn made two long visits to England, where he wrote his last 12 symphonies. He spent his last years in Vienna.

Hayes, Rutherford B.

Rutherford B. Hayes (1822–1893) was the 19th president of the United States. His presidency was important because it ended the bitter "reconstruction" of the South after the Civil War. He also stopped the corruption over government jobs that had become commonplace during the presidency of Ulysses S. GRANT.

Hayes was elected president only after a special "electoral commission" decided that many of the votes for his opponent, Samuel Tilden, were fraudulent. Later, his decisions to withdraw federal soldiers from the South and to give government jobs to Southerners angered many in the North but helped heal the wounds of the Civil War. Hayes was widely respected for his honesty.

RUTHERFORD B. HAYES

Nineteenth President 1877–1881
Born: Delaware, Ohio
Education: Kenyon College, Gambier, Ohio
Occupation: Lawyer
Political Party: Republican
Buried: Fremont, Ohio

Health

Good health is one of the most important things in life. It is something that allows a person to lead a happy, useful, and successful life. There are certain rules which help us to stay healthy.

We should eat a balanced diet of the right kinds of FOOD and drink plenty of water. All foods are fattening if we eat too much of them, but this applies especially to starchy foods, fats, and sweets.

We should have regular EXERCISE, if possible in the open air, and get enough sleep. The number of hours' sleep we need depends on our age. Young babies sleep from 20 to 22 hours each day; older people only need between 6 and 7 hours.

We should keep ourselves clean. Regular washing is important, especially of the hands after we have used the toilet. Teeth, of course, should be brushed night and morning.

Hearing

Hearing is the sense that allows us to pick up SOUND. The sense organ making this possible is the EAR. Some people cannot hear; they are *deaf*. Either they were born without hearing or, at some time, their ears became damaged by an illness or accident. Deaf people can "talk" by using special sign language.

Like people, all animals with backbones have hearing organs. Some can hear much better than people. CATS and DOGS, for example, pick up more sounds than we can. BATS hunt by sound, listening for echoes bounced back off flying insects.

Heart

The heart is a muscle in the body. It pumps BLOOD around the body through VEINS and ARTERIES. In an adult person, the heart goes on working at between

▲ *The range of vibrations that can be heard varies in different animals. In humans, the range is from about 20 (very low-pitched) to 20,000 cycles per second. A bat and a dog can hear high-frequency sounds that the human ear cannot detect. The frog cannot hear high-pitched sounds.*

▶ *Your heart is about the same size as your clenched fist and is made of strong muscle. It constantly pumps blood around your body, so that each cell gets the food and oxygen it needs. The areas shown in red in the illustration indicate where oxygen-rich blood travels. The areas shown in blue show where blood low in oxygen travels back to the lungs. The* atria *(plural of* atrium*) collect the blood flowing into the heart. The* ventricles *are strong muscles that pump blood into the arteries.*

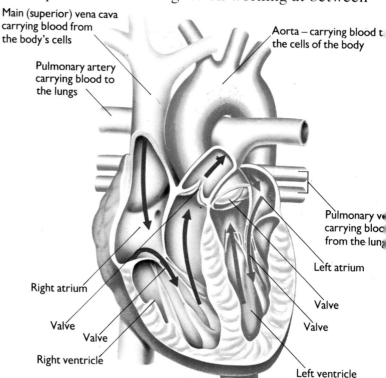

Main (superior) vena cava carrying blood from the body's cells

Aorta – carrying blood t the cells of the body

Pulmonary artery carrying blood to the lungs

Pulmonary v carrying bloc from the lung

Left atrium

Right atrium

Valve

Valve

Valve

Valve

Right ventricle

Left ventricle

70 and 80 beats a minute until death. It was the English doctor, William Harvey (1578–1657), who discovered how the heart works.

The blood carries OXYGEN from the LUNGS and energy from the food we eat. Arteries carry this rich red blood to feed the body. Veins carry away waste products and return the dark "tired" blood to the heart to be "recharged" with oxygen from the lungs.

When the heart stops beating, the body is starved of oxygen and quickly dies. But doctors can sometimes massage a stopped heart back to life. People with diseased hearts can be given "spare parts" to repair them and even a new heart, transplanted from someone who has just died.

Heat

Heat is a form of ENERGY. We can feel it, but we cannot see it. We feel heat from the SUN, or when we sit in front of a fire. When something burns, heat is produced. The Sun gives out enormous amounts of heat, which is produced by atoms joining together, or "fusing," inside the Sun. This same kind of energy can be released by a hydrogen bomb on Earth. It is because we get just the right amount

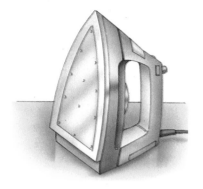

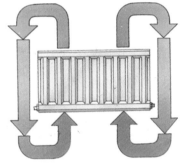

▲ Heat travels in three ways—by conduction, convection, and radiation. A conductor, such as a metal iron, allows heat to pass through it. When heat is carried from a radiator by convection, molecules in the air move, taking the heat with them. Heat from the Sun travels by radiation in the form of electromagnetic waves.

◄ The energy in heat can be used in many different ways. This picture shows a solar-powered car which converts the Sun's energy and uses it to drive along.

We need fuel to keep our body warm. This fuel is the food we eat. The human body contains a surprising amount of heat. It gives out about 100 calories of heat an hour. This is about the same as a 120-watt electric bulb. You can see, therefore, why it can become quite hot if a lot of people are gathered in a room.

of heat from the Sun that our Earth and ourselves are what they are. A few degrees less heat from the Sun, and our world would be a lifeless waste. A few degrees more heat, and life could not exist.

Most of the heat we use comes from burning fuels. But heat can also be made by FRICTION, or rubbing. Heat is also produced when electricity travels through a coil of wire. This is what makes the coils inside a toaster glow red.

We can measure how hot a thing is by finding its temperature. This is done with a THERMOMETER. When a substance gets hot, the molecules, or tiny particles, of which it is made move around more quickly. Often the substance expands (gets bigger) as this happens. Metals expand the most when they are heated.

Hebrews

In the early days of their history, the Jewish people were known as the Hebrews or Israelites. There were 12 tribes, descended from Abraham. The greatest Hebrew leader was Moses, who led his people out of slavery in Egypt to the Promised Land of Canaan. Hebrew is the national language of modern Israel.

Hedgehog

Like the American PORCUPINE, the European hedgehog has a coat of spines to protect it. When frightened, it curls up into a prickly ball.

▼ Hedgehogs need to fatten themselves up if they are to survive their period of hibernation in the winter. They are carnivorous and like dog or cat food.

Hedgehogs amble along snuffling for snails, slugs, worms, and insects to eat. They will often visit people's yards. During the winter, hedgehogs HIBERNATE. They live in northern Europe, Asia, Africa, and New Zealand.

Helen of Troy

Helen of Troy was said by the ancient Greeks to be the most beautiful woman in the world. She was the wife of Menelaus, King of Sparta, but ran away with Paris, Prince of Troy. Menelaus followed with a great army and so began the TROJAN WAR. The story is told by the poet HOMER.

▲ King Menelaus of Sparta with his wife, Helen of Troy. The war that started because of her went on for ten years, according to the story told by Homer.

Helicopter

The helicopter is an unusual and useful aircraft. It was invented in the 1930s, and today, it is used for all kinds of jobs, especially sea and mountain rescue. Helicopters can take off and land vertically and can therefore work in areas too small for ordinary aircraft. Helicopters can fly in any direction and hover in mid-air. Instead of fixed wings, they have a moving wing called a rotor, which acts as a wing and a propeller. The pilot controls the craft by changing the angle, or "pitch," at which the blades of the rotor go through the air. A smaller rotor on the tail keeps the helicopter from spinning around. Helicopters are also used for carrying passengers over short distances and for transporting troops to remote areas.

▼ The UH-1 Iroquois was used by the United States army in the Vietnam war. A similar type is still being made today. The Ka-26 Kamov Hoodlum is mainly used for farming purposes, although it is also used as an air ambulance. It has two sets of main rotors rotating in opposite directions.

Kamov Ka-26

Bell UH-1 Iroquois

▲ *Ernest Hemingway was a war correspondent in the Spanish Civil War, and was fascinated by bullfighting.*

Hemingway, Ernest

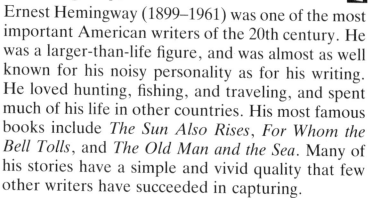

Ernest Hemingway (1899–1961) was one of the most important American writers of the 20th century. He was a larger-than-life figure, and was almost as well known for his noisy personality as for his writing. He loved hunting, fishing, and traveling, and spent much of his life in other countries. His most famous books include *The Sun Also Rises*, *For Whom the Bell Tolls*, and *The Old Man and the Sea*. Many of his stories have a simple and vivid quality that few other writers have succeeded in capturing.

Henry (kings)

Eight English kings have been called Henry. They were: Henry I (1069–1135), the youngest son of William the Conqueror; Henry II (1133–1189), the first of the Plantagenet kings; Henry III (1207–1272), a weak king ruled by powerful barons; Henry IV (1367–1413), or Henry Bolingbroke; Henry V (1387–1422), who was a brilliant soldier; Henry VI (1421–1471), the last of the Lancastrian kings; Henry VII (1457–1509), the first of the Tudors and a shrewd ruler; and Henry VIII (1491–1547), who had six wives.

▼ *Henry VI was a quiet and religious king, very different from his strong-willed wife, Margaret of Anjou. The Wars of the Roses were fought during his reign.*

◀ *These simple designs found on old heraldic shields are called* charges, or ordinaries. *The designs of many modern flags are based on these shapes.*

Heraldry

In the MIDDLE AGES, a knight in full ARMOR was hard to recognize, for his face was hidden by his helmet. So knights began to use special designs worn on their surcoats and shields. These designs became special family emblems, which no one else could wear. They were called coats-of-arms.

Heralds were officials who kept records of coats-of-arms and awarded new ones. The College of Heralds in London still does this. There are special names for the colors and patterns used in heraldry.

Herb

Herbs are plants with soft, rather than woody, stems. But the name herb is also given to certain plants which are added to food during cooking. They are valued for their scent and flavor. A common herb is mint, which can be bruised and used in iced tea.

Other herbs used in cooking include sage, thyme, parsley, garlic, chervil, rosemary, basil, fennel, and

SEE IT YOURSELF

You can preserve herbs by drying them. Spread them out in a warm, dry, dark place for 3 to 5 days. Place them in a strainer over a sheet of clean paper and rub the herbs through the strainer with the flat of your hand. Throw away the stalks, and pour the rubbed herbs back into the strainer. Do this until there are no more stalks. Store your dried herbs out of direct light in sealed glass jars.

▼ *These herbs are easy to grow and make attractive garden plants as well as being useful in cooking.*

Tarragon

Rosemary

Sweet marjoram

▲ *Slaying the Hydra was the second of the twelve tasks of Hercules. As soon as Hercules cut off one of its heads, two more grew in its place.*

A hibernating marmot may slow down its breathing from 16 to 2 breaths a minute, and its heartbeats from 88 to 15 per minute. In a test, the temperature of a hibernating ground squirrel fell to almost freezing. The creature later woke up unharmed.

chives. Most can be grown quite easily, although they came originally from the warm, sunny lands of the Mediterranean region.

Hercules

Hercules was a famous hero of ancient stories told by the Greeks and Romans. He was the son of the chief god, Jupiter, and a mortal princess. He was amazingly strong. As a baby, he strangled two snakes sent by Jupiter's jealous wife to kill him.

Later, Hercules went mad and killed his wife and children. To make amends, he had to perform twelve tasks, or labors. They included killing the Nemean lion and the many-headed Hydra; and washing clean the stables of King Augeas, where 3,000 oxen lived. In the end, Hercules was killed when he put on a poisoned shirt.

Heredity *See* Genetics

Hibernation

When an animal hibernates, it goes to sleep for the winter. It does this because, in winter, food is scarce. Going to sleep during the cold weather saves certain animals from starving to death.

Before hibernating, animals eat as much food as they can find. The woodchuck, for example, stuffs itself until it is fat and round. As fall approaches, it makes a snug nest, curls into a ball, and falls into a sound sleep. In fact, its heart beats so slowly, the woodchuck looks dead. Its body uses hardly any energy during hibernation, in order to make its store of fat last as long as possible. In spring, a thin and hungry woodchuck wakes up and comes out of its nest to look for food.

In cold countries, many animals hibernate. Not all sleep right through the winter.

Hieroglyphics

Hieroglyphics were an ancient form of writing. Our alphabet has 26 letters. However, 5,000 years ago,

the ancient Egyptians used picture-signs instead of letters. Later, these signs became hieroglyphics—marks which stood for things, people, and ideas. Egyptian hieroglyphics were sometimes written from right to left, and sometimes from left to right. Hieroglyphic writing was very difficult, and only a few people could do it. When the Egyptian empire died out, the secret of reading it was lost. No one could understand the hieroglyphics carved on stones and written on papyrus scrolls. Then, in 1799, a Frenchman found the Rosetta Stone, which is now in the British Museum in London. On it was something written in two known languages and also in hieroglyphics. By comparing the known languages with the hieroglyphics, experts were able to understand and translate the signs.

High Holy Days

The High Holy Days are the two most important Jewish holidays. The first is Rosh Hashanah, the first day of the new year on the Jewish calendar, which is about 6,000 years old. Yom Kippur, 10 days later, is the solemn Day of Atonement, when Jews ask forgiveness for any wrongdoings of the past year. Both holidays occur early each fall.

▲ Hibernating animals have to find a warm, safe place to spend the winter. They need to reserve their energy until the weather warms up.

▲ Many examples of hieroglyphic writing carved in stone have survived over thousands of years and can now be understood.

333

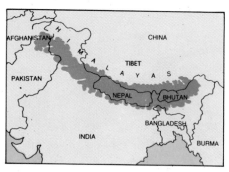

▶ The Himalayas form a great natural barrier between India and the large plateau of Tibet. The passes that run through the Himalayas are among the highest in the world. Few are lower than 16,500 feet (5,000 m).

▼ Hindus believe in many gods, all with different characters. Four-armed Shiva is often shown dancing. Kali (left) is a fierce giantess, and Ganesh, Shiva's son, has the head of an elephant and is believed to bring success when worshiped.

Kali

Shiva

Ganesh

Himalayas

The highest range of mountains in the world is the mighty Himalayas. The name means "land of snow." The Himalayas form a great barrier range across ASIA, dividing INDIA in the south from TIBET (part of CHINA) in the north. Many of Asia's greatest rivers rise among the Himalayas, fed by the melting snows.

Until aircraft were invented, few outsiders had ever been into the Himalayas. There are no roads or railroads. The only way to travel is on foot, over steep mountain tracks. Horses, yaks, goats, and even sheep are used to carry heavy loads.

The highest mountain in the world lies in the Himalayas. This is Mount EVEREST, 29,028 feet (8,848 m) high.

Hinduism

Hinduism is one of the world's great religions. Most Hindus live in ASIA, and particularly in INDIA. Their religion has grown over a period of 4,000 years.

Hindus believe that God is present in all things. Only priests (Brahmans) can worship the supreme God. Ordinary people worship other gods, such as Vishnu, God of Life. The most important holy books of Hindus are the *Vedas*. Hindus believe that certain animals, such as the cobra and the cow, are sacred and must never be killed or eaten.

Hippopotamus

The name hippopotamus means "river horse," but in fact, the hippo is related to the pig, not the horse. It is a huge, heavy animal and lives in Africa. Of all land animals, only the elephant is bigger.

Hippopotamuses live near rivers and lakes. They spend most of their time in the water and are good swimmers. In spite of their fearsome-looking jaws, hippopotamuses eat only plant food. They browse on water weeds and grasses, and at night, they often come ashore to feed.

These animals are not usually dangerous if left alone, but they can inflict serious wounds with slashes from the tusks in their lower jaws.

▲ Hippopotamuses have eyes on the tops of their heads so they can stand under water and peep out without being seen. They can stay submerged for almost ten minutes without coming up for breath.

▼ The history of ancient civilizations has to be pieced together from clues that have come to us over the years. This is a bronze head of a king who lived almost 4,500 years ago.

History

History is the story of the past. The people who write down history are called historians. They usually write about important events such as wars, revolutions, and governments, because these affect nations. However, historians are also interested in the lives of ordinary people and in what they did and thought about.

Nowadays, we think of history as being written down in history books. But in earlier times, before books and printing, history was passed on by word of mouth. People told stories about their kings, their wars, their adventures, and also about their

Continued on page 338

335

HISTORY

AFRICA

B.C.

3,000,000 Australopithecus is early ancestor of modern man

30,000 Human hunters in Africa

5000 Stone Age craftworkers in Nile Valley

4500 Metal working in Egypt

2780 First pyramid in Egypt

1400 Golden age of Egypt's power

500 Kushite kingdom in Africa

146 Romans destroy power of Carthage, a great North African city-state

A.D.

500 Kingdom of Ghana

850 Building of citadel at Great Zimbabwe

980 Arabs begin to settle on east coast

1000 Moslems control all of North Africa; Ife bronze art at its peak in West Africa

1307 Empire of Mali in central Africa reaches its height under Munsa Mali

1498 Vasco da Gama begins Portugese trade along east coast

1500 Empire of Gao

1591 Fall of Songhai empire (which had succeeded Mali)

1652 Europeans led by Jan van Riebeeck settle at Cape of Good Hope

1713 Height of slave trade between West Africa and the New World

1818 Chaka founds the Zulu empire

1821 Liberia (West Africa) founded as free state for ex-slaves from U.S.A.

1835–37 Great Trek by Boers to found Transvaal

1869 Opening of Suez Canal creates shorter sea route from Europe to Asia

1884 Berlin Conference allows European powers to divide Africa between them

1899–1902 Boer War; Britain defeats Boers

1936 Italy conquers Ethiopia, Africa's oldest independent African nation

1949 South Africa adopts policy of apartheid (separation of the races)

1956 President Nasser of Egypt nationalizes the Suez Canal; this leads to a brief war with Britain and France

1960 Civil war in Congo

1960s Many former European-ruled states become self-governing

1963 Formation of Organization of African Unity

1967 Civil war in Nigeria after Biafra breaks away

1974 Portugal gives up its last African colonies

1980 Zimbabwe (Rhodesia) becomes independent

1980s Apartheid in South Africa; civil war in parts of the continent; drought and famine are serious problems

ASIA

B.C.

9000 Beginnings of agriculture in "fertile crescent"

7000 Jericho is world's first town

3500 Copper working in Thailand

3100 Earliest known writing, cuneiform script from Sumer

2300 Mohenjo-daro civilization in the Indus River valley (modern Pakistan)

2100 Abraham migrates from Ur

1500 Chinese master the skills of bronze working

1230 Peak of Assyrian power

565 Birth of Buddha

551 Birth of Confucius

221–210 Reign of Chinese emperor Shihuangdi, builder of the Great Wall; China is the world's largest empire

A.D.

4? Birth of Jesus Christ

570 Birth of Muhammad

1000 Perfection of gunpowder in China

1100 Temples of Angkor Wat in Cambodia

1405–33 Chinese fleets led by Cheng Ho make voyages of exploration in Pacific and Indian oceans

1190 Genghis Khan begins to conquer an empire for the Mongols

1275 Marco Polo at the court of Kublai Khan

1498 Vasco da Gama sails from Portugal to India

1520s Mogul empire in India

1600 Shogun Ieyasu becomes ruler of Japan

1760 French and British fight for power in India

1854 Japan is forced to sign trade treaty with U.S.A.

1857 Indian Mutiny

1868 Meiji government begins to "westernize" Japan

1900 Boxer Rebellion in China

1905 Japan defeats Russians in war

1912 Sun Yat-sen leads new Chinese republic

1930s Rise of Japan as a military power

1939–45 World War II: first atomic bombs dropped on Japan

1947 India gains independence from British rule

1948 Creation of the state of Israel

1949 Mao Tse-tung's Communists win civil war in China

1954 French pull out of Indochina: beginnings of Vietnam War

1976 Vietnam War ends with victory for North Vietnam

1979 Shah of Iran overthrown; Iran becomes an Islamic republic

1980s Civil war in Lebanon; war between Iran and Iraq (ends 1988); China becomes more open

EUROPE

B.C.

6000 Planting crops and animal husbandry reach Europe from Asia

2000 Minoan bronze age civilization of Crete

1193 City of Troy destroyed by Greeks

331 Alexander the Great leads Greeks to victory over the Persian Empire

509 Foundation of the Roman republic

A.D.

43 Romans invade Britain

313 Christian religion tolerated throughout Roman Empire

330 Roman emperor Constantine founds Constantinople

476 Roman Empire collapses

732 Charles Martel leads Franks to victory over Moors

800 Charlemagne is crowned first Holy Roman Emperor

871 Alfred becomes king of Wessex in England

1066 William of Normandy conquers England

1096 First of six crusades by Christian armies against the Islamic rulers of the Holy Land (Palestine)

1215 English barons draw up Magna Carta

1300s The Renaissance in arts and sciences

1348 The Black Death kills millions

1453 Constantinople is captured by the Turks

1517 Martin Luther's protest begins the Reformation

1522 First circumnavigation by Europeans (Magellan's fleet)

1588 English defeat the Spanish Armada

1642 Civil War in England

1700s Revolutions in agriculture and industry; beginning of the Age of Machines

1789 French Revolution

1848 Year of revolutions in Europe

1854–56 Crimean War

1870–71 Prussia defeats France in Franco-Prussian War

1914–18 World War I: Germany and its allies are defeated by Britain, France, U.S.A., Russia and others. More than 10 million soldiers are killed

1917 Communist revolution in Russia

1933 Hitler becomes ruler of Germany

1936–39 Civil war in Spain

1939–45 World War II: Allies defeat Germany and Italy in Europe

1957 Treaty of Rome establishes European Community (E.C.)

1980s E.C. moves toward free market (1992); Gorbachev government brings new ideas in U.S.S.R.

AMERICA AND AUSTRALASIA

B.C.

100,000? Ancestors of Aborigines reach Australia

40,000 Ancestors of North American Indians migrate across "land bridge" from Asia

20,000 Indians complete settlement of South America

8400 First domesticated dog (Idaho)

3372 Earliest date in Mayan calendar (Mexico)

A.D.

1100 Maoris sail to New Zealand from Pacific islands

1400 Inca empire in Peru

1492 Columbus sails to "discover" America

1500 Cabral claims Brazil for Portugal

1518 Cortes begins conquest of Mexico, defeating Aztecs

1533 Pizarro conquers Inca empire for Spain

1584 Raleigh founds English colony in Virginia

1620 Voyage of the Pilgrim ship *Mayflower*

1626 Dutch found New Amsterdam (New York)

1642 Abel Tasman discovers Tasmania; French found Montreal in Canada

1763 Britain gains control of Canada after defeating France

1770 Cook explores coast of Australia and New Zealand

1776 American Declaration of Independence

1783 End of American War of Independence

1788 First British settlement in Australia

1789 George Washington first U.S. President

1824 South American republics break free from Spanish rule

1840 New Zealand becomes British colony

1861–65 American Civil War; Northern states defeat the South

1867 Canada becomes self-governing dominion

1901 Australia and New Zealand are independent

1917 U.S.A. enters World War I

1930s Depression and unemployment in U.S.A.

1941 Japanese attack on Pearl Harbor brings U.S.A. into World War II

1959 Fidel Castro leads Communist revolution in Cuba

1963 President John F. Kennedy is assassinated

1965 U.S. troops fight in Vietnam

1969 U.S. astronauts land on the Moon

1975 Last U.S. forces leave Vietnam

1980s U.S.A. is one of two strongest world powers; civil war in Nicaragua (Central America); Australia and New Zealand make new trade partners in Asia

HISTORY

▶ Historic moments are well documented today. Future historians will have no difficulty piecing together the past from pictures like this one, of Soviet leader Gorbachev and President Reagan signing a treaty.

▲ We know a great deal about the history of Europe, even in the Middle Ages. This type of ship, called a caravel, was used in the 15th century for voyages of discovery.

It is sometimes said, "Those who fail to learn the lessons of history are destined to repeat them." One of the best-known and most incorrect statements about history came from the famous American car manufacturer Henry Ford. He said: "History is bunk."

own families. It was in this way that the stories of ancient Greece were collected by the poet HOMER to form the *Iliad* and the *Odyssey*. Some early stories such as these were made up in verse and sung to music. This made it easier for people to remember the stories correctly.

In ancient Egypt, scholars recorded the reigns of the PHARAOHS and listed the victories they won in battle. Often, these accounts were written in HIEROGLYPHICS on stone tablets. The Chinese, Greeks, and Romans were also very interested in history. It was they who first took the writing of history seriously, and they wrote of how their civilizations rose to power. During the MIDDLE AGES in Europe, many people could not read or write, and printing had not been invented. The priests and monks preserved ancient books and kept the official records and documents. These records include the *Domesday Book* (1086), which tells us much of what we know about Norman England. History became an important branch of study in the 1700s and 1800s. Famous British historians were Edward Gibbon (1737–1794) and Lord Macaulay (1800–1859).

Historians get their information from hidden remains such as things found buried in old graves, as well as from old books. The study of hidden remains is called ARCHAEOLOGY. But history is not just concerned with the long distant past. After all, history is *our* story. What is news today will be history tomorrow. So modern historians are also interested in recording the present. They talk to old people about the things they remember, and they keep records on film and tape, often made for television news programs, of the events of today.

Hitler, Adolf

Adolf Hitler (1889–1945) was the "Fuhrer," or leader, of GERMANY during WORLD WAR II. An ex-soldier, born in Austria, he became leader of the Nazi Party which took over Germany in 1933.

Germany was still weak after its defeat in WORLD WAR I. The Nazis promised to avenge this defeat and create a new German empire. In 1939, Hitler led Germany into World War II and conquered most of Europe. Millions of people were killed in Nazi death camps. But, by 1945, Germany had lost the war. Hitler killed himself in the ruins of Berlin to avoid capture.

▲ *Hitler used to organize rallies, attended by thousands of people, to spread his ideas.*

Hobby

People today have more and more leisure time. Most people work fewer hours and have longer holidays than people did in the past. They retire at an earlier age and live longer. Housework takes less time because of modern household appliances. All this means that people have more free time for their

SEE IT YOURSELF

The hobby of paper-folding is called *origami*, a Japanese word. To make a paper penguin, follow the steps below: 1 and 2. Fold and crease a square along the dotted lines so C meets D. 3. Fold point B up. 4. Fold point B down along dotted line. 5. Fold and crease so that point F meets point E. 6. Fold point F along dotted line to make penguin's foot. 7. Turn over and fold point E to match other foot. 8. Fold point A down along dotted line to make head. 9. Unfold so head points up again. Separate folds of head and push inward along central crease. Cut to separate tail. Fold tail pieces back so penguin will stand. 10. Draw eyes.

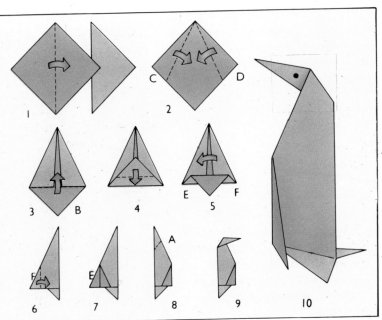

Most famous people have hobbies. George Washington collected different kinds of tea. Winston Churchill loved bricklaying. There is a long wall in the grounds of his former home built by the great man himself.

hobbies. Any activity that is enjoyed during your spare time is a hobby. It can be collecting things such as stamps, butterflies, bottles, or rocks. It can be a creative hobby, such as weaving, knitting, drawing, painting, or photography. Or it can be a playing hobby such as tennis, swimming, fishing, sailing, or chess. Part of the fun of any hobby is sharing it. The friendships that people gain from their hobbies are an important part of their interest.

Hockey

Hockey is one of the most popular, and fastest, team sports in North America. It is played indoors on ice rinks, and all the players wear ice skates. The rink is 200 feet long, with goal cages at either end. The object of the game is to knock a hard rubber disk called a "puck" into the opponent's goal using an L-shaped stick. Each team has six players; players can be substituted at any point during a game. All the players wear heavy padding to prevent injuries, but the goalie, a most important defender, wears the heaviest padding. The leading professional league is the National Hockey League.

▲ Ice hockey players, and particularly the goalkeeper, have to wear special padded clothing to protect them against injury.

Holography

Holography is a way of making very realistic three-dimensional pictures called *holograms*. It does this

► Holograms look very realistic because they are three-dimensional images. You can walk past a hologram and view it from different angles. Unfortunately, we cannot print a picture of a hologram in three dimensions here.

by using LASER light instead of a camera.

To make a hologram, a laser beam is split into two; one beam hits the object and is reflected onto a photographic plate; the other beam, angled by mirrors, strikes the plate directly. The photographic plate is developed, and a black-and-white pattern, the hologram, appears. When the hologram is lit by a laser beam and viewed from the other side, it produces a three-dimensional image of the original object. The image seems real, with width, depth, and height.

> One of the amazing things about a hologram plate is that it can be cut into pieces and each piece will give, not a part of the picture, but the whole picture.

Holy Roman Empire

For many years, a large part of Europe was loosely united as the Holy Roman Empire. At different times, it included Italy, Germany, Austria, and parts of France, the Netherlands, and Switzerland.

On Christmas Day in the year 800, Pope Leo III crowned CHARLEMAGNE as the first "Emperor of the Romans." The word "holy" was not added to the emperor's title until years later. After a while, the popes began to have more trouble than help from the emperors, and by the end of the thirteenth century, the emperor always came from the HAPSBURG family, the rulers of powerful Austria.

▼ *Homer's stories are full of excitement. In the* Odyssey, *Odysseus and his men encountered many dangerous monsters, including the Sirens, three bird-women whose beautiful voices lured sailors to their doom on the rocky shores. Odysseus had himself tied to the mast, and his men plugged their ears so they would not be tempted.*

Homer

Homer was a Greek poet and storyteller. He probably lived around 800 B.C., but we know nothing else about him. All we have are two great poems said to be by Homer: the *Iliad* and the *Odyssey*.

HONDURAS

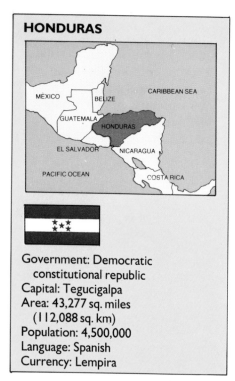

Government: Democratic
  constitutional republic
Capital: Tegucigalpa
Area: 43,277 sq. miles
  (112,088 sq. km)
Population: 4,500,000
Language: Spanish
Currency: Lempira

HONG KONG

Government: British Crown colony
Capital: Victoria
Area: Island 29 sq. miles (75 sq. km)
  New Territories, etc.
  375 sq. miles (971 sq. km)
Population: 5,300,000
Highest point: Tai Mo Shan 3,140 ft.
  (957 m)
Climate: Tropical monsoon
Rainfall average: 85 in. (2160 mm)

► *The name Hong Kong means "fragrant harbor." It is a crowded, busy place, and the famous Tiger Balm Gardens are a popular retreat.*

These poems tell us much of what we know about ancient Greek history and legend. The *Iliad* tells the story of the TROJAN WAR. The *Odyssey* tells of the adventures of Odysseus, a Greek hero, as he made his long journey home after the war.

Honduras

Honduras is a mountainous country in Central America. It has a long coastline with the Caribbean Sea and a short one along the Pacific. Most of the people are farmers. They live mainly in small villages in the west of the country and in the large banana plantations on the north coast. Columbus discovered Honduras in 1502. The country won its independence from Spain in 1821 and became a republic in 1838.

Hong Kong

Hong Kong is a tiny British colony off the coast of China. Part of it is a small island, and the rest is a narrow strip of land called the New Territories which is actually part of mainland China. Hong Kong has been governed by Britain since 1842. It is due to be handed over to Chinese rule in 1997.

Hong Kong has a fine harbor surrounded by

mountains. The capital is Victoria, and another busy city is Kowloon. Hong Kong is a fascinating mixture of East and West. The people live by trade, fishing, and farming. Tall apartment buildings have been built to house them, but there is still little room for the five million people who crowd this small colony.

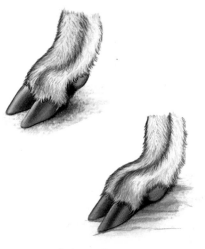

▲ *The ibex is a kind of wild goat. It has dual claws that can be brought down to give extra grip when scrambling up smooth rock faces.*

Hoof

A hoof is the hard covering of horn-like material that protects the feet of many animals. Animals that have hooves are divided into two main groupings: those that have an even number of toes; and those that have an odd number of toes. Those animals that have an even number of toes include DEER, GOATS, CAMELS, and SHEEP. All of these animals have either two toes or four toes. Animals that have only one toe include HORSES and zebras. All domesticated, or tame, horses have their hooves cut and trimmed and wear horseshoes. These are metal semicircles that are held in place by nails and that give valuable extra protection to the horse's hoof.

Hoover, Herbert Clark

Herbert Hoover (1874–1964) was president of the United States from 1929 to 1933. His presidency was dominated by the stock market crash of October 1929 and the Great Depression that followed it. The depression was the most severe in the history of the United States. Millions of people lost their jobs.

When Hoover became president, the United States had never been more prosperous. Most people expected that Hoover, who was a successful businessman, would help it to become richer still. Everyone was taken by surprise when the stock market fell only nine months after Hoover had become president. Few people knew what to do. Because Hoover believed that a country's economy should be allowed to regulate itself, he refused to give help to businesses or to pay unemployment to people who had lost their jobs. He became unpopular and was defeated in the next election by Franklin Roosevelt.

HERBERT C. HOOVER

Twenty-first President 1929–1933
Born: West Branch, Iowa
Education: Stanford University, Calif.
Occupation: Mining engineer
Political Party: Republican
Buried: West Branch, Iowa

▲ Hormones can affect how much—or how little—people grow. This jockey, shown here with his trainer, is exceptionally small.

Merino sheep

Markhor

Oryx

▲ The horns of some animals are very distinctive and decorative.

Hormone

Hormones are chemical messengers found in all animals and plants. In many animals, hormones are produced in organs called GLANDS. Glands are found in several parts of the body. From these glands, the different hormones are carried in the blood to other parts of the body. There, they make the parts do certain jobs.

The pituitary gland in the center of the head produces several hormones. These "master" hormones control the hormone secretion of several other glands. The thyroid gland in the neck, for example, is stimulated by the pituitary gland to make a hormone that controls how fast food is used up by the body. Too little of this hormone makes people overweight. The hormone adrenaline is controlled by nerve messages. When it flows, the heart beats faster, blood pressure rises, and the body prepares itself for strenuous physical exertion.

Many hormones can now be made in the laboratory and used to help people suffering from diseases caused by lack of certain hormones. Insulin is a hormone used in the treatment of diabetes, a disease in which too much sugar stays in the blood.

Horn

Many animals have horns or antlers. Horn is a special kind of hard SKIN. Finger and toe NAILS are made of horn. So are the FEATHERS and beaks of birds, and the scales of REPTILES.

Cattle, sheep, goats, and most ANTELOPES have curved horns. These are bony growths covered with a layer of horn, and they are fixed to the animal's skull. DEER have branched antlers, made of bone covered with skin. Every year, the antlers fall off, and the deer grows a new set.

Horse

The horse was one of the first wild animals to be tamed. Today, there are very few wild horses left. Many so-called "wild" horses are actually descended from domestic horses which have run wild.

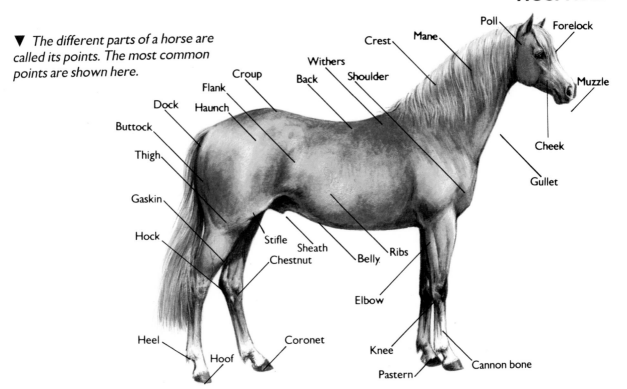

▼ *The different parts of a horse are called its points. The most common points are shown here.*

Poll · Forelock · Crest · Mane · Withers · Croup · Back · Shoulder · Flank · Muzzle · Dock · Haunch · Buttock · Cheek · Thigh · Gullet · Gaskin · Hock · Stifle · Sheath · Ribs · Chestnut · Belly · Heel · Coronet · Elbow · Hoof · Knee · Cannon bone · Pastern

The horse is valued for its speed and strength. But the first horse was a small, rather doglike creature, with a way of life quite unlike that of modern horses. Called *Eohippus*, or "dawn horse," it lived millions of years ago. It had four toes on its front feet and three toes on its back feet, and it probably hid from its enemies in the undergrowth.

Later, horses came out to live on the wide grassy plains. There was no undergrowth to hide in, so they escaped from enemies by running away. Gradually, their legs grew longer, and they lost all their toes except one. Finally, after millions of years of EVOLUTION, the modern horse appeared. It, too, has only one toe, and actually runs on tiptoe. Its toe has become a tough nail or HOOF.

Hospital

Hospitals are places where sick people, or patients, are cared for. Doctors and nurses look after the patients and try to make them better.

There are two types of hospital. One, the general hospital, deals with everything from accidents to contagious diseases. The other type of hospital specializes in certain conditions. For example, there

Today, horses are measured in hands from the ground to the highest point of the withers. A hand is 4 inches (10 cm), the width of a man's palm. But in the past a hand was only a little more than 3 inches because people's hands used to be smaller. Early horses were probably a lot smaller than those of today, seldom reaching 14 hands. Some of today's horses are over 17 hands and may even reach 20 hands.

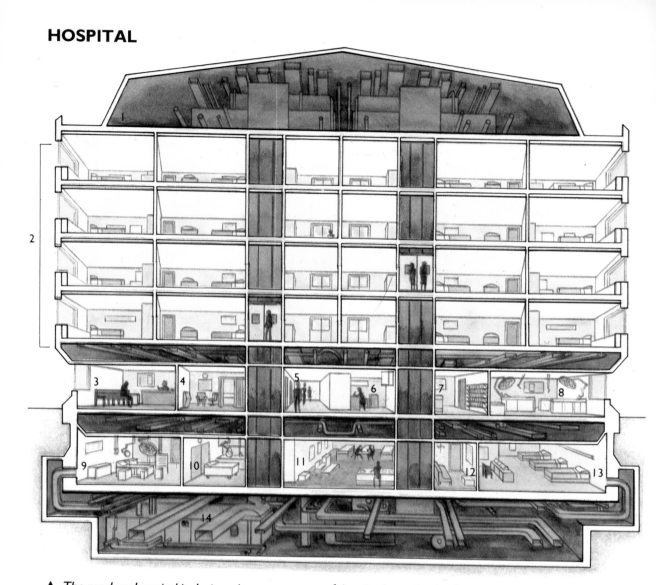

▲ The modern hospital is designed so that the needs of both patients and staff can be met in the most efficient way possible. Some of the most important parts are:
1 Heating and air conditioning
2 Patient floors 3 Waiting area
4 Consulting room 5 Corridor
6 Administration 7 Administration
8 Operating room 9 Operating room 10 Operating room
11 Staff restaurant 12 Chapel
13 Recovery room 14 Heating and air conditioning.

are *psychiatric* hospitals for people who are mentally ill; *maternity* hospitals where women have their babies; and *pediatric* hospitals that treat only children. In hospitals attached to medical schools, student doctors can gain experience through treating real patients.

In the ancient world, temples dedicated to the gods of healing used to have a hospital area. Sick people came there to pray and be treated. Later, in the Middle Ages, hospitals were attached to monasteries and run by monks and nuns. But in the last 200 years, non-religious hospitals have become the most common. In some countries, hospitals organized by the government provide inexpensive or free medical treatment for all people. Most hospitals are either owned by the community, the government, or are private and run like a business. Modern hospitals have a wide range of technical equipment.

Hotel

Hotels are places where travelers or people on vacation can stay. Before 1800, there were no hotels as we know them. Travelers spent the night at taverns or inns. Wherever people traveled, there were inns that gave food and shelter to the traveler and his horse.

Today, large hotels are like small towns. They provide people who are on business trips or are traveling for pleasure with all the comforts—swimming pools, television, restaurants, shops, travel agencies, and beauty salons.

Another kind of hotel is the "motel." This gives overnight housing for people who are traveling by car. Motels are found along major roads. Guests can usually drive their car right up to the door of their room.

▲ Hotel kitchens are usually run with great efficiency and discipline. In large hotels, the work is very specialized, with one person in charge of making sauces, for example, while someone else only makes desserts, etc.

House

Houses date back to prehistoric times. Some of the first were built in the Middle East. They were simple little boxes with flat roofs. Often, doors and windows were simply open spaces in the walls. (See pages 348–349.)

Hovercraft (Air Cushion Vehicle)

Depending on how you look at one, a hovercraft is either a plane with no wings or a ship that rides out of the water.

A hovercraft rides on a cushion of air, blown

Continued on page 350

▼ The cushion of air produced by powerful fans inside a hovercraft provides a fast ride across water or land.

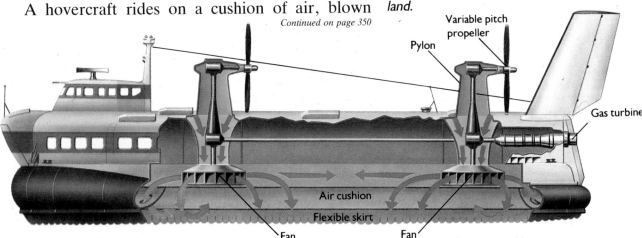

Variable pitch propeller

Pylon

Gas turbine

Air cushion

Flexible skirt

Fan

Fan

HOUSE

Prehistoric people lived in caves. The first houses were rough shelters, made of mud, branches, and leaves. Later, people learned how to make bricks by drying wet clay in the sun. Brick, wood, and stone were for thousands of years the materials from which almost all houses were built.

The modern house is built to keep out the cold and wet, and to keep in warmth. Insulation in the roof and walls helps to do this. Many homes have central heating and, in hot climates, air conditioning.

In most countries, a house is lived in by either a single family or a family group. A number of houses joined together form a row. Two houses joined side by side are called duplexes. A number of homes built on top of one another form an apartment building. In many big cities, there are not enough houses to provide homes for everybody. In some countries, poor people live in slums and shanty towns.

HOUSES AROUND THE WORLD

▶ *Although houses in cities around the world now look very much the same, there are still lots of differences in the way houses are built. Houses in North Africa and Arabia, for example, have thick mud-brick or cement walls and small windows. This helps to keep them cool. In Southeast Asia, many people live in houses built on stilts over the water. In Borneo, a whole village may live in one big dwelling called a long-house. In Canada, the U.S.A. and Scandinavia, many houses are built of wood, whereas in parts of Britain, you will see houses made of local stone, perhaps with a roof of thatch (reeds).*

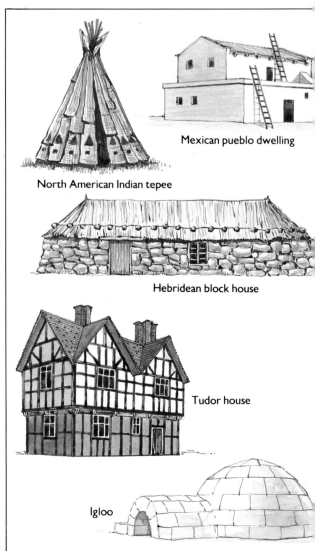

Mexican pueblo dwelling

North American Indian tepee

Hebridean block house

Tudor house

Igloo

HOW HOUSES AND APARTMENTS ARE BUILT

Houses are built in a different way from apartments. Both must have foundations, with pipes for water and sewage, and cables for electricity. A house often has walls of brick, covered on the inside with plaster or wallboard. The floors are made of concrete or wood. The roof is usually sloped, so that rain runs off easily and is covered with rows of shingles. An apartment building has a framework of steel girders to give extra strength. The walls may be factory-made panels, lifted into place by a crane. It will have an elevator, as well as stairs, and it may have a flat roof.

▲ *Traditional building techniques using timber, bricks, and tiles are still widely used, particularly for housing.*

▲ *Large-scale building projects often rely on advanced techniques and materials.*

Indonesian stilt house

Sudanese mud huts

Modern apartment building

English thatched cottage

Suburban house

HISTORY OF THE HOUSEHOLD

100 A.D. Wealthy Romans lived in houses with running water and underfloor heating.

1200s Only rich people could afford glass in their windows.

1500s The water closet was invented, but few people had real toilets until the 1900s.

1830 Edwin Budding invents lawnmower.

1840s Gas lighting replaced oil lamps and candles.

1858 Ferdinand Carré invents the refrigerator, allowing people to keep food fresh for later use.

1879 Electric light bulb invented.

1880s Gas stoves introduced to replace the old kitchen range.

1900s Invention of the vacuum cleaner.

1910 First electric washing machine.

1930s Electric stoves become popular.

1950s First dishwasher invented.

1953 Microwaves appear in the U.S. They cook food much faster than normal methods.

2000 The home run by a computer?

▼ *The Xanadu experimental house in Florida could be the shape of things to come. Built for maximum energy efficiency, it combines convenience with concern for the environment.*

BUYING AND RENTING HOUSES

People wanting to buy a house usually need to borrow most of the money, because houses are expensive. In the U.S., house buyers can borrow money from a bank or from a savings and loan. This is called taking out a mortgage. They have to repay the loan over a number of years. They will probably visit a realtor to see what houses are for sale.

Not all houses are owned by the people who live in them. Many people live in rented houses or apartments. They pay rent to the owner.

For information about how houses are built see ARCHITECTURE; BUILDING. For interesting and unusual houses, turn to AMERICAN INDIANS; CAVE DWELLER; ESKIMO; GYPSY. For the insides of houses, see FURNITURE; TAPESTRY.

HOVERCRAFT

A well-known use of the hovercraft principle is the "hovering" rotary lawnmower. The engine, besides rotating the grass-cutting blade, creates a cushion of air that raises the machine to the right height above the ground.

downward by fans, and held in by a skirt or side wall around the hovercraft. They work best over flat surfaces like water, but can also cross beaches and flat land. The only danger is that rough ground may snag their bottoms.

Hovercraft are much faster than ships. Since they do not have to push against any water, but simply skim smoothly through the air, they can easily manage speeds of 75 mph (120 km/hr). Their advantage over planes is the size of the load they can carry. A large craft can load dozens of cars and up to 400 passengers. And of course they do not need harbors or runways to land. They simply climb up the beach to settle on a simple concrete landing pad.

The hovercraft was invented in 1955 by a British engineer, Christopher Cockerell. The first working model appeared four years later and had soon crossed the Channel from England to France. Today, fleets of hovercraft shuttle back and forth every day carrying hundreds of cars and passengers.

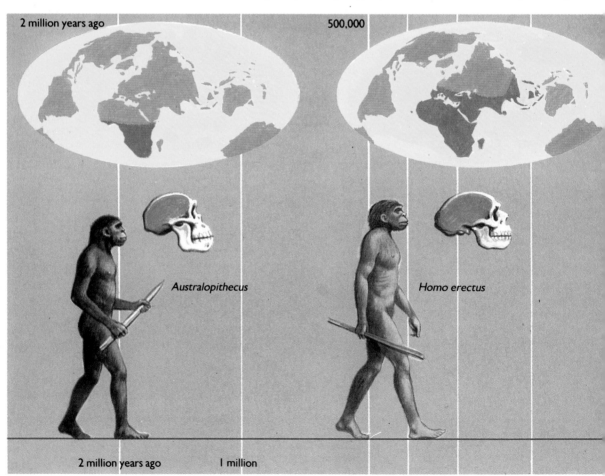

2 million years ago

500,000

Australopithecus

Homo erectus

2 million years ago

1 million

Human Beings

Human beings are mammals, but rather clever ones. They are very like their relatives, the apes. They have the same kind of bones, muscles, and other parts inside their bodies. But the main difference between people and any other animal is the size of their brain. The human brain is enormous, compared to body size. Some animals are stronger than human beings, others can run faster, hear and smell more acutely. But people use their brain to think things out, and when they have found an answer to a problem, they can talk about it with other people.

All scientists are now agreed that our ancestors were ape-like creatures who slowly, over millions of years, evolved (changed) into people. People something like ourselves have probably lived on Earth for about 500,000 years.

Today, all people belong to the same *species* (kind of creature). This creature is classified as

▼ *Our ancestors of two million years ago were very different from us, but the world, too, was very different. A series of ice ages meant that huge glaciers covered much of the northern half of the Earth. One of the most important events in the development of people took place about one million years ago, when our ancestors started to make tools. By about 10,000 B.C. people were beginning to understand how to grow and harvest crops. The red areas show how people spread all over the world.*

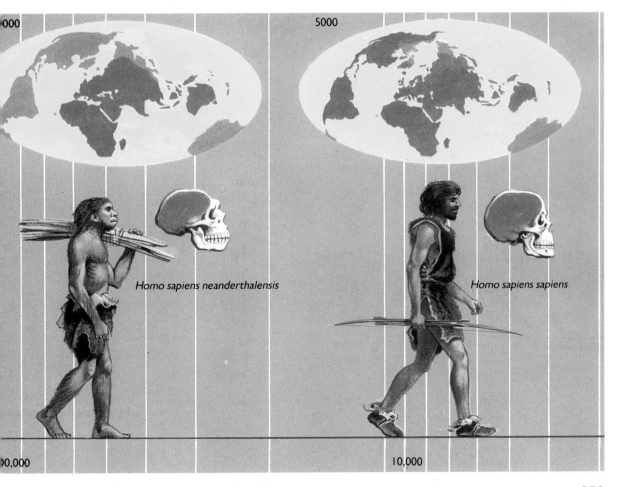

000

5000

Homo sapiens neanderthalensis

Homo sapiens sapiens

0,000

10,000

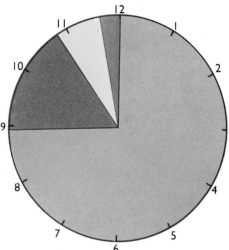

▲ If the history of the Earth to the present day were condensed into twelve hours, the earliest life in the sea would have begun just before nine o'clock. Life moved onto land at a quarter to eleven, and mammals appeared at twenty to twelve. Humans would have arrived just before the stroke of twelve.

▼ The body works through a series of interconnected systems that function all the time to keep us going.

Homo sapiens ("thinking man"). All people, in every country on Earth, whether black, white, brown, or yellow, are *Homo sapiens*.

Scientists divide human beings into three main *races*. The *Caucasoid* people are fair-skinned like the people of Europe and America or dark-skinned like the people of India, and others. The *Mongoloid* group takes in most of the yellow-skinned peoples of Asia, plus the American Indians. The *Negroid* group consists of the dark-skinned peoples of Africa and other regions.

Human Body

Your body is a wonderful machine with many parts. Each part has a special job, and all the parts work together to keep you alive and healthy. Like all machines, your body needs fuel—food. The OXY-GEN you breathe in from the air helps turn the food you eat into energy. This energy allows you to play, work, think, and grow.

Your body is made up of millions of tiny cells—many different kinds of cells. A group of cells that work together is called a *tissue*. For example, cells that allow you to lift things are called muscle tissue. Tissues that work together make up an *organ*. The HEART is an organ that pumps blood. Other organs are the LIVER, the LUNGS, the STO-MACH, and the SKIN.

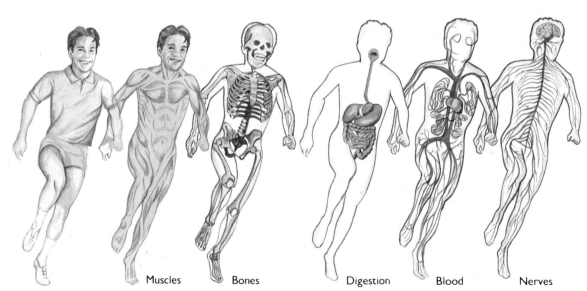

Muscles   Bones   Digestion   Blood   Nerves

Organs that work together are called *systems*. You have a *digestive system* (mouth, stomach, and intestines), a *circulatory system* (heart, arteries, and veins), and a *nervous system* (brain and nerves). The study of the body is called *anatomy*.

Humidity

All air has some water in it, although we cannot see it. Humidity is the amount of water in the air. If the air contains only a little water vapor, the humidity is low. When air holds a lot of moisture, we say the humidity is high. The warmer the air, the more moisture it can hold. Humidity affects the way we feel. When the humidity is high, we feel "sweaty" and uncomfortable. This is because the sweat does not evaporate easily from our skin. But too low a humidity is not very good for us. Some people use *humidifiers* in their homes to put more moisture into the air.

Hummingbird

These birds are among the smallest in the world. They are found only in the western hemisphere, from Canada to the tip of South America. The tiniest of the 320 kinds lives in Cuba. It is less than 2 inches (5 cm)—hardly bigger than a large bumblebee.

SEE IT YOURSELF

Scientists calculate the humidity with the help of an instrument called a hygrometer. You can make one by taping two identical outdoor thermometers to a brick. Cut a narrow strip about 8 inches (20 cm) long from an old towel and wrap it around the bulb of one thermometer. Fill a pan with water and put the other end of the strip in it. After a while, take the difference between the temperatures shown on the two thermometers in the shade outdoors. The less the difference, the higher the humidity. Keep a record of the humidity in your area.

▲ *The tiny hummingbird has a specially developed beak and tongue that enable it to feed from deep inside flowers.*

Some tiny hummingbirds spend 20 hours in the air and make journeys of up to 500 miles (800 km) over water.

The feathers of hummingbirds are colored in brilliant metallic hues of blue, green, red, and yellow. The colors flash in the sun, so they look like glittering jewels on the wing.

Hummingbirds can beat their wings up to 70 times a second. This is what causes their distinctive humming sound. It also lets them hover in mid-air and fly backward and sideways like a helicopter. In this way, they dart from flower to flower and feed while flying. They take nectar and tiny insects from deep within the cups of flowers.

Hungary

Hungary is a small, central European country. It covers an area about the size of Maine.

Hungary has no coastline. The mighty Danube river flows across the country on its way to the Black Sea, dividing it almost in two. Ships can sail up the river as far as Budapest, the capital and biggest city.

Hungary is low-lying and fairly flat. In the east, it becomes a vast grassy plain. Here herds of sheep, cattle, and horses graze. The climate is hot and dry in the summer, and bitterly cold in the winter. Agriculture is important, but more Hungarians work in industry than on farms. There are also rich sources of coal, oil, and bauxite for making aluminum.

HUNGARY

Government: Communist
Capital: Budapest
Area: 35,910 sq. miles (93,030 sq. km)
Population: 10,700,000
Language: Hungarian
Currency: Forint

▶ The capital of Hungary is actually made up of two cities—Buda and Pest, separated by the Danube.

After WORLD WAR I and the collapse of the Austro-Hungarian Empire, Hungary became an independent republic. After WORLD WAR II, it had a communist government and was closely linked with the Soviet Union. But, in 1989, the people demanded and achieved a more democratic form of government.

Huns

These were a group of fierce wandering warriors who swept into Europe in about A.D. 400 from the plains of Central Asia. They conquered large parts of Germany and France. Their famous general, Attila, attacked Rome and nearly destroyed the Roman Empire. However, the Huns' power grew less after his death in A.D. 453.

> When Attila, the great leader of the Huns, died in 453, his body was taken out into the plains and buried with much of his treasure. All those who had been at Attila's burial were put to death afterward so that his grave might never be discovered.

Hunting

In prehistoric times, hunting was the main way by which people lived. Nowadays, most hunting is done as sport or to keep down pests.

Big game hunting is the sport of tracking, stalking, and killing large wild animals. This kind of hunting is dying out, since people now want to preserve animals, not kill them. Another kind of hunting is with packs of hounds. The hunters may follow on foot or on horseback as the dogs chase deer, foxes, or hares through the countryside. Foxhunting is the most popular kind of hunting in the British Isles. In the United States, most hunting is done with guns.

▼ Hunting on horseback was a popular sport in ancient China. Cheetahs, dogs, and falcons were used in the chase.

▲ Satellite pictures can help to predict the route a hurricane will take. Hurricane Allen is shown here over the Gulf of Mexico. You can clearly see the "eye" in the center of the storm.

Hurricane

A hurricane is a severe storm. To be called a hurricane, a storm must have wind speeds of at least 75 miles (120 km) an hour. People who live around the Pacific Ocean call hurricanes *typhoons*. People who live on the Indian Ocean call them *cyclones*. Hurricane winds whirl around in a huge circle and can reach speeds of over 200 miles (320 km) per hour. The largest hurricanes have measured 1,000 miles (1,600 km) across. Hurricanes form over oceans near the Equator, where the air is very moist. The center of a hurricane is a narrow column of air that spins very slowly. This is the "eye" of the hurricane.

Hydroelectric Power

More than a quarter of the world's electricity is produced by using the energy of fast flowing water. This is called hydroelectric power. Most hydroelectric plants are found below dams, but some are powered by waterfalls.

Water is heavy. When it falls down through large pipes from a high dam, it can be made to turn TUR-BINES with paddle-shaped blades. Shafts connected to the blades turn electric generators, as in ordinary coal- or oil-fired POWER PLANTS.

▶ The huge turbine blades in a hydroelectric power plant are turned by water as it flows down from a dam. They in turn rotate a shaft connected to generators, which produce electricity in the same way as in ordinary power plants.

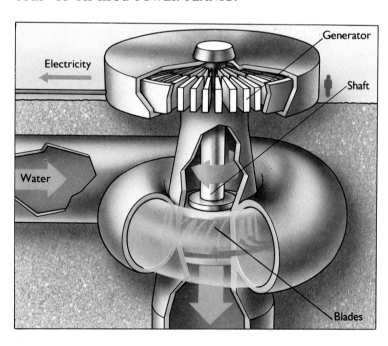

Hydrofoil

Much of a ship's engine power goes into overcoming the drag of the water around the ship's hull. A hydrofoil solves this problem by lifting the ship right out of the water. It does this with a set of underwater struts attached to the hull of the craft at the bow and stern. These "water wings" can lift the hull as the ship gathers speed. As the water's drag grows less, the craft shoots ahead, traveling far faster than an ordinary vessel can.

▲ At rest, a hydrofoil lies in the water like a normal ship, but once it starts moving, the hull rises up and the vessel is supported on its underwater struts.

Hydrogen

Hydrogen is a gas. It is thought to be the most abundant ELEMENT in the whole universe. It is the single most important material from which stars, including our SUN, are made.

Hydrogen is the lightest of all elements. It is more than 14 times as light as air. It is colorless and has no smell and no taste. Hydrogen burns very easily. Great masses of hydrogen are always being burned in the Sun. It is this fierce burning that gives us light and heat from the Sun.

Coal, oil, and natural gas all contain hydrogen. It is also a very important part of all plant and animal bodies.

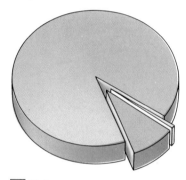

◻ Hydrogen
◻ Other gases
◻ Helium

▲ This pie chart shows the proportions of the gases that make up our Sun. Hydrogen is the main component by a long way.

Hyena

Hyenas are a small group of flesh-eating MAMMALS. Although they look a lot like dogs, they are more closely related to the cat family.

Hyenas feed on dead flesh, or carrion. They scavenge their meals from the kills of other animals such as lions. They have very powerful teeth and jaws for crushing the bones and making the most of their source of leftover food. Hyenas hunt in packs. They feed at night. By day, they sleep in holes and caves.

The spotted hyena lives in southern Africa. It is famous for its wild laughing cry, which resembles a hysterical human laugh, and is sometimes known as the laughing hyena. The striped hyena lives in India, southwest Asia, and northeast Africa.

▼ A pack of hyenas can drive away most hunting animals from their kill, which the hyenas then finish off.

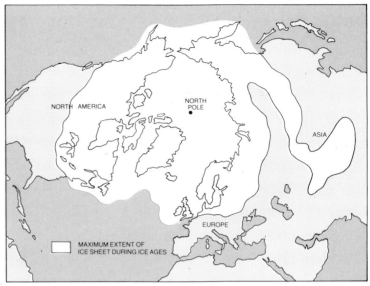

▶ *The glaciers that spread over large parts of the Earth during the Ice Ages carried huge rocks and boulders with them as they went. Geologists can trace the path of the glaciers by studying these rocks and figuring out where they came from.*

MAXIMUM EXTENT OF
ICE SHEET DURING ICE AGES

Ice Ages

The Ice Ages were times when vast sheets of ice covered parts of the Earth. Each period lasted for thousands of years. In between were warmer periods. The last Ice Age ended about 10,000 years ago, but the ice might return again.

During the Ice Ages, the weather was very cold. Endless snow fell, and GLACIERS grew and spread. At times, the glaciers covered much of North America and Asia, and Europe as far south as London. In some places, the ice piled up 3,300 feet (1,000 m) high. This made the sea level lower than it is today. A land bridge was formed between Asia and North America. The first people in America came across this land bridge from Asia.

▼ *Huge icebergs float in the sea because, when water freezes, it expands, so ice is less dense than water.*

Iceberg

Icebergs are pieces of GLACIERS and ice shelves that have broken away and float in the sea. They are found in the waters of the ARCTIC and the ANTARCTIC.

Icebergs can be very big. Some weigh millions of tons. Most of an iceberg is hidden under the surface of the sea. Some icebergs may be 90 miles (145 km) long. They can be 400 feet (120 m) high above water. An iceberg this high would be another 3,170 feet (960 m) deep under water.

Icebergs are dangerous to ships. Some icebergs

float south from the Arctic into the Atlantic Ocean. In 1912, a ship called the *Titanic* hit an iceberg in the Atlantic. It sank, and 1,500 people in it were drowned.

Iceland

Iceland is a small, mountainous island. It was first discovered by VIKINGS in A.D.874. The island lies just south of the Arctic Circle in the north Atlantic, between Greenland and Norway. Warm waters from the GULF STREAM keep most of the harbors free of ice all year round.

Iceland has many VOLCANOES. About 25 of its volcanoes have erupted. There are many hot springs, too. Some are used to heat homes. The north of Iceland is covered by GLACIERS and a desert of stone

ICELAND

Government: Constitutional republic
Capital: Reykjavik
Area: 39,768 sq. miles (103,000 sq. km)
Population: 241,000
Language: Icelandic
Currency: Krona

◀ *These two volcanic hills rising out of the landscape are typical Icelandic features.*

and lava (cooled volcanic matter).

Most people live in the south and east where the land is lower. They live by farming and fishing. It is light almost 24 hours a day in June, and dark nearly all the time in December.

Iceland became an independent country in 1944 after breaking its ties with Denmark.

Idaho

Idaho is one of the most spectacularly beautiful states. It is in the northwest of the country, on the Canadian border, and is dominated by the northern

IDAHO

Capital: Boise
Population: 1,000,000
Area: 83,557 sq. mi. (216,412 sq. km)
State flower: Idaho Syringa
State bird: Mountain Bluebird
State tree: White Pine
Statehood: July 3, 1890
    43rd state

▲ *Snake River Gorge, Idaho.*

ILLINOIS

Capital: Springfield
Population: 11,550,000
Area: 56,400 sq. mi. (146,075 sq. km)
State flower: Illinois Native Violet
State bird: Cardinal
State tree: White Oak
Statehood: December 3, 1818
  21st state

▼ *Lincoln's house in Springfield, Illinois.*

end of the Rocky Mountains. In the south is the rushing Snake River. It flows through Hells Canyon, which is 7,900 feet (2,400 m) deep, deeper than the Grand Canyon.

Idaho's most famous product is potatoes, but many other important agricultural products are grown, too, including wheat and sugar beets. Almost 40 percent of the state is forested. Paper, which is made from wood, is one of the state's most important products. Idaho also has enormous mineral reserves, and produces more silver than any other state. Gold, lead, and other minerals for industry are also produced.

Illinois

Illinois lies in the center of the Midwest. It is one of the most important industrial and agricultural states. Most industry is centered in and around Chicago, the largest city; over one half of the population lives in this area. Much of the rest of Illinois is rich agricultural land. The rolling prairie lands produce high-quality beef, pork, and dairy goods. With the Great Lakes to the north and the Mississippi running to the south, Illinois also lies in the center of many important transportation routes.

The French were the first people to settle Illinois. In 1763 it was taken over by the British. It became a U.S. territory in 1783. European settlers flooded into the state in the 1800s.

Immunity

You have probably been vaccinated against the disease called polio. The substance the doctor or nurse put into your body contained polio germs, but these germs had been made harmless, so you only caught a very mild case of polio. Your body did not know that the polio germs had been weakened, and it got to work fighting them. Your body produced *antibodies*—substances that attack certain disease-causing germs. These antibodies stay in your body to stop more of the same kind of germs from invading your body again. This kind of long-term protection against diseases is called immunity.

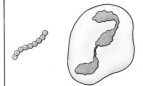  

1. A white blood cell is moving to attack a bacterium.

2. It surrounds the bacterium and takes it in.

3. The bacterium is killed by chemicals inside the cell.

4. The bacterium is expelled in the form of pus.

People also have *acquired* immunity to disease. This happens when they have a disease and produce antibodies to fight it off. After that, the antibodies are waiting to ward off these germs if they appear again. If you had measles, you are unlikely to get measles again.

However, some diseases are very difficult or impossible to vaccinate against. Your body stops making antibodies against the common cold almost as soon as you are over it. The VIRUS that causes AIDS damages the body's immune system so that it stops making antibodies against diseases at all.

▲ *The presence of bacteria in the body stimulates the white blood cells, which are always present to move in to attack them.*

Impressionism

In the 1860s in France, some young artists began to paint in a new way. Most artists worked indoors, but these young men began to paint outdoors. They

The Impressionists were so interested in light that they never used black. Black is the absence of light. If you look at an Impressionist painting, some things seem to be black, but look closely and you will see that they are dark brown, green, or blue.

◀ *Some of Monet's most famous paintings are of his garden at Giverny.*

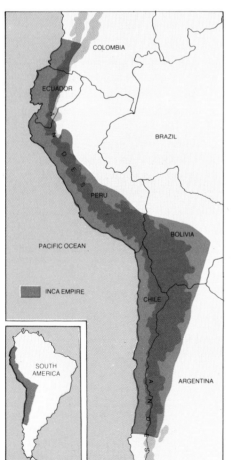

The Incas worshiped the Sun and other nature gods in elaborate ceremonies, at which their priests would offer sacrifices of animals.

▼ The Inca empire, when the Spaniards first encountered it, stretched for about 2,000 miles (3,200 km) north to south on the west coast of South America.

painted scenes from nature and tried to catch the ever-changing light.

In 1874, the group held an exhibition in Paris. Their work was laughed at, and one newspaper poked fun at a painting called *Impression: Sunrise* by Claude Monet. It called the group "Impressionists," and the name stuck.

Now, people recognize the Impressionists as being among the greatest artists of all time. In addition to Monet, the most important Impressionists were Edouard Manet, Camille Pissarro, Edgar Degas, Alfred Sisley, and Pierre Auguste Renoir.

Incas

The Incas were people who lived in SOUTH AMERICA. They ruled a great empire from the 1200s until the 1500s. The center of their empire was in PERU. In the 1400s, the empire grew. It stretched thousands of miles, from Chile in the south to Ecuador in the north.

The Inca king and his nobles ruled over the people in the empire. They were very strict and told the farmers and craftsmen what to grow and make. The Incas built many roads through the empire.

In the 1500s, Spanish soldiers led by Francisco Pizarro reached South America. They captured the Inca king Atahualpa and said they would free him in return for gold. Incas brought their treasure to free the king, but the Spanish still killed him. By 1569, the Spaniards had conquered the whole Inca empire.

Independence Day

Independence Day—July 4—is one of the most important holidays in the United States. It commemorates the acceptance of the Declaration of Independence by the Continental Congress in Philadelphia on July 4, 1776. It was first celebrated in Philadelphia on July 8, 1776, the day the Declaration of Independence was read in public. It was not until after the War of 1812 that people across the country began to celebrate Independence Day. And it was only in 1941 that Congress made it a national holiday. Today, people celebrate Independence Day with parades, parties, and fireworks.

John Adams, the second president, said that Independence Day "ought to be solemnized with pomp and parade, with shows, games, sports, guns, bells, bonfires, and illuminations, from one end of the continent to the other, from this time forward for evermore."

India

India has a population of nearly 800 million. It has more people than any other country except China. India is part of ASIA.

In the north of India are the HIMALAYAS. Many people live in the fertile northern plains, which are crossed by the great Ganges and Brahmaputra Rivers. The south is high, flat land, with mountains called the Ghats along the coast.

India is very hot and dry in summer. Parts of the country are almost DESERT. But winds called *monsoons* bring heavy rain to the northeast every year.

Most Indians are farmers. They live in small villages and grow rice, wheat, tea, cotton, and jute.

INDIA

Government: Federal republic
Capital: New Delhi
Area: 1,269,340 sq. miles
  (3,287,590 sq. km)
Population: 784,000,000
Languages: Hindi, English
Currency: Rupee

◀ *The Ganges river is sacred to Hindus because, in legend, it flows from the head of the god Shiva.*

India has some of the wettest places in the world. The Shillong Plateau in eastern India has an average of 427 in. (1,087 cm) of rain each year. New York has about 39 in. (99 cm).

India is also a fast-growing industrial country. Cities such as Calcutta and Bombay are among the world's biggest.

Hindi and English are the two main languages, but there are hundreds of others. Most Indians practice HINDUISM, but many follow the religion of ISLAM. There are also many other religions in India.

Indiana

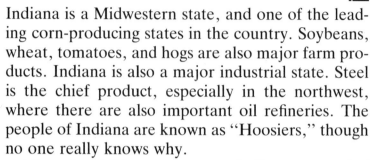

Indiana is a Midwestern state, and one of the leading corn-producing states in the country. Soybeans, wheat, tomatoes, and hogs are also major farm products. Indiana is also a major industrial state. Steel is the chief product, especially in the northwest, where there are also important oil refineries. The people of Indiana are known as "Hoosiers," though no one really knows why.

Like other Midwestern states, Indiana was settled first by the French, then by the British. It became a U.S. territory in 1783. In 1811, William Harrison fought an important battle against the Indians, the Battle of Tippecanoe. After this, many people settled in the state. Many famous writers have come from Indiana, including Theodore Dreiser and Booth Tarkington.

INDIANA

Capital: Indianapolis
Population: 5,500,000
Area: 36,291 sq. mi. (93,986 sq. km)
State flower: Peony
State bird: Cardinal
State tree: Tulip Tree
Statehood: December 11, 1816
    19th state

▶ Indiana's most famous annual event is the Indianapolis 500 automobile race.

Indian Ocean

The Indian Ocean is the third largest ocean, with an area of 28,350,000 sq. miles (73,426,500 sq. km). Two very large islands lie in the ocean—Madagascar, off southern Africa, and Sri Lanka, off the southern tip of India. Strong winds from the ocean called *monsoons* bring moisture to Southeast Asia each summer.

Indian Wars

The Indian Wars were the struggles between white settlers and the American Indians for control of the United States. The wars began almost as soon as white people landed in America in the 1600s. They continued until about 1900, when the Indians across the country were demoralized and defeated. As settlers moved farther west, the fighting moved west, too. Many people today believe that the settlers were cruel to take the Indians' land, and they claim that the Indians should have been respected because they had lived in America for thousands of years. But at the time, most people thought the Indians were savages who had to be defeated. Because many Indians were also cruel and often fought, white settlers felt that force was the best way to get rid of them. Because the settlers often outnumbered the Indians, and had better guns and equipment, they were able to defeat them quite easily.

When white people first came to America, about one million Indians lived there. By 1900 there were only about 200,000 Indians left in the whole United States.

Indonesia

Indonesia is a country in Southeast Asia. It is a chain of about 3,000 islands around the equator. The islands stretch over a distance of 3,000 miles (4,800 km).

Indonesia has 177 million people. More than half of them live in Java. Java is the biggest island. The capital city, Jakarta, is in Java. Most Indonesians are farmers. They grow many things, including rice, tea, rubber, and tobacco. Indonesia also produces minerals, including petroleum, and timber from its forests. Once ruled by the Dutch, Indonesia fought for and won independence in 1949.

INDONESIA

Government: Independent republic
Capital: Jakarta
Area: 782,657 sq. miles
(2,027,087 sq. km)
Population: 177,000,000
Language: Bahasa Indonesian (Malay)
Currency: Rupiah

▼ The spinning jenny was one of many machines invented during the Industrial Revolution. It altered work methods that had not changed for hundreds of years.

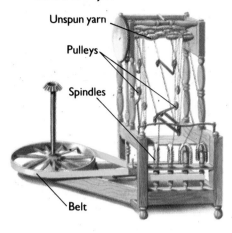

Unspun yarn

Pulleys

Spindles

Belt

Industrial Revolution

The Industrial Revolution was a great change which took place in Europe in the 1700s and 1800s. People began to make things on machines in factories. The new machines were run by STEAM ENGINES. They made things much faster than people could by hand. Mining and metalworking became more important, and the RAILROADS began. Many people moved from the countryside and began to work in factories in the towns.

Inflation

Inflation is a word used to mean rapidly rising prices. Every time prices go up, MONEY is worth less, because people need more money to buy the same things. In turn, people ask for higher wages. If wages rise, then the cost of making things in factories goes up. This often makes prices rise again. Because prices and wages affect each other like this, inflation is hard to stop. There are many reasons why inflation starts. If inflation becomes very bad, money can become worthless.

▼ Enormous social changes took place in the 1800s in Europe. Improved farming methods replaced traditional ways, and many peasant farmers had to move to towns where the conditions were crowded and unhealthy.

Infrared Rays

When you feel the heat from a fire or the Sun, you are feeling infrared rays. They are also called *heat*

rays. Although you cannot see infrared rays, they behave in the same way as light rays. They can be reflected and refracted. Photographers use film that is sensitive to infrared rays to take pictures in total darkness.

Inoculation

Inoculation is a way of protecting people from disease. It is also called *vaccination*.

Inoculation works by giving people a very weak dose of a disease. The body learns to fight the GERMS which cause the disease. In this way, the body becomes protected, or *immune*, from the disease.

IMMUNITY from a disease may last from a few months to many years, depending on the kind of disease and vaccine. There are many kinds of inoculation. They are used against diseases such as typhoid, cholera, measles, and polio. Many people used to become ill and die from these diseases. Now more people are saved every year through inoculation. A pioneer of inoculation was Edward JENNER.

Insect

There are millions of different kinds of insects in the world. Every year, thousands of new kinds are found. (See pages 368–369.)

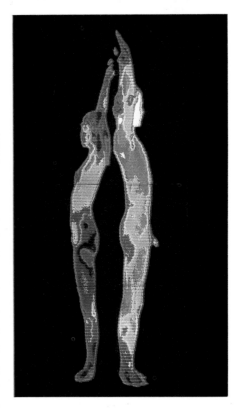

▲ Infrared sensitive film can be used to take pictures in which areas of heat and cold show up as different colors. White areas are the hottest, and blue are the coolest.

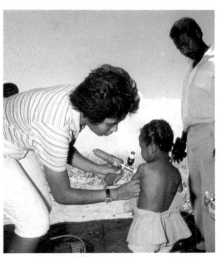

▼ Inoculation programs are vital in Third World countries, where diseases can be prevented and thousands of lives saved.

INSECTS

Insects live all over the world. They are by far the most numerous of all animal species. More than 850,000 different kinds of insects are known. Roughly eight out of ten of all the Earth's animals are insects!

Insects range in size from tiny fleas which can be seen only through a microscope to beetles as big as your hand. Many have interesting life stories, or cycles. Some insects, such as the desert locust of Africa, are destructive pests. But many others are helpful. Without bees and other flying insects, flowering plants would not be pollinated, and fruit trees would not bear fruit.

Among the most fascinating insects are the social insects, which live in highly organized communities or colonies. These include ants, bees, and termites. Many insects make regular journeys. Some butterflies, beetles, and dragonflies migrate at certain times every year.

▼ *These are just a few of the hundreds of thousands of different kinds of insects alive on Earth. Their success as a living species is due to the fact that they are small, they can adapt to many environments, and they reproduce rapidly.*

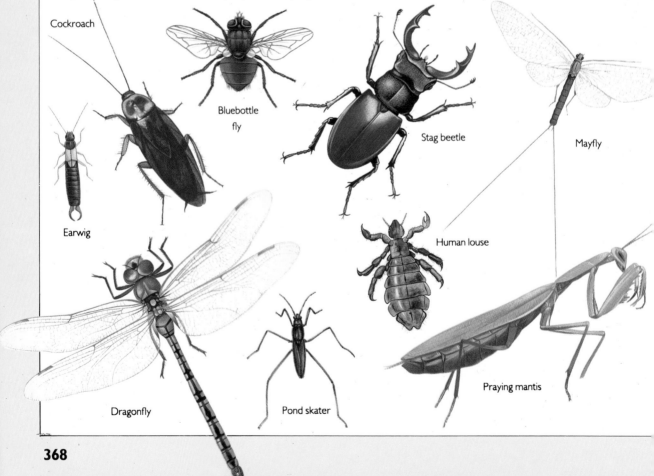

Cockroach

Bluebottle
fly

Stag beetle

Mayfly

Earwig

Human louse

Dragonfly

Pond skater

Praying mantis

INSECT HELPERS

elpful insects include bees, which pollinate flowering
ants and also give us honey. The silkworm (the larva of
e silk moth) is reared for the silk it spins when turning
to a pupa. Ladybugs are the gardener's friends because
ey prey on the aphids which attack roses and other
ants. Insects such as the ichneumon wasp prey on
ther insects, controlling pests. Scavenging insects, such
burying beetles, feed on dead matter and help to
ake the soil fertile.

◀ *The seven-spot ladybug feeds on aphids,*
ests in our gardens.

INSECT PESTS

armful insects are those that carry disease and
estroy food grown by farmers. The mosquito
which carries malaria) and the tsetse fly (which
preads disease in people and cattle) are pests. Flies,
e, fleas, and cockroaches live close to people, often
side houses, damaging food and spreading disease.
he Colorado beetle destroys potato crops. Locusts
e feared by farmers in Africa because they swarm
such vast numbers that they blacken the skies. The
custs eat every plant in their path.

▶ *The locust travels long distances in*
estructive swarms.

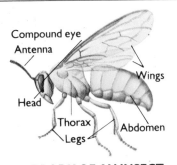

THE BODY OF AN INSECT

All insects have a similar body
plan. An insect's body is in three
parts: a head, thorax, and
abdomen. The head has eyes,
jaws, and feelers (antennae).
The middle part, or thorax,
carries three pairs of jointed legs
and sometimes wings. The
abdomen contains the stomach,
reproductive organs, and
breathing tubes called spiracles.

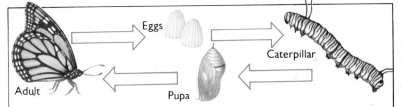

THE LIFE CYCLE OF INSECTS

All insects start life as eggs. In the most advanced insects, there are four
stages in the life cycle. The egg hatches into a larva or grub. This larva
grows by shedding its skin and finally turns into a pupa or chrysalis. The
pupa looks lifeless, but inside many changes are taking place. The pupa
finally splits apart, and a fully-formed adult insect emerges.

Some insects, such as grasshoppers, hatch from eggs not as larvae, but
as nymphs. Grasshopper nymphs do not yet have wings, but otherwise
look much like their parents. Nymphs grow by molting their skins. The
most primitive insects, such as silverfish, hatch from the egg looking
exactly like adults, only much smaller, and shed their skins many times as
they grow.

For more information turn to these articles; ANT; BEE; BEETLE; BUTTERFLY; FLEA; FLY; GRASSHOPPER; LOCUST; PARASITE; TERMITE.

Instinct

People have to learn to read and write, but bees do not learn how to sting. They are born knowing how to sting when there is danger. This kind of behavior is called instinct. Parents pass on instincts to their young through HEREDITY.

Animals do many things by instinct. Birds build nests this way. Simple animals, such as insects, do almost everything by instinct. They have set ways of finding food, attacking enemies, or escaping. Animals that act entirely by instinct do not have enough INTELLIGENCE to learn new ways of doing things and cannot easily change their behavior.

Insulin

Insulin is a HORMONE that controls the body's use of sugar. It is produced in a part of the pancreas GLAND. When not enough insulin is produced, the body cannot use or store sugar properly. This condition is called *diabetes*. Many people with diabetes have to be given insulin daily.

Insurance

Insurance is a way of safeguarding against loss or damage. A person with an insurance *policy* pays a little money to an insurance company every year. If they lose or damage something they have insured, the company gives them money to replace it or to pay for its repair.

▼ *Instinctive behavior is seen in humans and animals alike. Three examples are shown below. Bees sting as an instinctive reaction to danger, a newborn baby will grasp tightly enough with its hands to support its own weight, and a weaver bird makes an elaborate hanging nest out of grasses.*

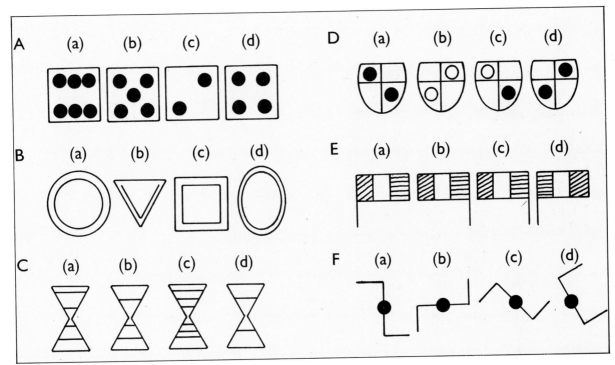

▲ An example of a test for measuring intelligence. The idea of this reasoning problem is to spot the "odd-one-out" in each group. Answers on page 373.

Intelligence

Intelligence is our ability to think and to learn. Creatures that act only by INSTINCT lack intelligence.

Human beings are the most intelligent animals. Apes and whales are also quite intelligent. No one knows why some people are more intelligent than others, or why some people are better at some subjects. Some people think that our environment—where we live—determines intelligence. Others think that intelligence is something that individual people have when they are born. Some think, too, that it can be inherited from our parents. A person's intelligence can be measured by an IQ test, but not very accurately.

A person's intelligence quotient, or IQ, is a number based on the person's score compared with others on the same test. The value of 100 is given to the average score and people tested are given IQs above or below 100.

Internal Combustion Engine

In internal combustion engines, FUEL burns inside the engines. The most common internal combustion engines are gasoline engines and DIESEL ENGINES. In the gas engine, fuel mixes with air inside a cylinder. A spark sets the mixture alight, and it explodes. This happens over and over again. Hot gases from the explosions push a piston to and fro inside the cylinder. Most engines have several cylinders. The

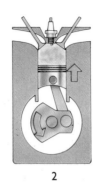
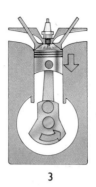
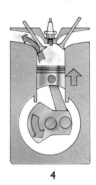

| 1 | 2 | 3 | 4 |

THE FOUR-STROKE ENGINE

In a four-stroke engine, the inlet valve opens (1) and the fuel mixture is drawn into the cylinder by the downward movement of the piston. Then both valves close, and the mixture is compressed (squeezed) (2) by the rising piston. The spark plug ignites the mixture (3) forcing the piston down. Finally, the exhaust valve opens and the rising piston pushes out the burned gases (4).

GREAT INVENTIONS

A.D. 105 Paper (from pulp) (Chinese)

1100 Magnetic compass (Chinese)

1440 Printing press Johannes Gutenberg (Ger.)

1608 Telescope Hans Lippershey (Neth.)

1765 Condensing steam engine James Watt (Scot.)

1822 Camera Joseph Niepce (Fr.)

1831 Dynamo Michael Faraday (Eng.)

1837 Telegraph Samuel F. B. Morse (U.S.)

1876 Telephone Alexander Graham Bell (Scot.)

1877 Phonograph Thomas Edison (U.S.)

1888 Kodak camera George Eastman (U.S.)

1895 Radio Guglielmo Marconi (It.)

1903 Airplane Wilbur & Orville Wright (U.S.)

1925 Television John Logie Baird (Scot.)

1948 Transistor John Bardeen, Walter Brattain, & William Shockley (U.S.)

1960 Laser Theodore Maiman (U.S.)

---

pistons work very quickly in turn. They move the crankshaft. This movement turns WHEELS or propellers.

Gasoline and diesel engines are used in AUTOMOBILES and trucks, and in ships and some planes.

Invention

An invention may be the creation of something completely new or an improvement of something that someone else has produced. Many important inventions have come from the work of one person; others have been created by many people working as a team. We will never know who thought of many of the very early inventions, such as the wheel and the plow.

Invertebrate

Invertebrates are animals that have no spine, or backbone. There are more than a million different invertebrates. They include all the WORMS from the flat worms and round worms to the worms with joints, or segments, like earthworms, SHELLFISH, OCTOPUSES, INSECTS, SPIDERS, CRABS, STARFISH, and many others.

Iowa

IOWA

Capital: Des Moines
Population: 2,850,000
Area: 56,290 sq. mi. (145,780 sq. km)
State flower: Wild Rose
State bird: Eastern Goldfinch
State tree: Oak
Statehood: December 28, 1846
 29th state

Iowa is a Midwestern state and among the most important agricultural states in the country. Its rich prairie lands grow corn, oats, and soybeans. Hogs and cattle are also raised in large numbers. There is little major industrial activity. Most industries supply farming equipment. Because it is such an important agricultural state, Iowa has a relatively low population for its size.

Iowa became a part of the United States in the Louisiana Purchase of 1803. But few settlers lived there until the 1830s, when much of the state was purchased from Indians after the Black Hawk War. Many of its settlers came from Scandinavia and Germany. It quickly developed into the important agricultural region it is today.

Iran

IRAN

Government: Islamic republic
Capital: Tehran
Area: 636,293 sq. miles
 (1,648,000 sq. km)
Population: 47,000,000
Language: Farsi (Persian)
Currency: Rial

Iran is a country in Asia. It lies between the Caspian Sea in the north and the Persian Gulf in the south. The country is a little bigger than Alaska. It has a long coastline along the Persian Gulf and the Arabian Sea. Deserts, snowy mountains, and green valleys cover most of the land. Much of the country has hot, dry summers and cold winters.

Iranians speak Persian. (Persia is the old name for Iran.) Their religion is Islam. Tehran is the capital.

Alexander the Great conquered Persia about 330 B.C. Later, the country was ruled by Arabs and Mongols. During this century, Iran was ruled by emperors, or *shahs*. In 1979, the government of Iran changed, and the shah left the country. Religious leaders now rule this Islamic Republic.

In 1980, Iran went to war against Iraq, and this bitter war lasted for eight years.

Iraq

Iraq is an Arab country in southwest Asia. Much of Iraq is a dry, sandy, and stony plain. It is cool in winter and very hot in summer. The Tigris and Euphrates Rivers flow through the plain to the Persian Gulf. Their water helps the farmers to grow

Answers to Intelligence Test on p.371: A(b); B(b); C(b); D(c); E(a); F(d).

IRAQ

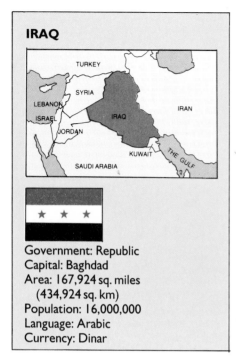

Government: Republic
Capital: Baghdad
Area: 167,924 sq. miles
  (434,924 sq. km)
Population: 16,000,000
Language: Arabic
Currency: Dinar

rice, cotton, wheat, and dates. Iraq is also one of the biggest oil producers in the world. Pipelines carry the oil from the north of the country across the desert to ports in Syria and Lebanon.

Many Iraqis are NOMADS. They live in the deserts with their sheep and goats. But nearly 4 million of the 16 million people work in Baghdad.

Some of the first cities in the world were built near Iraq's big rivers. Ur was one of the earliest cities. It was built by a BRONZE AGE people called the Sumerians. Later, the Babylonians built their famous city, BABYLON, in Iraq. The ruins of Babylon can still be seen. Modern Iraq is a republic. It was at war with IRAN from 1980 until 1988.

Ireland

Ireland is the second largest island of the BRITISH ISLES. Mountains rim the edges. The middle is a low plain. Through this flows the Shannon, the longest river in the British Isles. Irish weather is often mild and rainy. Meadows and moors cover much of the land. Southern Ireland is the Republic of Ireland, or Eire. It occupies five-sixths of the island. Its capital city is Dublin. Northern Ireland is part of the United Kingdom of GREAT BRITAIN and Northern Ireland. Its capital city is Belfast.

Iron and Steel

Iron is the cheapest and most useful of all metals. Much of our food, clothes, homes, and cars are made with machines and tools made from iron.

Iron is mined, or *quarried*, as iron ore, or MINERALS. The ore is melted down, or *smelted*, in a blast furnace. The iron is then made into cast iron, wrought iron, or mixed with a small amount of CARBON to form steel.

Cast iron is hard, but not as strong as steel. Molten cast iron is poured into molds to make such things as engine blocks. Wrought iron is softer, but tough. It is used for chains and gates. Steel is hard and strong. Steel ALLOYS containing metals such as tungsten and chromium are used to make many different things, from bridges to nails.

IRELAND (EIRE)

Government: Parliamentary republic
Capital: Dublin
Area: 27,136 sq. miles (70,283 sq. km)
Population: 3,600,000
Languages: English, Irish (Gaelic)
Currency: Irish pound (punt)

Shaduf

The shaduf was used for irrigation, as long ago as 5000 B.C.

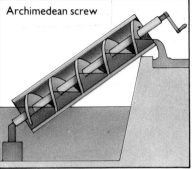

Archimedean screw

The Archimedean screw uses a rotating spiral to raise water.

King Sennacherib's canals

King Sennacherib of ancient Assyria built canals for irrigation.

Irrigation

Farmers and gardeners who water plants are irrigating them. Irrigation makes it possible to grow crops and flowers in dry soils, even in a DESERT. Farmers

▼ *To produce iron from iron ore, the ore is mixed with coke and limestone, then heated at a very high temperature. A poor quality iron, called pig iron, is made first. It can then be made into steel or steel alloys, which are much stronger.*

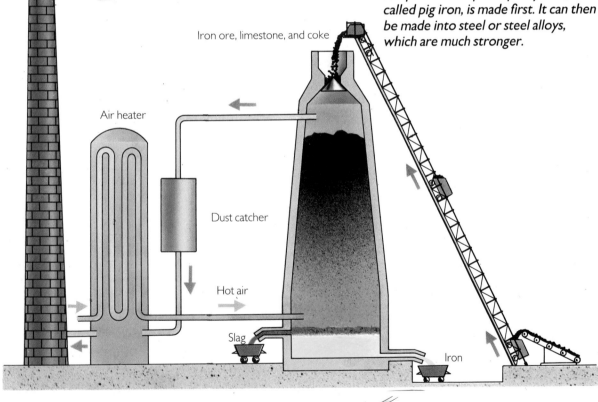

Iron ore, limestone, and coke

Air heater

Dust catcher

Hot air

Slag

Iron

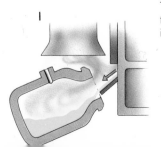

1

The furnace is filled with scrap iron and molten iron

2

Impurities escape with exhaust gases

Oxygen blown in

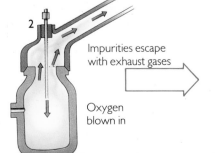

3

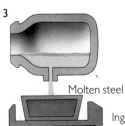

Molten steel

Ingot

▲ *Islamic styles of building are very graceful and well suited to hot climates. Mosques, the Islamic places of worship, often have a high tower from which a priest calls the people to prayer.*

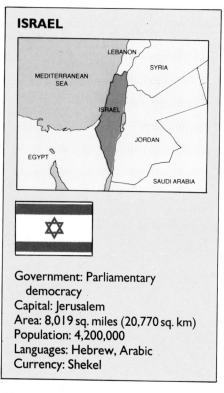

ISRAEL

Government: Parliamentary democracy
Capital: Jerusalem
Area: 8,019 sq. miles (20,770 sq. km)
Population: 4,200,000
Languages: Hebrew, Arabic
Currency: Shekel

in China, Egypt, and Iraq have been irrigating large areas of land for thousands of years.

Many countries store water in lakes made by building DAMS across rivers. CANALS take water from the lakes to farms. One irrigation canal in Russia is 530 miles (850 km) long. Ditches or pipes carry water from each canal to the fields. In each field, the water flows between the rows of plants. Sometimes it spurts up from holes in the pipes. It sprinkles the plants like a shower of rain.

Islam

Islam is a religion started in A.D.622 by MUHAMMAD. It has more followers than any other religion except Christianity. Islam means "submission." Its followers are called Muslims. Muslim means "submissive one." Muslims believe they must submit, or give in, to God's will. They believe in one God and in Muhammad as his prophet. Muslims pray five times a day and give gifts to the poor. They go without food until dark for one month a year and try to visit Mecca, Muhammad's birthplace, before they die. They also try to obey the rules for good living set out in the KORAN, the holy book of Islam.

Islam began in Arabia. Today it is the main religion in North Africa and most of southwest Asia.

Israel

Israel is a country in southwest Asia, on the shores of the Mediterranean Sea. Though people have lived here for thousands of years, Israel itself is a modern nation. It was founded in 1948 as a homeland for Jewish people from around the world. Its short history has been difficult. Many Arabs lived in what is now Israel, and they fiercely opposed the Jews who wanted to settle there. The Israelis have had to fight wars to survive. Israel is a holy land to Jews, Christians, and Muslims. It was in Israel that Jesus lived. More than half the land is dry mountain or desert. On the rich lands by the sea, farmers grow oranges, cotton, and grain. There are important industries here, too. But Israel imports more goods than it exports.

Italy

ITALY

Italy is a country in southern EUROPE. It is shaped like a boot stuck out in the Mediterranean Sea to kick the island of Sicily. Sicily and Sardinia are Italian islands.

Much of Italy is mountainous. The sharp, snowy peaks of the ALPS cross northern Italy. The Apennines run like a backbone down the middle. Between the Alps and Apennines lies the plain of

Government: Republic
Capital: Rome
Area: 116,313 sq. miles
(301,252 sq. km)
Population: 57,200,000
Language: Italian
Currency: Lira

◀ *Venice was a wealthy trading city in the 16th and 17th centuries. This beautiful city of canals is full of art treasures.*

Lombardy. Italy is famous for its hot, sunny summers. Rain falls mostly in winter.

Crops grow on almost half the land. Italy produces more pears and olives than any other country. The farmers also grow a lot of grapes, lemons, wheat, rice, and oranges. Big factories in northern Italy make cars, chemicals, and machines.

The capital is ROME. Many tourists visit Rome to see the VATICAN and ruins of the ROMAN EMPIRE.

Italy is the world's largest producer of wine, with nearly 2 billion gallons a year out of a world production of 35 billion bottles. Italians drink more wine than any other nation—over 24 gallons (90 liters) per head of the population in a year.

Ivan the Terrible

Ivan IV, the Terrible (1530–1584), was the first emperor, or *tsar*, of RUSSIA. He was a cruel man who killed his son with his own hands. But he helped to make Russia great. During his reign, Moscow became the Russian capital and Russia began trading with Western countries.

Ivory Coast *See* Côte d'Ivoire

ANDREW JACKSON

Seventh President 1829–1837
Born: Waxhaw, South Carolina
Education: Mostly self-educated
Occupation: Lawyer
Political Party: Democratic
Buried: Nashville, Tennessee

Jackson, Andrew

Andrew "Stonewall" Jackson (1767–1845) was the 7th president of the United States. He was one of the most influential presidents of the 1800s, and changed the style of American politics in several important ways. He was the first president to come from one of the frontier states, (as they then were) Tennessee. And he was the first president who was elected through a modern democractic system. People talk of "Jacksonian democracy" to describe the new political ideas introduced under him. Jackson had been a successful soldier before he became president. The popularity he gained then helped him when he ran for president. In office, he was tough and resolute. His biggest problem was the rights of individual states as opposed to the federal government. Though his political opponents said he behaved more like a king than a president, he remained popular.

Jaguar

No other American wild CAT is as heavy or perhaps as dangerous as the jaguar. From nose to tail, a jaguar is longer than a man and may be nearly twice his weight. The jaguar is yellow with black spots. The LEOPARD also has spots, but many of the jaguar's spots are in rings. Jaguars live in the hot, wet forests of Central and South America. They leap from trees onto wild pigs and deer. They also catch turtles, fish, and alligators.

▶ *Jaguars look like the leopards of Asia and Africa but they are heavier.*

Jamaica

Jamaica is a tropical island in the Caribbean Sea. The name Jamaica means "island of springs." It is a beautiful island, with hundreds of streams flowing from springs on the sides of its green mountains.

There are more than two million people in Jamaica. Most of them are of African ancestry. Many work on farms that grow bananas, coconuts, coffee, oranges, and sugarcane. Jamaica also mines bauxite. The country's beautiful beaches and pleasant climate attract many tourists.

JAMAICA

Government: Constitutional
  monarchy
Capital: Kingston
Area: 4,244 sq. miles (10,991 sq. km)
Population: 2,300,000
Language: English
Currency: Jamaican dollar

James (kings)

James was the name of two kings of Great Britain. James I (1566–1625) was the son of Mary, Queen of Scots. He was the first king of Scotland and England. James II (1633–1701), the grandson of James I, tried to restore the Roman Catholic Church to Britain but was forced to resign his throne in 1688.

Japan

Japan is a long, narrow string of islands off the mainland coast of Asia. Altogether they make a country slightly smaller than California.

▼ *There is very little spare land in Tokyo, so overhead trains are an ideal way of coping with commuter travel.*

JAPAN

Government: Parliamentary democracy
Capital: Tokyo
Area: 143,750 sq. miles (372,313 sq. km)
Population: 121,400,000
Language: Japanese
Currency: Yen

Mountains cover most of Japan. The highest is a beautiful volcano called Fujiyama, or Mount Fuji. Parts of Japan have forests, waterfalls, and lakes. Northern Japan has cool summers and cold winters. The south is hot in summer and mild in winter.

Japan is a crowded country. It has more than 120 million people. To feed them, farmers grow huge amounts of rice and fruit. The Japanese eat a lot of fish and seaweed. They catch more fish than any other country.

Japan does not have many minerals, so the Japanese buy most of their minerals, such as iron ore, from other countries. But no other country makes as many ships, television sets, radios, videos, and cameras as Japan does. The Japanese also make a lot of cars.

Jazz

Jazz is a kind of music. The players use unexpected rhythms. They can play any notes they like, but they must fit the music made by the rest of the band. In this way, jazz musicians often *improvise*, or make up music as they go along. Jazz began in the United States in the 1800s.

THOMAS JEFFERSON

Third President 1801–1809
Born: Albemarle County, Virginia
Education: College of William and Mary, Williamsburg, Virginia
Occupation: Planter and lawyer
Political Party: Republican
Buried: Charlottesville, Virginia

Jefferson, Thomas

Thomas Jefferson (1743–1826) was the 3rd president of the United States, and one of the most important founders of the country. He was a champion of democracy and liberty and is best remembered because he wrote the Declaration of Independence. But he was more than just a politician. He was interested in many things—architecture, farming, music, painting, philosophy, and science. Though he said he disliked politics, he spent most of his life as a politician. He was governor of Virginia, a Congressman, ambassador to France, secretary of state, and vice president. His most important acts as president were the LOUISIANA PURCHASE of 1803, which doubled the size of the country, and keeping the country out of the Napoleonic Wars in Europe. He retired to his home in Virginia. In 1819, he founded the University of Virginia.

Jenner, Edward

Edward Jenner (1749–1823) was a British doctor and the first man to discover how INOCULATION works. He inoculated a young boy with cowpox germs. Cowpox is a disease like smallpox, but less dangerous. Then Jenner injected the boy with smallpox germs. Because the cowpox germs protected the boy, he did not develop smallpox. Today, millions of people all over the world are inoculated against many diseases.

Jerusalem

Jerusalem is the capital of ISRAEL. It is a holy city of the Jews, Christians, and Muslims. David, Jesus, and other famous people in the Bible lived or died here. Jerusalem stands high up in hilly country. It has many old religious buildings. Huge walls surround the city's oldest part. In 1948, Jerusalem was divided between Israel and Jordan, but Israel took the whole city during a war in 1967.

▲ An old street in Jerusalem. In the distance is the Dome of the Rock, a Muslim shrine built on the spot where Muhammad is said to have ascended to heaven.

▼ The Baptism of Christ was painted by the Italian Renaissance artist Piero della Francesca in the 1400s. Many masterpieces of Western art have had the life of Jesus as their inspiration.

Jesus

Jesus was a Jew who started CHRISTIANITY. The New Testament of the BIBLE says that Jesus was God's Son. He was born in Bethlehem. His mother was called Mary. When he grew up, he traveled around, teaching and healing sick people. Some Jewish priests were jealous of Jesus. They told their Roman rulers that he was making trouble. The Romans killed Jesus on a cross, but the New Testament says that he came to life and rose to heaven. Followers of Jesus spread his teachings worldwide.

Jet Engine

A swimmer swims forward by pushing water backward. A jet engine works in a similar way. It drives an AIRCRAFT forward by pushing gases backward. Engines that work like this are called *reaction* engines. ROCKETS are also reaction engines. The main difference between jets and rockets is that jets take in oxygen from the air to burn their fuel, but

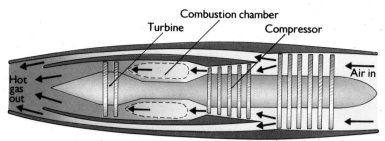

► Jet engines provide a powerful thrust to drive both passenger and military planes.

▲ Joan of Arc successfully took on the role of soldier to lead the French into battle against the English.

rockets have a supply of oxygen in their fuel.

There are four main kinds of jet engine. These are turbojets, turboprops, turbofans, and ramjets.

Jet engines have replaced propeller-driven piston engines in many kinds of plane. There are many reasons for this. Jet engines weigh less than piston engines. They also break down less often. Their moving parts spin instead of moving to and fro. This stops the plane from shaking. Jet engines burn cheap kerosene instead of costly gasoline. Jet engines can also carry planes faster and higher than piston engines can.

Joan of Arc

Joan of Arc (1412–1431) was a French girl who believed that God told her to free France from its English invaders. At 17, she left the farm where she worked, and persuaded France's King Charles VII to let her lead his army. She won five battles. Then she was captured and burned as a witch. But she had saved France. In 1920, the Pope made her a SAINT.

Johnson, Andrew

Andrew Johnson (1808–1875) became president of the United States when Abraham Lincoln was assassinated. He was immediately faced with serious problems arising from the division of the nation after the Civil War. Congress opposed many of Johnson's policies and accused him of being too friendly with the South. The division became so wide that the Representatives voted to impeach the president (charge him with conduct unworthy of his position). Eventually, the Senate found Johnson "not guilty."

Andrew Johnson came from a very poor family

ANDREW JOHNSON

Seventeenth President 1865–1869
Born: Raleigh, North Carolina
Education: Mostly self-educated
Occupation: Tailor
Political Party: National Union-
   Republican
Buried: Greeneville, Tennessee

and he received little schooling. People are still undecided whether he was a good or bad president.

Johnson, Lyndon Baines

Lyndon Johnson (1908–1973) became president of the United States after the assassination of John F. Kennedy. He ran again for the presidency in 1964 and was elected by a large majority. Johnson set about the task of fighting poverty, improving education, and enforcing civil rights laws.

Johnson faced problems in foreign affairs, especially the war in Vietnam, which he supported. The war aroused opposition throughout the country, and in 1968 Johnson announced that he would not seek re-election and urged peace talks. "LBJ" retired to his ranch in Texas.

LYNDON B. JOHNSON

Thirty-sixth President 1963–1969
Born: Stonewall, Texas
Education: Southwest Texas State Teachers College
Occupation: Teacher and legislator
Political Party: Democratic
Buried: LBJ Ranch, Stonewall, Texas

Jordan

Jordan is a small Arab country in the northwest corner of the Arabian Peninsula. Most of the country lies on a plateau 3,300 feet (1,000 m) above sea level. The Jordan River and the salty Dead Sea lie west of the plateau. The Jordanians and the Israelis have for many years been unfriendly neighbors. In 1967, Israel captured Jordanian land west of the Jordan River. This land is known as the West Bank.

JORDAN

Government: Constitutional monarchy
Capital: Amman
Area: 37,728 sq. miles (97,740 sq. km)
Population: 2,800,000
Language: Arabic
Currency: Jordanian dinar

Judaism

Judaism is a religion that believes in one God and has as its holy book the Bible. The Hebrew Bible

◄ *Many Jewish religious traditions, such as those involved in this wedding, are very ancient.*

The total number of Jews in the world is estimated to be 16,000,000. Nearly half of that number, 7.3 million, live in North America. There are 2 million Jews in the New York area alone. In Israel, there are nearly 3.5 million, while the British Jewish population is nearly 400,000.

consists of the first five books of Moses (the Torah), historical accounts of the tribes of Israel, and books written by prophets and kings. (Christians include all this material in their Bible, calling it the Old Testament.) Judaism's followers are called Jews. They observe the Ten Commandments. They believe God gave the Law to Moses on top of Mount Sinai after Moses led their ancestors out of Egypt, where they had been slaves. The commemoration of this Exodus from Egypt is one of Judaism's most important festivals and is called PASSOVER. Today, Jews live all over the world, but regard Israel as their spiritual and historical home.

JUPITER FACTS

Average distance from Sun:
483 million miles (778 million km)
Nearest distance from Earth:
391 million miles (630 million km)
Average temperature: −238°F (−150°C)
Diameter across equator:
88,734 miles (142,800 km)
Atmosphere: Hydrogen, helium
Number of moons: 14 known
Length of day: 9 hours 50 minutes
Length of year: 11.9 Earth years

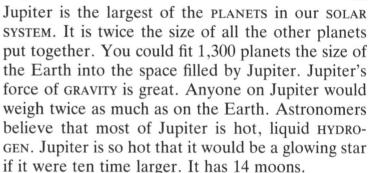

Earth

Jupiter

Jupiter

Jupiter is the largest of the PLANETS in our SOLAR SYSTEM. It is twice the size of all the other planets put together. You could fit 1,300 planets the size of the Earth into the space filled by Jupiter. Jupiter's force of GRAVITY is great. Anyone on Jupiter would weigh twice as much as on the Earth. Astronomers believe that most of Jupiter is hot, liquid HYDROGEN. Jupiter is so hot that it would be a glowing star if it were ten time larger. It has 14 moons.

Jupiter spins so fast that a day and night last less than ten Earth-hours. But a YEAR on Jupiter is 12 times longer than one of ours. This is because Jupiter is farther from the SUN than we are.

If an astronaut managed to "land" on Jupiter, he or she would find that there are no seasons. The faint Sun, so distant as to be just a flickering star, would rise and set every nine and three-quarters hours. Jupiter's biggest moon, Callisto, is bigger than the planet Mercury.

▶ The planet Jupiter appears to have light and dark belts around it in its atmosphere.

Kampuchea (Cambodia)

Kampuchea is a country in southeast Asia. It changed its name from Cambodia to Kampuchea in 1976 and back to to Cambodia in 1988. Most of Kampuchea's people live in small villages and grow rice, fruit, and vegetables. The country was formerly part of the French colony of Indochina. It became independent in 1955. Since then, Kampuchea has seen bitter civil war and starvation.

Kangaroo

Kangaroos are MARSUPIALS that live in New Guinea and Australia. Most of them live on grassy plains and feed on plants. They move around in troops, springing along on their big, powerful hind legs and large feet. Their long tails help them to balance.

There are more than 50 kinds of kangaroo. Red and gray kangaroos are the largest. A red kangaroo may be taller and heavier than a man. Gray kangaroos can bounce along at 25 mph (40 km/hr) if chased. Wallabies are smaller kinds of kangaroo. The smallest of all are rat kangaroos. They are about the size of a rabbit. Tree kangaroos live in New Guinea.

KAMPUCHEA

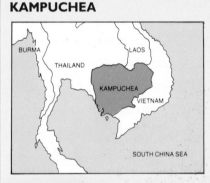

Government: Coalition
Capital: Phnom Penh
Area: 69,898 sq. miles
    (181,035 sq. km)
Population: 6,400,000
Language: Khmer
Currency: Riel

◀ *Kangaroos are considered pests in Australia, and to keep their numbers down, they are sometimes hunted.*

KANSAS

Capital: Topeka
Population: 2,460,047
Area: 82,264 sq. mi. (213,047 sq. km)
State flower: Sunflower
State bird: Western Meadowlark
Statehood: January 29, 1861
  34th state

▲ *A restoration of Front Street,
Dodge City, Kansas.*

JOHN F. KENNEDY

Thirty-fifth President 1961–1963
Born: Brookline, Massachusetts
Education: Harvard University
Occupation: Author and legislator
Political Party: Democratic
Buried: Arlington National
  Cemetery, Arlington, Va.

Kansas

The state of Kansas, located in the heart of the continental United States, is the breadbasket of America. Agriculture has always been its mainstay, either crop growing, or, especially in its early days, cattle rearing. In the 1860s and '70s, the cowboys of Kansas were famous. This was the Wild West, when thousands of cattle passed through Kansas towns such as Dodge City and Abilene on their way from Texas to the East. Lawmen such as Wild Bill Hickok and Wyatt Earp became well known. Before it became a state, people argued fiercely about whether Kansas should allow slavery. There were so many violent battles that Kansas became known as "bleeding Kansas." In the end, it was decided that slavery should not be allowed.

Kennedy, John Fitzgerald

John F. Kennedy (1917–1963) was the 35th president of the United States. He was only 43 when he was elected, the youngest man ever to win the office. When he was killed, he was the youngest president to die in office. The "Kennedy era" was a time of great optimism and prosperity in the United States. To many people, Kennedy was a symbol of this strength. His death was seen as the end of a vigorous period, as well as a great tragedy. The greatest challenge he faced as president was with the Soviet Union. It wanted to put nuclear missiles in Cuba. Kennedy bravely forced it not to. Afterward, relations with the Soviet Union improved. Kennedy also agreed with the Soviet Union to stop testing atomic bombs. He was assassinated in Dallas, Texas.

Kentucky

The state of Kentucky is known for tobacco, bourbon, whiskey, coal mining, and horseracing. It lies just to the west of the Appalachian mountains, and was one of the first frontier areas to be settled in the late 1700s. After it became a state in 1792, people began to breed horses in the lush pastures of the

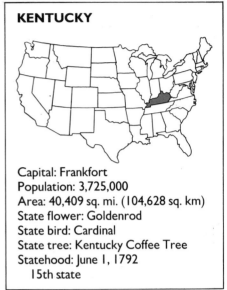

KENTUCKY

Capital: Frankfort
Population: 3,725,000
Area: 40,409 sq. mi. (104,628 sq. km)
State flower: Goldenrod
State bird: Cardinal
State tree: Kentucky Coffee Tree
Statehood: June 1, 1792
     15th state

bluegrass region. By the 1830s, tobacco and cotton became major crops. These tied it closely to the industries of the South. Kentucky suffered badly in the Civil War. Though it fought on the Union side, many people supported the South. After the war, the economy slumped. Coal became an important industry around 1900.

Kenya

Kenya is a country in east AFRICA. It is just a little smaller than Texas. The southwest border touches Lake Victoria. The Indian Ocean is on the southeast. The EQUATOR goes across the middle of the country. Much of the land is covered by mountains and flat-topped hills. The rest looks like a huge open park. It is a hot, dry country.

KENYA

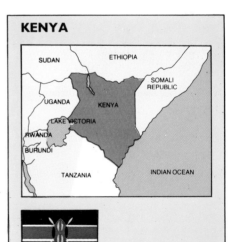

Government: Republic
Capital: Nairobi
Area: 224,960 sq. miles
     (582,646 sq. km)
Population: 21,000,000
Languages: Swahili, English
Currency: Shilling

◄ *Sisal, used to make rope, is made from the agave plant, which is widely grown in Kenya.*

▼ *The kidneys are part of a vital system for cleaning the blood of impurities and excess liquid. They are drained off through the ureters into the bladder and leave the body as urine. Blood flows in through the renal artery and back to the heart through the renal vein.*

Kenya is a member of the British COMMONWEALTH. Most of the 21 million Kenyans are African. They belong to a number of different tribes. Some tribes, like the Masai, keep cattle. Kenyan farmers grow corn, tea, and coffee. Kenya sells a lot of tea and coffee abroad. Many tourists visit Kenya to see the wild animals roaming the huge nature reserves. Britain ruled Kenya until it became independent in 1963.

Kidney

All VERTEBRATES (animals with a backbone) have two kidneys. Kidneys look like large, reddish-brown beans. Human kidneys are about the size of a person's fist. They lie on each side of the backbone, at just about waist level.

Kidneys clean the BLOOD. They filter out waste matter and strain off any water that the body does not need. Blood pumped from the HEART flows into each kidney through an artery. Each kidney contains tubes that act as filters. Blood cells, tiny food particles, and other useful items stay in the blood to be used by the body. Filtered blood flows out of the kidney through a vein. All the waste matter and extra water mix together to make urine.

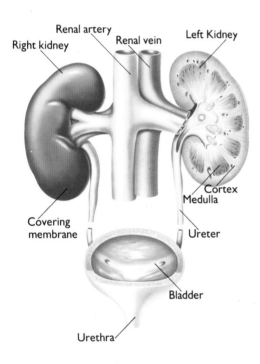

Renal artery
Right kidney
Renal vein
Left Kidney
Cortex
Medulla
Covering membrane
Ureter
Bladder
Urethra

King, Martin Luther

Martin Luther King (1929–1968) was an American civil rights leader who worked for racial justice through peaceful means. He was born in Altanta, Georgia, and became a Baptist minister like his father. It was in Montgomery, Alabama, where he was pastor, that he began his CIVIL RIGHTS crusade. One of King's first actions was to organize a boycott of buses in Montgomery in 1956 as a protest against unfair treatment of black passengers. During the next ten years, he led many peaceful demonstrations and meetings all over the country. Success came when Congress passed CIVIL RIGHTS laws in 1964 and 1965.

In 1964, King won the Nobel Peace Prize for his campaigns of non-violence. In 1968, at the age of 39, he was assassinated in Memphis, Tennessee.

▼ *When Martin Luther King Jr. was assassinated, President Johnson declared a day of national mourning.*

Kiribati

Kiribati is one of the smallest countries in the British Commonwealth. It is a string of islands in the Pacific Ocean, northeast of Australia. The islands were a British protectorate from 1892 until 1979, when they became independent. The people live simply, fishing and growing coconuts.

Kiwi

This strange bird from New Zealand gets its name from the shrill cries made by the male. The kiwi is a stocky brown bird as big as a chicken. It has tiny wings, but cannot fly.

Kiwis are shy birds that live in forests. By day, they sleep in burrows. At night, they hunt for worms and grubs. Kiwis can hardly see. They smell their food with the help of nostrils at the tip of their long beaks. The females lay very large eggs.

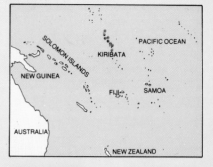

KIRIBATI

Government: Republic
Capital: Tarawa
Area: 360 sq. miles (931 sq. km)
Population: 63,000
Languages: Gilbertese, English
Currency: Australian dollar

Knot

Knots are a way of fastening rope, cord, or thread. They are especially important for sailors and climbers. But everyone needs to tie a knot at some time.

Knots are used to make a noose, tie up a bundle, or join the ends of small cords. There are also *bends* and *hitches*. A bend is used to tie the ends of a rope together; a hitch is used to attach a rope to a ring or post. Common knots are the square knot and bowline, both true knots; the clove hitch, half hitch, and sheet bend. Rope ends can also be joined by weaving them together. This is called a *splice*.

▼ *There are many different types of knots for various purposes. Choosing the right knot is half the skill of knot-tying.*

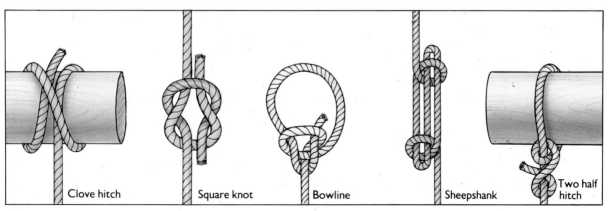

Clove hitch   Square knot   Bowline   Sheepshank   Two half hitch

NORTH KOREA

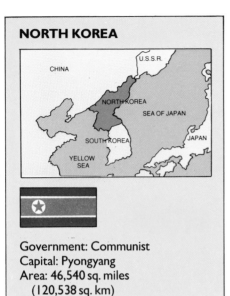

Government: Communist
Capital: Pyongyang
Area: 46,540 sq. miles
    (120,538 sq. km)
Population: 21,000,000
Language: Korean
Currency: Won

SOUTH KOREA

Government: Republic
Capital: Seoul
Area: 38,025 sq. miles (98,484 sq. km)
Population: 43,500,000
Language: Korean
Currency: Won

▶ *The Olympic Stadium in Seoul was the location of the 1988 games. Superbly equipped, it saw many record-breaking achievements.*

Koran

The Koran is the sacred book of ISLAM. Its name means "a recitation." It has 114 chapters of Arabic verse and teaches that there is one God whose prophets (messengers) included Abraham, JESUS, and MUHAMMAD. The book teaches Muslims to be humble, generous, honest, courageous, and just. It is said that the Koran was revealed to Muhammad through the angel Gabriel. Parts of the Koran resemble the Bible. The way it is written has influenced Arab literature.

Korea

Korea is a peninsula in ASIA which juts out from CHINA into the Sea of Japan. The land has many mountains and small valleys. Forests cover most of the country. Korean farms produce much rice and silk. Korean factories make steel and other products.

Korea was divided into two separate nations in 1945. They are known as North Korea and South Korea.

War between North and South Korea broke out in 1950, with Soviet and Chinese forces supporting the North and United Nations (mostly American) forces helping the South. There is now an uneasy peace between the two countries.

◀ *The view across Red Square to the Kremlin and St. Basil's Cathedral must be one of the most impressive in the world.*

▼ *The fifth chief Khan of the Mongol race, Kublai Khan, established the Mongol dynasty in China. Although he was a Buddhist, he was interested in Christianity and allowed missionaries to come to China.*

Kremlim

This is the oldest part of Moscow. Some of its buildings date from the 1100s. The Kremlin was once the fortress home of Russia's *tsars*. Inside the high wall that surrounds it stand old palaces and cathedrals crowned by golden domes. For most of its history, the Kremlin has been the seat of the Russian government; it still is today.

Kublai Khan

Kublai Khan (1216–1294) was the grandson of GENGHIS KHAN. Kublai became Great-Khan in 1259. Under his rule, the Mongol empire reached its peak of power. He conquered CHINA and set up his capital at Cambulac, modern Beijing. It was the first time that China had been completely overcome by outside forces. Neighboring countries in Southeast Asia were forced to recognize Kublai as their ruler. He also tried to conquer Japan and Java, but failed. Kublai encouraged art, science, and trade. Among his many foreign visitors was MARCO POLO.

Kuwait

The tiny nation of Kuwait is one of the richest in the world. It lies at the northwestern end of the Persian Gulf. All Kuwait's wealth depends on oil. Except for the capital city, Kuwait, the country is almost all desert. The climate is one of the world's hottest.

KUWAIT

Government: Constitutional monarchy
Capital: Kuwait
Area: 6,879 sq. miles (17,818 sq. km)
Population: 1,780,000
Language: Arabic
Currency: Dinar

Lake

Lakes are large areas of water surrounded by land. The world's largest lake is the salty Caspian Sea. It lies in the Soviet Union and Iran. The largest freshwater lake is Lake Superior, one of the GREAT LAKES.

Many lakes were formed in the ICE AGES. They began in valleys made by glaciers. When the glaciers melted, they left behind mud and stones that formed DAMS. The melted water from the glaciers piled up behind the dams.

Language

Language is what we use to talk to, or communicate with, one another. Many animals have ways of communicating. These may include special body movements and sounds. But the speaking of words is something that so far only human can do. Spoken language came first; later people invented a way of writing it down. This is known as written language. Language is always changing, as some words are forgotten and others are added.

Today, there are about 3,000 languages in the world. They can be grouped into a number of language families. Some of the most widely spoken languages are English, French, German, Russian, Chinese, Hindi, Arabic, and Spanish.

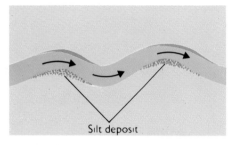

Silt deposit

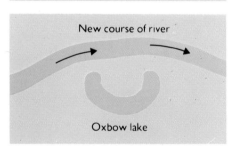

Silt deposit

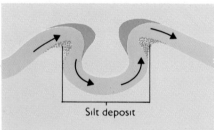

New course of river

Oxbow lake

▲ Rivers can gradually form bends by erosion of one bank and a build-up of material on the other. After a time the river cuts a straight channel through the neck of the bend. The loop of leftover water is called an oxbow lake.

▶ This bewildering array of newspapers from countries all over the world gives an indication of how difficult international relations can be when people are divided by alphabet, language, and culture.

Laos

Laos is a country in Southeast Asia. It is slightly smaller than Wyoming. The country's capital and largest city is Vientiane on the Mekong River. Most of Laos is covered with forests and mountains. Nearly all the people earn their living by farming—especially rice. Laos became a French protectorate in 1893, but gained its independence in 1949. It has a communist government.

Lapland

Lapland is a region in the ARCTIC. It lies in the far north of Sweden, Norway, Finland, and Russia.

Some Lapps are nomads. They travel with herds of reindeer. They sleep in tents and eat reindeer meat. Other Lapps are fishermen or farmers. They live in small huts in villages. Lapps speak a language related to Finnish. They keep warm by wearing clothes made from wool and reindeer skins. Their clothes are brightly colored.

LAOS

Government: Communist
Capital: Vientiane
Area: 91,428 sq. miles
   (236,800 sq. km)
Population: 3,700,000
Language: Lao
Currency: New kip

Laser

A laser is a device that strengthens light and makes it shine in a very narrow beam. Many lasers have a ruby CRYSTAL or gas inside them. Bright light, radio waves, or electricity are fed into the laser. This

▼ *In this Los Angeles studio, experiments are being carried out into the use of lasers in games for the future.*

Laser light is being used more and more to carry telephone conversations. A narrow cable containing 144 hairlike glass fibers can carry 40,000 telephone conversations at the same time.

makes the ATOMS of the crystal or gas jump around very quickly. The atoms give off strong light.

The light of lasers can be used for many things. Doctors use small laser beams to burn away tiny areas of disease in the body. They also repair damaged eyes with laser beams. Dentists can use lasers to drill holes in teeth. Some lasers are so strong they can cut through DIAMONDS. Lasers are used in factories to cut metal and join tiny metal parts together.

Lasers can also be used to measure distance. The laser beam is aimed at objects far away. The distance is measured by finding the time it takes for the light to get there and back. Laser beams can also carry radio and television signals. One laser beam can send many television programs and telephone calls at once without mixing them up.

Latitude and Longitude

Every place on Earth has a latitude and a longitude. Lines of latitude and longitude are drawn on MAPS. Lines, or *parallels*, of latitude show how far north or south of the *equator* a place is. They are measured in degrees (written as °). The equator is at 0° latitude. The North Pole has a latitude of 90° north, and the South Pole is 90° south.

▼ *Some of the lines of latitude and longitude are marked on globes or atlases. They form a kind of network that can be used to pinpoint specific places.*

Latitude is a measure of the distance of a point on the surface of the Earth to the north or south of the equator.

Longitude is the measure of the distance of any point east or west of the imaginary line running from the north pole, through Greenwich, in London, England, to the south pole.

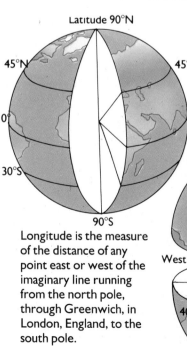

Lines, or *meridians*, of longitude show how far east or west a place is. They are also measured in degrees. Greenwich, in London, is at 0° longitude. A place halfway around the world from Greenwich is at 180° longitude.

Law

Laws are rules made by a country's leaders. Laws are made to help people live together in peace. They control many of the things people do. The laws of each country are often different. Some countries have very strict laws about things which other countries do not worry about. Every country has judges and POLICE. They help to make sure that people obey the law. When people break the law, they are often punished. They may have to pay money (fines) or go to prison. Sometimes people are put to death for breaking laws.

The people of BABYLON had written laws over 3,000 years ago. The ancient Greeks and Romans also made laws. In Europe, many important laws were made by kings and the Church. Today, laws are made by governments.

▲ *This carved stone block dates from about 1800 B.C. and is inscribed with laws made up by a king of Babylon called Hammurabi.*

Lead

Lead is a soft, heavy, blue-gray metal. It does not RUST. Lead is used for many things, but its greatest single use is in car batteries. Lead shields protect ATOMIC ENERGY workers from dangerous radiation. Lead is mixed with TIN to make pewter or *solder*. Solder is used for joining pieces of metal. Many items are now made without lead, because lead can become poisonous.

Leaf

Leaves are the food factories of green PLANTS. To make food, leaves need light, carbon dioxide, and water. Light comes from the Sun. Carbon dioxide comes from the air. Air enters a leaf through little holes called *stomata*. Water is drawn up from the ground by the plant's roots. It flows up the stem and into the leaf through tiny tubes called veins. Inside

▼ *In the past, lead was often used to make toys and, in particular, model soldiers, but for reasons of safety, it is no longer used.*

LEATHER

▶ *Leaves come in many shapes, sizes and even colors. You can identify a tree by looking at one of its leaves, once you learn a little about them.*

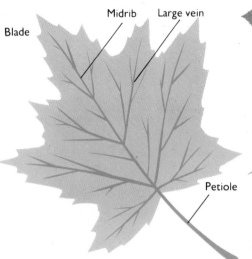

Blade · Midrib · Large vein · Petiole

▲ *Most leaves have the same basic parts. Of great importance are the veins that carry water and food to all parts of the plant.*

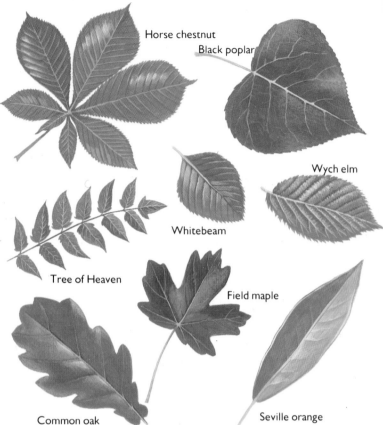

Horse chestnut · Black poplar · Wych elm · Whitebeam · Tree of Heaven · Field maple · Common oak · Seville orange

the leaf is a green coloring called chlorophyll. The chlorophyll uses light, water, and carbon dioxide to make SUGAR. The way it does this is known as *photosynthesis*. The sugar then passes through tubes to the other parts of the plant.

In the fall, many trees lose their leaves. First they shut off the water supply to the leaves. This destroys the green color and gives the leaves yellow, red, and orange tints.

Leather

Leather is made from the skin, or hide, of animals. The skins are treated to make them strong and waterproof (for the soles of shoes) or flexible (for furniture and luggage). The process of treating them is called *tanning*. Before tanning, the skins are *cured* by being soaked in salt water. Then, the remaining hair and meat is taken off. Next, the skins are treated with a chemical called *tannin*, which comes from tree bark. Then, the leather is oiled to soften it and dyed different colors. It is now ready to be cut, shaped, and stitched or glued into the final product.